Savoring Disgust

Savoring Disgust

The Foul and the Fair in Aesthetics

CAROLYN KORSMEYER

OXFORD
UNIVERSITY PRESS

2011

Oxford University Press, Inc., publishes works that further
Oxford University's objective of excellence
in research, scholarship, and education.

Oxford   New York
Auckland   Cape Town   Dar es Salaam   Hong Kong   Karachi
Kuala Lumpur   Madrid   Melbourne   Mexico City   Nairobi
New Delhi   Shanghai   Taipei   Toronto

With offices in
Argentina   Austria   Brazil   Chile   Czech Republic   France   Greece
Guatemala   Hungary   Italy   Japan   Poland   Portugal   Singapore
South Korea   Switzerland   Thailand   Turkey   Ukraine   Vietnam

Published by Oxford University Press, Inc.
198 Madison Avenue, New York, New York 10016

www.oup.com

Oxford is a registered trademark of Oxford University Press.

Library of Congress Cataloging-in-Publication Data
Korsmeyer, Carolyn.
Savoring disgust : the foul and the fair in aesthetics / Carolyn Korsmeyer.
    p.   cm.
Includes bibliographical references and index.
ISBN 978-0-19-975694-0; 978-0-19-975693-3 (pbk.)
1. Aversion. 2. Aesthetics. I. Title.
BH301.E45K67   2010
111'.85—dc22   2010014969

9 8 7 6 5 4 3 2 1

Printed in the United States of America
on acid-free paper

Preface

I began the work that became this book a number of years ago, and I have accumulated many debts along the way. The first lecture I delivered on aesthetic disgust was in 1998 at the International Congress of Aesthetics in Ljubljana, Slovenia. Subsequently, I presented lectures on various aspects of the topic at a number of professional meetings, including a conference on Ethics and the Arts at Arizona State University; the Society for Literature and Science; the Nordic Society for Aesthetics, Uppsala; the American Philosophical Association; and the American Society for Aesthetics. In addition, I delivered lectures at Siena College; Baruch College, CUNY; Queen's University, Ontario; Loyola College in Maryland; the University of Missouri, St. Louis; Trinity University, San Antonio; Alfred University; and my home institution, the University at Buffalo (SUNY). I thank my hosts and the members of those audiences, whose interest and queries helped to hone my thinking about matters disgusting and pleasant. I also thank the students in two courses I taught as a guest lecturer at the University of Helsinki and the Jagiellonian University, Krakow.

Certain ideas in this book originally were developed in article form, though they have been redistributed and revised here. A pilot study, "Disgust," appeared in *Aesthetics as Philosophy: Proceedings of the XIV Congress for Aesthetics*, ed. Aleč Erjavec. Some of chapter 3 was published as "Delightful, Delicious, Disgusting," *Journal of Aesthetics and Art Criticism* 69, no. 3 (2002). Portions of chapters 5 and 6 were developed in "Fear and Disgust: The Sublime and the Sublate," *Revue Internationale de Philosophie* 62, no. 246 (December 2008). And the possible kinship between aesthetic disgust and beauty, advanced in chapter 7, was first articulated in "Terrible Beauties," published in *Contemporary Debates in Aesthetics and Philosophy of Art*, ed. Matthew Kieran. I gratefully acknowledge these journals and Wiley-Blackwell, publisher of the last-mentioned volume, for permission to use material that appeared in their publications.

My colleague Barry Smith first acquainted me with the essay by Aurel Kolnai that I make use of in this study, and I thank him for introducing me to phenomenological perspectives on emotion. Our joint introduction to Kolnai's *On Disgust* (2004) provided the foundation for some of the analysis here.

A number of people patiently read drafts of this book, in part or in whole. Foremost among them are the stalwart members of my writing group: Ann Colley, Carrie Tirado Bramen, and Regina Grol. I also thank Joe Palencik for suggestions on portions of chapter 1. Peg Brand helped me think through the uses of disgust in feminist art; Susan Feagin introduced me to ossuaries and their grisly charms; and Cynthia Freeland contributed insights into numerous aspects of my argument and shared her robust fund of examples of disgusting art. Others who lent their assistance in various ways include Jorge Gracia, Mary Wiseman, and Sandra Firman. My editor at Oxford University Press, Peter Ohlin, was efficient and helpful in the acquisitions process, and Lucy Randall and Liz Smith were invaluable with advice concerning the many details required to get a book into press. I also thank three anonymous readers for the press, who offered useful critical suggestions as the manuscript took final shape.

Given the subject matter of this book, a dedication would be a dubious honor. Therefore, I end with thanks to my friends and family for putting up with—and occasionally sharing—the art, movies, and television that fed my imagination as I wrote.

Contents

Savoring Disgust

Introduction

Disgust may seem at first to be among the simpler human affective responses—one that functions in a basic, visceral manner to repel us from noxious substances. It often manifests a strongly reactive character, rather like sensations and reflexes such as startle, and as such it seems as much physical reaction as emotion. Disgust indeed has a striking corporeal character; its signature marker is nausea. This physicality makes disgust immediate, powerful, and difficult to override. All the same, like any emotion, disgust can be the occasion for reflection, for it provides insight about its objects in a manner peculiar to itself. Moreover, although this emotion seems to represent pure aversion, disgusting objects can also fascinate—and even attract. Disgust can exert a paradoxical magnetism, as those theorists who have studied this emotion have struggled to understand.

This attraction is especially evident in the forms that may be called "aesthetic disgust." By this term I do not mean disapproval or rejection but rather an emotion appropriately aroused by certain works of art—and by other objects as well—that signals appreciative regard and understanding. As will be evident from the examples to come, this emotive reaction can assume many forms. Generally speaking, aesthetic disgust is a response that, no matter how unpleasant, can rivet attention to the point where one actually may be said to *savor* the feeling. In virtue of this savoring, this dwelling on the encounter, the emotion constitutes a singular comprehension of the value and significance of its objects. This book analyzes the nature of this emotion and the various forms that disgust can manifest, investigating in particular the meanings that disgust assumes in our engagement with art—and even on occasion with food.

With a few notable exceptions, theoretical investigations of disgust have been relatively scanty in the past. Recently, however, the subject has gained the attention of many, including psychologists, evolutionary biologists, philosophers, literary scholars, art theorists, and artists. The investigations of this emotion and its significance for psychological, moral, and aesthetic life have produced an impressive range of analyses. Those who study the neurobiology or the evolution of emotions often conclude that disgust is a primitive, protective aversion with strong reactive properties, making it recalcitrant to change. In contrast, moral philosophers tend to treat it as a sophisticated, educable, and potentially dangerous emotion that produces value judgments of great power; whether those judgments should be trusted is a matter of controversy. Perhaps most noticeably, in the heterogeneous worlds of art one finds numerous works that deliberately evoke disgust in their audiences by means of pictures, installations, performances, films, and videos. The human body in all its fleshly frailty has become the postmodern artistic object par excellence.[1] Artistic arousal of disgust can be turned to political, social, religious, and aesthetic ends, and it may be mingled with horror, humor, sorrow, or satire.

The term "disgust" and kindred labels are used in a variety of contexts. I may report my disgust at the slime that has accumulated in a clogged drain, at the taste of spoiled meat, or at the sight of an infected wound; and I may claim to be disgusted by the hypocritical behavior of a colleague. The immense range of objects of disgust has prompted many theorists to formulate two categories of the emotion: literal "core" or "material" disgust that is viscerally responsive to foul and contaminated objects in close proximity, and "moral" disgust that takes as its objects persons or behaviors that transgress social norms. It is the first type that chiefly interests me here. The two categories, however, are not always easy to separate, and some of the examples that ground this study will have both visceral and moral dimensions.

Nonetheless, it will be helpful to indicate some limits to the scope of this book. I believe that often the language of disgust is applied to moral situations to indicate emphatic disapproval in a manner that is more metaphorical than literal. Since disgust is a strongly negative emotion, and since deeply immoral behavior prompts condemnation, it is tempting to interpret moral censure in terms of an appropriately strong affective reaction. Without doubt there are types of behaviors, such as those that involve sadistic injury or twisted sexuality, that do prompt disgust inasmuch as they occasion the visceral, nauseous recoil

---

1. Arthur C. Danto, "Beauty and the Beastly," *Nation* 272, no. 16 (April 23, 2001): 25–29. See also Danto, *The Abuse of Beauty: Aesthetics and the Concept of Art* (Chicago: Open Court, 2003); Carole Talon-Hugon, *Goût et dégoût: L'art peut-il tout montrer?* (Nîmes: Éditions Jacquelin Chambon, 2003), 10–14.

that is the signature of the emotion. Disgust clearly can be aroused in morally laden situations, and examples to come will bear this out. But there is little reason to think that literal disgust is either a foundational or a typical response of moral disapproval generally.[2]

What is more, when the language of disgust is more than metaphorical, its operation becomes itself morally questionable. Disgust is an affective response that can be mustered to patrol social boundaries and norms—for instance, to reinforce proscriptions on what should be eaten or on sexual behavior. But many have noted that in this role disgust can also have some nasty applications insofar as it is used to categorize persons in unpopular minority groups as "disgusting." This is not the place to debate this matter, for the literature on disgust as grounds for moral (and legal) judgments is a complex subject of its own, with some theorists defending disgust as a sound basis for disapprobation and others arguing that the emotion is apt to motivate unjust and exclusionary judgments.[3] In any event, the occasions for aesthetic disgust that interest me most are those for which I want to claim a strong degree of insight and truth about human frailty and mortality, for which disgust in its material, visceral version plays a far-reaching and subtle role. Therefore, while there doubtless can be moral resonance in instances of aesthetic disgust, most of this study focuses on core or material disgust, the kind of emotion that typically follows encounters with sour milk, sewage, and slime; slugs, maggots, and lice; infected sores, gangrened flesh, and decomposing corpses. These things prompt unqualified visceral disgust and may include unpleasant involuntary responses, including the gag reflex, nausea, and even vomiting. But even if we do not reach the latter stages of reaction, the physical recoil of disgust is palpable. That said, oftentimes visceral disgust is aroused in situations entangled with moral, social, or religious precepts, and part of its meaning will derive from those values. This feature, shared by emotions in general, will enhance the cognitive role of aesthetic disgust, a point to be explained in the chapters to come.

Disgust in the core sense of visceral revulsion seems to represent the very bedrock of aversion. Yet at the same time, that which disgusts sometimes exerts a peculiar allure. Plato used the attraction of disgust in one of his most powerful pictures of the warring factions of the soul when he described Leontius, who admonished his own eyes for desiring to look upon the corpses of

2. For a scientific attempt to ground morality in distaste and disgust, see H. A. Chapman, D. A. Kim, J. M. Susskind, and A. K. Anderson, "In Bad Taste: Evidence for the Oral Origins of Moral Disgust," *Science* 323 (February 27, 2009): 1222–26.

3. John Kekes, "Disgust and Moral Taboos," *Philosophy* 67 (1992): 431–46. Martha Nussbaum argues that disgust is an emotion that precludes empathy and whose reliability should be doubted. See Nussbaum, *Hiding from Humanity: Disgust, Shame, and the Law* (Princeton, NJ: Princeton University Press, 2004); also her *Upheavals of Thought: The Intelligence of Emotions* (Cambridge: Cambridge University Press, 2001).

executed criminals. The upsetting fascination with disgusting objects has long been observed, though differently diagnosed. Julia Kristeva notes a "vortex of summons and repulsion," and phenomenologist Aurel Kolnai describes an "eroticism of disgust."[4] No matter how one labels the phenomenon, the presence of allure packaged with aversion calls for explanation.

Perhaps, however, the preceding list of disgusting items has already inspired dispute. Things such as lice and slugs are not really disgusting, not in themselves, one might say. Rather, it is we the disgusted who have learned to classify them as such. People in other cultures might not do so—indeed, they might eat things with relish that others consider revolting. In discussing this subject over the last several years, I have encountered a difficulty in theorizing about disgust that stems from this agnostic attitude. So widespread is the assumption that objects of disgust are culturally and individually relative, that many people seem to think that the emotion merely signals unworthy squeamishness, that it does not deserve to be taken seriously, or that it should be resisted and overcome. This attitude is twinned with skepticism about the reliability of disgust to register insight about its objects. I find this assumption curious, as examples of typical triggers for other emotions rarely inspire such opposition. The fervor to insist that venomous snakes and earthquakes are not really worthy of fear, for instance, is not nearly so ready to hand. Nor is anyone even tempted to argue that the loss of a loved one is not truly an object of grief or sorrow. I believe that in its own way disgust is a conduit for accurate if unsettling insights, a feature of the emotion exploited in multifarious aspects in art.

It will take some time to sort through these issues, so at this point I only set out my approach. The objects that come to be recognized as disgusting are indeed at least partly a product of culture, and insofar as this obtains, the occasions for the emotion will be culturally variant. The fact that foods that are considered delicacies in one culture may be sickening to members of another supports the idea that this emotion is built up from education and habit. But there are grounds for stressing the fixity of the response as well. Disgust involves visceral reaction and appears to be more or less hardwired into human physiology. I take seriously the scientific studies that locate pancultural responses of disgust to objects in very similar categories, though just which particular objects belong in those categories remains variant—sometimes highly so. Indeed, studying disgust affords an opportunity to see a physiological aversion that becomes culturally molded to different situations, including those that transform it into a terrible attraction. However, if disgust is taken to

4. Julia Kristeva, *The Powers of Horror: An Essay on Abjection*, trans. Leon S. Roudiez (New York: Columbia University Press, 1982), 1; Aurel Kolnai, *On Disgust* (1929), ed. Barry Smith and Carolyn Korsmeyer (Chicago: Open Court, 2004), 60.

be only a matter of cultural practice unrelated to constants in human life, its power and significance are subverted. Therefore, I resist the impulse to disqualify objects as truly disgusting, for this inadvertently divests them of their power. Especially in the varieties exploited in art, eliciting the palpable reaction of disgust—literally a gut response—contributes tremendously to their aesthetic impact.

In short, the great diversity of objects of disgust and the emotion's elastic aesthetic uses indicate how complex the manifestations of this emotion can be. Disgust is a protean emotion that is anchored in automatic physical reactions. If there were no cultural variety to disgust, we would not have the panoply of aesthetic disgust that art and eating practices provide. All responses would be automatic and similar, rather like startle or the gag reflex. On the other hand, without noting the immediate and fundamentally physiological reaction that marks this emotion, we cannot account fully for the profound power of objects that evoke disgust. Studying disgust reveals a physical, visceral aversion that becomes a culturally powerful—and manipulable—aesthetic response.

The original meaning of the term "aesthetic" in modern philosophy pertains to sense experience and to the immediate insight about an object that such experience delivers. In one of its earlier usages it referred to an inferior type of knowledge that was too particular to be brought under the abstractions of reason—and hence generalization and reliable grasp of concepts. At the same time, it was appropriated to refer to impressions of pleasure and pain that later become articulated in terms of the singular experience of beauty.[5] Emphasis on the cognitive elements of the aesthetic diminished with the rise of the field of aesthetics during the European Enlightenment, when the majority of philosophers sought to understand beauty as a particular type of pleasure. Hedonic analyses of beauty further necessitated distinguishing aesthetic pleasure from merely sensuous pleasure, which in turn confirmed the venerable hierarchy of the senses, whereby the distance senses of vision and hearing were considered true aesthetic senses, while taste, smell, and touch were designated senses that provide bodily but not aesthetic pleasure. As we shall see in chapter 2, the exclusion of the bodily senses from what were deemed properly aesthetic activities is one element that helped to overdetermine the exclusion of disgust from among the emotions that could be turned to positive use in artistic representation.

The legacy of this complicated history is presently undergoing considerable revision, and more and more theorists now include the bodily senses among those that are capable of delivering a kind of experience that counts as "aesthetic." Similarly, the emotion of disgust is receiving far more interest than it

---

5. See David Summers, *The Judgment of Sense: Renaissance Naturalism and the Rise of Aesthetics* (Cambridge: Cambridge University Press, 1987), esp. chap. 10, for the complicated history of analyses of sense and cognition.

previously did. Many theorists who now argue on behalf of the bodily senses seek to show how they can furnish a pleasure that qualifies as aesthetic; apologists for disgust similarly tend to focus on the covert pleasures hidden in this unseemly emotion. In this study I take an alternative approach, though one that I believe is complementary to the latter. Rather than putting the stress on pleasure—an overused concept in my view that obscures stubborn philosophical problems—I shall return to the notion of "aesthetic" that connotes immediate apprehension or understanding of its object. In other words, I shall emphasize the capacity of disgust to impart an intuitive, felt grasp of the significance of its object. As Paul Guyer puts it in a summary of the contribution of Alexander Baumgarten, who introduced the term "aesthetics" into modern usage: "The particular feature of sensory perception that is exploited for the unique pleasure of aesthetic experience . . . is its *richness*, the possibility of conveying a lot of information through a single pregnant image, a possibility that is sacrificed by logical or conceptual cognition for the sake of greater clarity."[6] This somewhat cognitivist—as opposed to hedonist—focus leads me to use the terms "aesthetic apprehension" or "aesthetic encounter" as a rule rather than the more common phrase "aesthetic appreciation," which has become an unfortunately anemic term. Pleasure often attends such experiences, but its evocation is not necessarily their purpose; the magnetism or allure of disgust sometimes but by no means always indicates a degree of pleasure in the event. Moreover, a theoretical focus on pleasure is apt to neglect the profound cognitive aspects of sensory apprehension. Disgust affords a powerful means by which difficult truths are conveyed with maximum aesthetic impact. The fact that, fundamentally, disgust is a supremely unpleasant visceral emotion sustains my claim that pleasure is a limited concept to employ in the philosophical investigation of aesthetics.

Once nearly overlooked in theories of emotion and aesthetic apprehension, disgust is now given center stage in many analyses. The philosophical status of this emotion reached a nadir at the time that aesthetic theory itself made huge strides in the eighteenth century, as it was the sole emotion shut out from positive aesthetic uses (a subject to be reviewed in chapter 2). Now the tables have turned. Many contemporary artists almost routinely exploit the disgust response; movies and television strive with ever more shocking special effects to nauseate and repel; and theorists plumb psychoanalysis to account for the allure of the disgusting. Moreover, as a "basic" emotion with its own neural signature, disgust has also been at the center of a good deal of psychological research and attendant evolutionary speculation. All this attention has had some paradoxical results: disgust is considered at one and the same time the

---

6. Paul Guyer, *Values of Beauty: Historical Essays in Aesthetics* (Cambridge: Cambridge University Press, 2005), 268–69.

most primitive of emotions, a modular response similar to the emotions that we share with other animals, yet it appears to be uniquely human. It is a pan-cultural, hardwired reaction designed for protection against contamination, and it is also the site of cultural distinction—a "culture-creating passion," as one commentator remarks.[7] When it was refused attention as a robust and aesthetically profound element of art, it was regarded as unique in its disquali-fication, the one emotion that could not be incorporated into an experience of beauty. And now that it is the subject of eager critical attention, it is still treated as unique among the emotions aroused by art—signaling the abject or that which resides outside the boundaries of the aesthetic. Whether neglected, rejected, or embraced by theorists and researchers, disgust receives a kind of attention that sets it apart from other emotions.

One reason for this, I surmise, is that disgust is almost always taken to be an extreme emotion—an absolute recoil from its object. A goal of this study is to disclose the more subtle variants of disgust and to argue for their aesthetic indispensability. For this reason, I spend relatively little time on the more obvious examples of disgust in our contemporary cultural products, those especially found in the genres of horror and in forensic and medical dramas, though these are not entirely neglected. My emphasis will be on the ways in which disgust becomes part of deep aesthetic apprehension of difficult experiences, including some that might even qualify as beautiful—and even more surprisingly as delicious.

This book occupies a shelf alongside several other studies of disgust, including Aurel Kolnai's long essay "Disgust" from 1929, the first dedicated philosophical study of this emotion; William Ian Miller's *Anatomy of Disgust* (1997); and Winfried Menninghaus's compendious *Disgust: The Theory and History of a Strong Sensation* (2003). It bears affinity with certain theoretical applications such as Martha Nussbaum's *Hiding from Humanity: Disgust, Shame, and the Law* (2004) and Julia Kristeva's examination of the abject in *The Powers of Horror: An Essay on Abjection* (1982), as well as the many analyses of the disgusting in art such as Robert Rawdon Wilson's *The Hydra's Tale: Imagining Disgust* (2002). Carole Talon-Hugon's *Goût et dégoût: L'art peut-il tout montrer?* (2003) covers some of the same territory as this study, including aspects of the history of aesthetics and of the contemporary art scene, though she is more inclined than I am to endorse the traditions that exclude disgust from positive aesthetic deployment. Despite—or perhaps because of—their different theoretical allegiances, all these works shed light on the complex manifestations of disgust.[8]

---

7. William Ian Miller, *The Anatomy of Disgust* (Cambridge, MA: Harvard University Press, 1997), xii.

8. As this book was entering production, I learned of another philosophical study in the works, Colin McGinn's *The Meaning of Disgust: Life, Death, and Revulsion*, Oxford University Press, forthcoming 2012. McGinn's emphasis on death as an essential object of disgust supports my analysis here.

Since my own examination is directed to the phenomenon of aesthetic disgust, I concentrate on the occasions when this aversion constitutes a form of apprehension and understanding of artworks. Whether scientist or philosopher, those who have studied disgust tend to find this affective response an all-or-nothing affair, an utter recoil complete with gagging sensation and grimace. (Kolnai is a noteworthy exception.) There seems to be little space recognized for mild disgust or for noting a continuum of strength of affect that virtually all other emotions admit. I believe that this either-or understanding of disgust, as though the emotion operates like an on-off switch, has both led to some exaggerated claims about its significance and blinded us to the subtleties of its artistic usage, a case I hope to make with the chapters that examine specific examples where art exploits this peculiar aversion.

This book proceeds from a general discussion of disgust and theories that have traditionally sidelined this emotion from philosophical aesthetics, to a set of speculations about how aversion becomes attraction. I begin the latter examination with the most unlikely case, that of food, and from there proceed to a series of examples from art, including a sustained discussion of one highly complex theme that combines horror, cruelty, even sublimity—the eviscerated human heart. Finally, I shall extend the valence of disgust as far as I find plausible into the domain of the classic aesthetic virtue: beauty.

Chapter 1 presents a broad picture of disgust, drawing together theoretical insights from philosophy, psychology, and neurobiology. Here we find that a good deal of opinion emphasizes the automatic, reactive nature of this emotion and hence its qualifications to be pancultural. According to some approaches, disgust figures as one of the so-called basic emotions. Basic affective responses are relatively invariant across cultures; they are manifest in standard display postures and facial expressions and can be measured by characteristic microchanges in the body (e.g., heart rate, galvanic skin response, increased electrochemical activity in distinctive regions of the brain). Supporting arguments align basic emotions with the adaptations of evolution and the survival of the species. From such a perspective, disgust is widely analyzed as a relatively simple aversive response, deeply rooted in sensory experiences, to substances that are foul and thereby dangerous to contact through touch, taste, or smell. The idea that disgust is a pure and simple aversion, however, is hardly adequate to the actual experiences of disgust and their complexity, a point acknowledged even by those who stress its physiological components. Disgust is synonymous with neither nausea nor distaste, though it shares their immediacy and physicality.

One of the most intransigent complexities of this emotion is the fact that, paradoxically, even this profound bodily aversion can present features that allure. Before demonstrating the entanglement of aversion with attraction, I discuss the formidable philosophical tradition that has regarded disgust as aesthetically disreputable. This is the subject of chapter 2. Other "negative" emotions such as fear have long been recognized as contributing to the aesthetic import of tragedy and the sublime, as many theorists have observed. But until recently disgust has not been regarded as aesthetically manipulable into a positive component in art. As Kant famously asserts, it is the only emotion that cannot be converted into aesthetic liking by means of artistic representation. But only a little reflection illuminates the extent to which disgust is evoked as an appreciative aesthetic response in artworks from ancient tragedy to postmodern photography. This chapter reviews the classic arguments against disgust and argues that, traditional opinion to the contrary, the arousal of disgust often has a positive value in appreciation and understanding of artworks. In addition to its role as the opposite pole to beauty—the paradigm of the "anti-aesthetic" as some would have it—there are many ways that disgust converts from pure aversion to paradoxical attraction while retaining its trademark visceral shock.

One might assume that disgust exerts positive aesthetic appeal only when it is safely contained in works of art, but in fact it has an interesting role to play in a venue where the visceral response is most literal: actual eating. This is the subject of chapter 3. How did something like a snail, a clot of fish eggs, a leech, or an animal's brain ever end up on a dinner plate? What induces someone to overcome the rotting smell of decay and cultivate a taste for "high" meat? This chapter addresses the most basic sort of disgust: the visceral disgust that is a response to foods that violate one's sense of the edible. Even this reactive type of disgust, I argue, is philosophically revealing, for foods and eating present a paradox of aversion fully as complicated as those paradoxes familiar from meditations on tragedy or horror. Those who attempt to understand sophisticated eating and the "art" of cuisine usually approach the subject by considering the pleasures of taste. Some of the most recondite pleasures of the table, however, are actually disgusting on first exposure, offering not invitation but repulsion. This suggests that certain kinds of particularly difficult eating originate not in the search for pleasure but in exploring the meaning of extreme and difficult emotions, a phenomenon that ties eating with the experience of the sublime. This chapter explores some examples of terrible eating, arguing that segments of the borderline between the terrible and the tasty, the disgusting and the delicious, are slim indeed.

I continue to assemble examples where this emotion operates in aesthetic contexts in chapter 4. Sometimes appreciative disgust is a sort of grisly relish; other times it requires an uncomfortable cognitive assessment in order to frame appreciation. It can carry an unsettling eroticism; sometimes it is funny, sometimes sad, sometimes outrageous, and of course oftentimes just revolting. (And it should not be forgotten that sometimes disgust plays its standard role of rejection; not all disgusting art can be savored, nor for that matter valued.) This chapter surveys examples of disgust in different art forms to amplify the range of disgust aroused as part of appreciation and comprehension.

Representative artworks discussed include paintings, literary narratives, photography, science fiction, and horror. Considering the deployment of disgust on the part of feminist artists indicates the deep social meanings that surround certain objects of disgust, including the female body. I argue that the positive and negative valence of the disgust aroused by art is specific to objects that both trigger and partially constitute that emotion.

Discussion of theories that seek to account for this attractive aversion has been postponed until a full set of examples has been presented, for the plausibility of explanations for the allure of disgust varies quite a lot depending on the kinds of objects one has in mind. Chapter 5 reviews a range of theories that seek to explain why this powerful aversion can also be the occasion for "enjoyment" of some sort or other, including approaches that make use of psychoanalysis, phenomenology, and cognitive science. While there is considerable agreement about the objects that typically trigger disgust, there is no such unity when it comes to speculations that try to account for its paradoxical allure. I spend some time sorting through confusions regarding the concept of pleasure before arguing for a position that seeks to accommodate many of the insights from other approaches. Despite the considerable differences of these various theorists, each of them contributes some insight into the aesthetic uses of disgust, though I believe none adequately covers all of them, a conclusion that reinforces the particularism advanced in chapter 4. In the pages to come, I try to honor the myriad varieties of disgust, including the rare times when its objects evoke reverence and awe, engendering an aesthetic quality comparable to the sublime. If the result is less systematic than a philosopher might be expected to endorse, it is (I hope) more adequate to account for the individual cases of disgust, especially as they arise in art and other aesthetic contexts.

Having reviewed a number of exemplary cases of aesthetic disgust and considered a set of theoretical speculations that seek to illuminate them, in chapter 6 I explore one widespread theme that can be found—in both disgusting and nondisgusting modes—in narrative and graphic art: the representation of the eviscerated human heart. The heart is an object of horror and revulsion when it is ripped from the body still warm and pulsing and bleeding—a scene frequently employed in horror movies. And yet there is no organ of the body more invested with meaning both secular and religious. Indeed, one need not turn only to representational art for support; historical practice itself provides ample evidence, as with the phenomenon of heart burial. Multifarious artistic renditions from ancient to contemporary artworks all make use of the resonant meanings of the heart, including when it is an object of disgust. This chapter demonstrates the subtle varieties of visceral response to this one theme, a range that extends from humor to horror, reverence to love, and where aesthetic qualities may extend to the gruesome, tender, delicate, crude, brutal, and transcendent.

Once one recognizes the tremendous range of valence that the arousal of disgust possesses, the rich function of this emotion in aesthetic encounters becomes apparent. Thus even though from some perspectives disgust represents in principle an aesthetic antithesis, I shall make the case that it occasionally contributes profoundly to experiences of artistic beauty. This is the thesis of chapter 7, where the varieties of aesthetic disgust are revisited to explore what role some might play in the achievement of the classic pinnacle of aesthetic value that beauty represents. Here I strive again to show the affinity of aesthetic disgust with traditional categories such as beauty and sublimity, and in so doing to explore the underlying meanings that encounters with this visceral aversion disclose.

I

What Is Disgust?

What kind of an emotion is disgust? What are its objects? What function does it have in our mental makeup, and what roles does
it play in our grasp of the world around us? This chapter aims to discover how disgust compares with other emotions in terms of its
structure, its operation, and the circumstances that prompt it. I begin
with a brief review of the reigning options for philosophical treatments of emotion before turning to the particular case of disgust and
the kind of theory that best suits its analysis.

Current philosophical theories of emotion are aligned very
roughly into two camps, one that stresses the connection of emotional responses to belief systems and cultures, and one that focuses
on their physical, reactive character. Those who emphasize the role
that emotions play in the social order are apt to connect affective
dispositions with patterns of learned behavior that reflect and per-
petuate ideologies, moral codes, and religious precepts. This line of
thinking stresses the degree to which emotions vary across societies
and throughout history. In contrast, those who emphasize the distinctive physiological features of emotional response are more disposed to take an approach that emphasizes the continuity of human
emotions with those of other animals, and to speculate about the
roles that emotions play—or once played—in the survival of the species. The latter theories tend to treat emotions as relatively constant
and uniform across different populations. I shall maintain that disgust, because of the immediacy and physicality of its operation, is
importantly analyzed in terms that stress its reactive, automatic

nature and its sensory triggers. This emphasis foregrounds the visceral power of this affect in both its ordinary contexts and its operation in art. However, I shall also argue that this approach by no means precludes acknowledgment of the cultural plasticity of this palpably embodied emotion, which, in its very physical and reflexive function, yet manifests extraordinary diversity.

Colloquially, emotions are spoken of as "feelings." However, feelings are subjective states that can be extremely difficult to describe, making this aspect of emotions by itself a tough subject for analysis. Partly because of this, philosophers tend not to stress subjective feeling in their treatments, focusing instead on physiological changes correlated with the advent of affective states, typical objects that trigger emotions, and the contributions of cognitive states such as beliefs and attitudes. Nonetheless, the quality of feeling induced by an emotion remains one of its most significant aspects, especially if one is interested in the aesthetic import of an emotion. I begin by examining the standard elements that are candidates for components of emotion, especially an emotion such as disgust.

Objects and Intentionality

Emotions are intentional. The philosophical use of the term "intention" in this context is not to be confused with its usual meaning of having an aim or purpose. "Intentional" refers to the directedness of mental states and events to some object or state of affairs.[1] Peter Goldie describes the intentionality of emotion as "feeling towards." "Feeling towards is *thinking of* with feeling, so that your emotional feelings are directed towards the object of your thought."[2] If one is afraid, one fears certain objects or occurrences; if one is angry, one is angry at some person or situation. Intentional states also may be directed inward, as is the case with shame when the object of shame is oneself. Indeed shame, like jealousy, envy, and guilt, has more than one object component. Minimally, the emotion is directed toward oneself plus the action of which one is ashamed. Envy is directed toward a person who possesses something one would like to have, but it spreads to include thwarted desire for the object and an awareness of oneself as lacking it. Often the intentional object of emotion may be expressed in propositional form. One might worry that one will not get home in time for a party, or be disappointed that the weather turned nasty, or anxious that one will not have enough money to provide for a family. In short, intentional objects can be physical things, persons, events, states of affairs, hypotheses, or ideas.

1. This modern usage was initiated by Franz Brentano, *Psychology from an Empirical Standpoint* (1874), ed. Linda L. McAlister (New York: Humanities Press, 1973).
2. Peter Goldie, *The Emotions: A Philosophical Exploration* (New York: Oxford University Press, 2002), 19.

Sometimes the intentional object of an emotion is also its triggering cause. If I am angry that you lost my watch, then your losing the watch is also the immediate cause of my anger.[3] But it is possible for there to be an underlying, even unacknowledged cause of the emotion, such as anxiety about money or attachment to the person who gave me the watch. In this case, the object of the emotion and its cause need to be distinguished, for the galvanizing influence for arousal has been displaced from its immediate object. I shall set aside issues of hidden or mediate causes for disgust until later in this study, for they enter most interestingly into interpretations of the meaning of the emotion. But even in cases where the cause and the object are identical, emotions require some preexisting condition that disposes one to respond. Human beings share many general dispositions, such as a preference for safety over danger (daredevils aside). Other dispositional states, such as a tendency to be phobic or irascible, are part of individual character and vary accordingly.[4]

Emotions can be individuated with reference to the characteristic properties of their exemplary intentional objects.[5] The typical intentional object of fear is something that has the property of being dangerous or fearsome, for example. In any particular instance of fear it is a specific dangerous thing, such as a menacing stranger or a rattlesnake. The general property that inspires disgust is rottenness or foulness, for this emotion is vividly focused on the sensory qualities of things one might ingest or touch. Intentional objects may be large and vague ("I am worried about the state of the world economy") or very specific ("I am angry about the dent in the fender of my new car"). They may be recurrent (frustration at a child's messiness) or single-instance (surprise at one's birthday party). If there is no specific object of an affective state, many theorists reclassify that state from an emotion to a mood. Depression, for example, can be considered a general lens through which the entire world seems glum. But to call the whole universe an "object" invokes so vast a scope that it hardly counts as naming an object at all, and hence the mental state is considered a mood rather than an emotion. (This issue is disputable; some theorists are inclined to consider the objects of moods vague and dispersed rather than absent.)

Feelings and Physiology

Emotions are also distinguished by how they feel to the person experiencing them. Emotions involve feelings because of the way they alter our subjective

---

3. Or, more precisely, the immediate external cause. For the moment I am not considering the various neural events that are necessary for an emotion to be triggered.

4. Amélie Rorty speaks of "magnetizing dispositions" as the context in which emotions are triggered. See her "Explaining Emotions," in *Explaining Emotions*, ed. Amélie Oksenberg Rorty (Berkeley and Los Angeles: University of California Press, 1980), 103–6.

5. Ronald de Sousa, *The Rationality of Emotions* (Cambridge, MA: MIT Press, 1987), chap. 5.

being, the way they agitate or enervate or energize, the way they clutch at the heart or constrict the throat or make us smile, the way they . . . well . . . *feel*. However, being intimate, subjective events, they are directly accessible only by introspection and are therefore hard to measure and assess; moreover, they may be inchoate and difficult to describe precisely.[6] As mentioned earlier, the suspicion that feelings are elusive and indeterminate has led many theorists to formulate definitions based upon other components of emotions. Indeed, some have gone so far as to argue that all emotions occur with undifferentiated arousal of the nervous system, and that the emotions become distinguished from one another not phenomenally but through cognitive assessments that appraise objects and environments.[7] It would be ironic if that which is experienced as the most important aspect of emotions, the way they feel, is too imprecise to contribute to their analysis. Luckily, that conclusion is not necessary, for no matter how private they may feel and no matter how we might guard against their betrayal on occasion, emotions are correlated with characteristic physiological reactions, including some that are apparent to others such as weeping or trembling.[8] There are other less public physical changes that summon attention when one is moved, such as the upset stomach that marks anxiety, or the hot rush of adrenaline that indicates anger, or the pounding pulse that is characteristic of both these agitations. Emotion can alter behavior, such as changes in posture or gait, comportment, and eating. While such manifestations of affect may be misinterpreted, they also provide familiar guides by which the "inner" states of other persons are apprehended, thus providing some public key to what individuals experience as subjective feelings.

In addition, there are many physiological markers of emotions that are difficult or impossible to recognize even by the person undergoing them. These require scientific instruments to discern: the measurement of the skin's conductance of electrical charge, for example, which is a subtle gauge of perspiration, or the activation of certain parts of the brain that can be observed through functional magnetic resonance imaging. While much of this research is still in early stages, scientists have documented some distinctive profiles of the neurophysiological changes that occur with specific emotions. The role of the amygdala in fear is well established, for instance.[9] One does not experience the amygdala per se, so while brain functions there have a causal role in fear, they are not part of the subjectivity of fear. However, sometimes physical correlates do appear to explain subjective aspects of emotion. For example, the metaphor "cold fear,"

6. Though introspection is often considered unreliable, it has its defenders. See Peter Vermersch, "Introspection as Practice," *Journal of Consciousness Studies* 6, nos. 2/3 (1999): 17–42.

7. For a history of developments within this approach and its eventual rejection, see Randolph R. Cornelius, *The Science of Emotion* (Upper Saddle River, NJ: Prentice-Hall, 1996), 78–94.

8. For a fine-tuned discussion of the relationship between feelings and expressions of emotions, see Anthony Kenny, *Action, Emotion and Will* (London: Routledge and Kegan Paul, 1963), chap. 3.

9. Joseph LeDoux, *The Emotional Brain* (New York: Simon and Schuster, 1996).

often used to describe the first-person subjective state ("It made my blood run cold!"), is not just poetic. Temperature measurably drops when one is afraid.

Disgust manifests its own characteristic bodily changes. Negative emotions and withdrawal responses are controlled by processes on the right hemisphere of the cerebral cortex, and disgust activates this region.[10] Recognition of disgust expressions in others occasions activity in the insula and the basal ganglia regions of the brain, and these areas also appear to govern the experience of disgust.[11] The insula is also implicated in the control of taste aversion and the perception of nauseating tastes, supporting the speculation that the emotion of disgust evolved from protective taste responses. When disgust is aroused, the heart rate slows, and blood pressure drops.[12] I doubt that many of us are aware of a decreased pulse when experiencing disgust, but we may be aware of a certain pause in the recoil, a tendency to dwell, albeit with loathing, over the disgusting object. This feature of disgust will be considered later in this chapter.

There is another quite evident element to the subjective component of emotions: most of them are either "positive" (such as joy) or "negative" (such as fear). In recognition of this fact, many emotion theorists include a positive-negative valence when unpacking the elements of emotions. Spinoza in his *Ethics*, for example, argued that all emotions are a mixture of desire, pleasure, and pain, mixed with the idea of an intentional object, an early version of the idea that emotions begin with undifferentiated arousal and become particularized according to their objects. Also included in the valence of emotions is the comfort or discomfort they prompt, and a consequent desire that the intentional object persist, disappear, or change.[13] Those who strive to program computers to recognize emotions stipulate positivity or negativity when they specify which emotion is to be registered.[14] By any account, the pleasure-pain valence of disgust is strongly weighted on the pain side, for it is an aversion with built-in physical recoil. As one researcher notes, "It would be difficult to generate approach tendencies toward an object that elicits disgust. Similarly, it would be difficult to develop withdrawal tendencies toward stimuli that are strongly appetitive."[15] Aversive it is, but one of the enigmas of disgust lies in the fact

10. Cornelius, *Science of Emotion*, 230. The appendix to Cornelius's book, "The Neurophysiology of Emotion," is a useful general guide to the nervous system and emotional activities.

11. Andrew J. Calder, Andrew D. Lawrence, and Andrew W. Young, "Neuropathology of Fear and Loathing," *Nature Reviews: Neuroscience*, May 2001, 359–60.

12. Experiments show differentiated autonomic nervous system activity for six basic emotions: anger, fear, sadness, happiness, surprise, and disgust. See Paul Ekman, Robert W. Levenson, and Wallace V. Friesen, "Autonomic Nervous System Activity Distinguishes among Emotions," *Science* 221 (September 1983): 1208–10; Robert W. Levenson, Paul Ekman, and Wallace V. Friesen, "Voluntary Facial Action Generates Emotion-Specific Autonomic Nervous System Activity," *Psychophysiology* 27, no. 4 (1990): 363–84.

13. Patricia S. Greenspan, *Emotions and Reasons: An Inquiry into Emotional Justification* (New York: Routledge, 1988).

14. Rosalind Picard, *Affective Computing* (Cambridge, MA: MIT Press, 1997).

15. Richard J. Davidson, "Complexities in the Search for Emotion-Specific Physiology," in *The Nature of Emotion*, ed. Paul Ekman and Richard J. Davidson (New York: Oxford University Press, 1994), 239.

that the emotion can also attract; therefore the occasions when it beckons and fascinates are especially intriguing.

Cognition

That emotions are intentional states directed toward objects is a widely accepted thesis of both philosophical and scientific theories. So is the fact that they often feel a certain way to us, and the presence of distinctive physiological and behavioral profiles for different emotions helps us to understand them beyond what we experience and strain to describe subjectively. However, the next candidate for a requisite emotion component has become a matter of considerable contention. Presently researchers disagree about whether cognitive states such as beliefs and propositional attitudes are also necessary to ground emotions and regulate their occurrence.

Certainly there are propositional objects of emotions, as is the case when one hopes that the sun will shine tomorrow. This is indisputable. The controversy arises over the thesis that, no matter what its intentional object, a full emotion also typically comprises elements that include beliefs or propositionally formed "thoughts." An emotion such as grief, for example, may be directed to a person, but it also presupposes a belief that a terrible loss has occurred. But there are other emotions such as surprise that occur without any pertinent grounding belief. Surprise and certain kinds of fear employ the startle reflex, which is virtually involuntary even when one expects a startling event to happen.[16] What is more, emotions may occur despite the presence of a countervailing belief. One may experience fear in the presence of a snake that one knows to be harmless, for instance, or apprehension in a bouncing airplane even though one believes the situation to be no more dangerous than a bumpy road.

To understand the relative importance given such examples, we need to place the examination of emotions in a larger context, for the dispute over the propositional content of emotions pivots around theories of the role of emotions in the acquisition of knowledge and the grounds for their defense as intelligent and vital aspects of mental life. Explaining this comment requires some history.

Traditionally, emotions have enjoyed a spotty reputation. Most Western philosophy has exalted reason as the supreme human capacity that separates us from other animals and makes possible the development of abstract knowledge, moral judgment, science, technology, and culture. Emotions are often regarded as rivals to reason and therefore as forces of irrationality that interrupt the progress of knowledge or morality or sound judgment. One thinks of insane jealousy or paralyzing fear or blind love as examples that capture in

---

16. Jenefer Robinson, "Startle," *Journal of Philosophy* 92, no. 2 (1995): 53–74. Robinson argues that startle should be understood at least as a "proto-emotion."

their very descriptions the competition with reason that emotions can represent. It is by no means the case that all philosophers have dismissed emotion or recommended that it be expunged from one's mental landscape, though some schools of thought such as Stoicism have reached that conclusion. The majority have either counseled the cultivation of emotions in judicious and moderate form, such as Aristotle did, or have simply neglected to consider them worthy of extended philosophical interest. Even the most sympathetic philosophical treatments almost unanimously have maintained that emotions require the governance and guidance of reason. This point of view has sometimes led to the idea that emotions are *only* to be governed, at best providing energy and motivation to act at the behest of reason.

When interest in emotions reignited in the latter part of the twentieth century, philosophers often began by arguing against the traditional bad reputation of emotions in comparison to reason.[17] The recognition of a propositional component of emotions is one means to correct the view that emotions are unreliable upheavals of the mind. What are sometimes called "cognitivist" theories argue that a full, complete emotion arises in a context where some propositionally formulated thought grounds and explains its occurrence. By such accounts fear, for instance, entails holding a belief that one is in danger. I may be in danger from an approaching stranger, but if I do not recognize this fact, I do not fear him. No belief, no emotion. Conversely, I may fear an apparently rabid dog that is simply drooling from the heat. In this case, my belief is incorrect, but the fear is prompted by it anyway. An advantage of the requirement of belief is that it provides a clear way to certify emotions as reasonable or to discredit them as irrational. If the belief prompting the emotion is warranted, then the emotion is warranted—is "rational" if you will. If the belief is crazy or ill founded, then so is the emotion. A proposition need not be true in order for an emotion to be justified. It is sufficient that there be reasonable grounds for believing that it is true. Moreover, theorists do not always require that the propositional attitude be as strong as a belief. We might simply entertain a thought that something is the case or is a possibility. (Indeed some emotions occur only without belief that the situation described by their propositional objects is true, such as a hope that one is not ill.)[18] Whether propositions are believed or simply held in mind, they are important components to full-fledged emotions, according to this line of thought.

---

17. Examples: Robert C. Solomon, *The Passions* (Garden City, NY: Anchor/Doubleday, 1976); William E. Lyons, *Emotion* (Cambridge: Cambridge University Press, 1980); Robert M. Gordon, *The Structure of Emotions: Investigations in Cognitive Philosophy* (Cambridge: Cambridge University Press, 1987); Greenspan, *Emotions and Reason*; De Sousa, *Rationality of Emotions*. It should be noted that the rise of general philosophical attention to emotion at this time significantly correlates with the rise of feminist philosophical critiques of the discipline, many of which are directed to the centrality of rationality in philosophical systems.

18. See Robert Gordon's distinction between "epistemic" and "factive" emotions in *The Structure of Emotions*, chap. 2.

As the foregoing review indicates, the commonly used term for theories that maintain a propositional component to emotions is "cognitivism."[19] However, there is much confusion bought with this term, for the rival approach that holds that at least some emotions occur in the absence of propositional thought also recognizes them as important sources of information and insight. To call these "noncognitivist" theories would suggest that they do not recognize the intelligence of emotions and their role in the formation of knowledge, which would be inaccurate. To avoid this implication, some prefer the term "propositional attitude" theories to designate those otherwise called "cognitivist."[20] And indeed, the outright dismissal of emotions as irrational does not represent a viable position. That is to say, no serious theorist, whether scientist or philosopher, social constructionist or evolutionary biologist, considers emotions simply to be dumb. The question is not *can* emotions provide insight but, rather: *What form* does the "intelligence" of emotions take? In what way does "cognition" or "knowledge" enter into their formation and motivate the behavior they generate?

The propositional requirement is flatly denied by those who argue that cognitivism has gone too far in its strategy to vindicate emotions, and that certain emotions—including fear and disgust—are better understood as modular reactions to immediate stimuli. A rabbit freezes in fear in the presence of a fox, but lacking language, it is unlikely to entertain propositional beliefs. Rational assessment is relatively slow and therefore counterfunctional for a creature in danger. If the rabbit were to take the time to formulate a proposition about the proximity of the fox before reacting in fear, it would be dinner. Therefore the "intelligent" element of emotions does not lie in higher-order cognition but in dispositions to react appropriately to galvanizing circumstances. This point of view gains further support from research indicating that emotional responses can occur from stimuli that appear to the subject too fleetingly to be registered consciously, suggesting that what emotions respond to need not always be available for propositional formulation.[21] According to this approach, while human brains are more complex than those of other animals, permitting us to refine the representation of emotions and their objects in language and other expressive forms, the emotions themselves unfold from aspects of neurophysiology that are antecedent to an ability to articulate them in propositional form.

From this thumbnail sketch it is clear that the two ways to understand cognitive elements in emotions differ considerably. The first places cognition

19. John Deigh, "Cognitivism in the Theory of Emotions," *Ethics* 104 (1994): 824–54. Jesse Prinz reviews several possible meanings of "cognitive," noting that even cognitive science has neglected to clarify this key term. See Prinz, *Gut Reactions: A Perceptual Theory of Emotions* (Oxford: Oxford University Press, 2004), 41–45.

20. This is the usage suggested by Paul Griffiths, *What Emotions Really Are* (Chicago: University of Chicago Press, 1997), 2–3.

21. J. S. Morris, A. Ohman, and R. J. Dolan, "Conscious and Unconscious Emotional Learning in the Human Amygdala," *Nature* 393 (1998): 467–70. See also Jenefer Robinson, *Deeper Than Reason: Emotion and Its Role in Literature, Music, and Art* (Oxford: Oxford University Press, 2005), pt. 1.

in conscious understanding that can be articulated in language. So understood, it would be an aspect only of human emotions, on the assumption that only humans (and perhaps a few other primates) are capable of formulating propositions and entertaining beliefs or belief-like intentional states. The second position stresses the continuity of emotional life with dispositions shared with other animals.[22] We might consider the latter account to provide a poor defense against the charge that emotions are unreliable rivals to reason. However, quick reactions are neither irrational nor stupid. Fleeing from danger is a smart thing to do, though it does not necessarily bespeak higher cortical functions. And of course rapid responses may be the basis on which propositional understanding is founded. Here is another way to state the disagreement: whether the propositional attitude is a prerequisite for the emotion to come into being, or whether the emotion occurs first, and the belief is formulated later if at all.

Where does disgust fall within the terms of this controversy? Does it presuppose beliefs about the loathsomeness of certain types of objects? Some instances of disgust clearly are grounded in beliefs, and those beliefs themselves are embedded in cultural values. Therefore, however automatic and reactive the disgust response is, at least some of its activity requires a cultural account to understand. Living within a religious milieu that prohibits the eating of pork, for example, inculcates the belief that pork is inappropriate food. The relevant cognitive assessments become exceptionally strong evaluations, such as "pig products are abominable." The assessment also takes a strong visceral form: the smell of bacon is nauseating, the sight of a pork chop repulsive. Upon discovering that one has accidentally eaten pork, perhaps in the form of a hot dog or other composite food believed to have been made of something else, one may feel retrospective nausea and be disgusted by the past event of eating pork. (Let us set aside for the moment the possibility that such disgust may be accompanied by a furtive desire to transgress dietary laws.) In this sort of case, the emotion depends upon a preexisting belief that certain substances are foul and in the "inedible" category.

However, there is little reason to think that disgust permits a solely cultural account. Disgust has a strongly reactive or reflex character; it can be more immediate than conscious rational assessment, as, for example, when one recoils from the reek of decomposing flesh before actually recognizing what it is. In a case such as this it is unlikely that one is reacting from a belief that something is in the category of foul and revolting objects. The disgust is the first response, and propositional assessment of the foulness of the intentional object is premised upon the emotive reaction rather than vice versa.

What is more, disgust is stubborn, often persisting despite knowledge that its object does not merit the response—unlike grief, for instance, where the

22. John Deigh raises the problem of accounting for intentionality in humans and animals in the same terms in "Primitive Emotions," in *Thinking about Feeling*, ed. Robert Solomon (Oxford: Oxford University Press, 2004), 9–27.

discovery that one was mistaken that a grievous event occurred causes the emotion to vanish. Psychologist Paul Rozin and his colleagues have conducted wicked experiments that offer subjects chocolate shaped like feces. Even when subjects learn that the shapes are made from a substance that is acceptable—even delicious—they refuse to transfer them to the "nondisgusting" category.[23] When disgust lingers in the face of contrary corrective knowledge, it displays the old rivalry between reason and emotion.

In short, many of the traits that define disgust qualify it as a basic emotion strongly inflected by sensory reactions and automatic physical responses. This is a feature of disgust that needs foregrounding in order to account for both the aesthetic power of this emotion and the philosophical discredit it has received—a discredit that (as we shall see in the next chapter) far exceeds the discipline's traditional suspicion of emotions in general. The following section considers what type of emotion theory best accommodates disgust, moving from there to consider the panoply of objects considered disgusting and the distinctive subjectivity of disgust.

The Physiology of Disgust

As this study progresses into the worlds of art, the examples of disgust will become more complicated and more obviously reliant on cultural understanding. But even for those cases, it is important to retain attention to the somatic power of this emotion and therefore its governing physiology.

Disgust is on the list of what some psychologists label "basic" emotions, which also include versions of anger, fear, surprise, joy, and sadness.[24] Basic emotions are pancultural, meaning that they are experienced by members of all societies, and that aspects of their expression are recognized by social groups throughout the world.[25] They are accompanied by standard physical reactions, including cringing, blinking, heart rate, skin conductance of electrical charge, and a typical facial expression that displays the emotion to others. For disgust, this expression features a wrinkled nose and a pursed or open mouth pulled down at the corners. As a rule patterns of display of these emotions are common across cultures, and their facial expressions are readily recognized. Because of their activation in the limbic system and their distinctive profiles in autonomic nervous system activity, basic emotions are considered more automatic and involuntary than complex, reflective emotions.

23. Paul Rozin, Jonathan Haidt, and Clark R. McCauley, "Disgust," in *Handbook of Emotions*, ed. Michael Lewis and Jeannette M. Haviland (New York: Guilford Press, 1993), 583. For a cautionary view, see Richard J. McNally, "Disgust Has Arrived," *Anxiety Disorders* 16 (2002): 561–66.
24. The number of basic emotions varies by theorist. There are many who dispute the soundness of the idea of basic emotions at all. See Ekman and Davidson, *The Nature of Emotion*, 5–47. In this volume Klaus R. Sherer notes that most languages include terms for what are considered basic emotions: "Toward a Concept of Modal Emotions," 25.
25. Paul Ekman, "Facial Expressions of Emotion: An Old Controversy and New Findings," *Philosophical Transactions: Biological Sciences* 335, no. 1273 (1992): 63–69.

Those who focus on the physiology of emotions tend to be sympathetic to evolutionary perspectives, which analyze basic emotions as adaptive patterns of response that are sensitive to objects with significance for an organism's well-being. In the case of the highly sensory disgust response, natural selection has programmed us for quick, protective recoil from things that smell or taste foul or are repellent to touch, and where ingestion or contact may be dangerous or noxious.[26] Evidence for this surmise can be found in the fact that objects identified as disgust elicitors across the globe, such as feces, pus, sexual fluids, and parasites, are also disease-bearing substances.[27] Because it is difficult to ascertain when a substance is actually poisonous or unhealthy, the scope of objects that provoke disgust is protectively greater than is necessary in any given instance. Better to avoid safe substances unnecessarily than to risk contamination. Thus what appears to be an irrational aspect of disgust, namely, that its range of objects far exceeds those that are truly infectious or toxic, is in fact a kind of protective umbrella with an important adaptive function.

Though all agree on the strongly sensory nature of disgust, there is dispute about just which sense is the core trigger. Following Darwin, who posited that the facial expression typical of disgust is a variation of the gape that accompanies vomiting,[28] many theorists treat disgust as a response to tastes that signal inedible substances; others consider smell more central. Taste and smell, of course, are highly coordinated senses.

Appeals to evolution focus on emotions that admit relatively simple versions, which disgust (in contrast to embarrassment, pity, or nostalgia) in fact does. Support for this approach is provided by the fact that such emotions are governed from a part of the brain that is considered to have evolved long before the cerebral cortex: the region sometimes called the limbic system that contains the cingulate gyrus, the hypothalamus, the amygdala, the insula, and the basal ganglia.[29] Only minimal sensory stimuli are needed to trigger responses in this area. For instance, a baby chick with no experience of birds of prey will duck and hide its head when a broad-winged shadow passes above it. The chick has no beliefs about hawks and a very small birdbrain, yet it displays an immediate

26. Carroll Izard surmises that "in evolution, disgust probably helped motivate organisms to maintain an environment sufficiently sanitary for their health and to prevent them from eating spoiled food and drinking polluted water." Izard, *Human Emotions* (New York: Plenum Press, 1977), 337. Nico Frijda observes that the functional role of disgust "reduces sensory contact with distasteful substances in the mouth cavity and tends toward expelling those substances." Frijda, *The Emotions* (Cambridge: Cambridge University Press, 1986), 11.

27. Valerie Curtis and Adam Biran, "Dirt, Disgust, and Disease: Is Hygiene in Our Genes?" *Perspectives in Biology and Medicine* 44, no. 1 (2001): 17–31. See also the massive Internet-based study conducted in Britain in 2003, reported at www.bbc.co.uk/science/human body/mind/surveys/disgust.

28. Charles Darwin, *The Expression of Emotions in Man and Animals* (1872) (Chicago: University of Chicago Press, 1965), 256–58.

29. This region manages what neurologist Antonio Damasio terms "primary" emotions, those that require little reflective consciousness and appear to be rather hardwired in the brain, since they substantially involve the autonomic nervous system. By the designation "primary" Damasio refers to innate, "preorganized" responses of avoidance or confrontation that can develop into fully formed emotions in human awareness (at which point higher conscious activity is required). Damasio, *Descartes' Error: Emotion, Reason, and the Human Brain* (New York: Avon Books, 1995), 131–34.

fear reaction to appropriate stimulation. Insofar as human emotions display this sort of automatic response, their arousal bypasses rational processes.

The brand of emotion theory that puts the greatest stress on their physiological triggers and their independence from conscious assessment is affect program theory.[30] "Affect" refers to the changes an organism undergoes in response to circumstances of arousal; "program" connotes an inborn propensity to respond and behave more or less automatically. Affect programs, so understood, are subject to a degree of learning, but they set patterns of rapid response that do not depend on higher-level cognitive systems. As such, they are "modular" mental activities, prompting quick response to a situation before slower rational deliberation can make its assessment. Paul Griffiths offers this picture of the affect program emotions:

> These emotions consist of complex, coordinated, and automated responses. . . . There is a flow of perceptual information to the mechanisms controlling these responses which is separate from the flow of information from perception to the higher cognitive processes responsible for intentional action. . . . In some cases higher cognitive processes may be able to trigger emotional responses directly, but in other cases the associations which lead to the response must be separate from the evaluations made by higher cognition.[31]

Affect program theory emerges from contemporary psychology, but the idea that emotions are faster and more automatic than reason is not new. In 1757 Edmund Burke wrote:

> Whenever the wisdom of our Creator intended that we should be affected with any thing, he did not confide the execution of his design to the languid and precarious operation of our reason; but he endued it with powers and properties that prevent the understanding, and even the will, which seizing upon the senses and imagination, captivate the soul before the understanding is ready either to join with them or to oppose them.[32]

In other words, the function of emotions to convey particularly pressing information speedily has been recognized for a long time.

---

30. This is the term used by psychologist Paul Ekman; he attributes its origin to Sylvan Tomkins (Ekman, "Biological and Cultural Contributions to Body and Facial Movement in the Expression of Emotions," in Rorty, *Explaining Emotions*, 101 n. 8). The term is adopted by philosopher Paul Griffiths in *What Emotions Really Are* to refer to emotions that are rooted in limbic-centered responses. Griffiths argues that "emotion" is not a term that survives scientific scrutiny, since the many mental states we refer to as emotions differ too much to be usefully categorized as instances of a single genus. See also Griffiths, "Are Emotions Natural Kinds?" in Solomon, *Thinking about Feeling*.

31. Griffiths, *What Emotions Really Are*, 93. Griffiths adopts the term "modular" from Jerry Fodor, *The Modularity of Mind* (Cambridge, MA: MIT Press, 1983).

32. Edmund Burke, *A Philosophical Enquiry into the Origin of Our Ideas of the Sublime and Beautiful* (1757), ed. James T. Boulton (Notre Dame, IN: University of Notre Dame Press, 1968), 107.

Affect program theory aptly captures the immediacy and physicality of disgust, and portions of this analysis are useful to retain in our understanding of this emotion. However, the reactive aspects of disgust have also led some theorists erroneously to conclude that it is a relatively simple and primitive response, a judgment that does not do justice to its complexity.[33] Moreover, an approach that stresses modularity is also disposed to insulate emotions from cultural variation. Griffiths, for instance, describes affect programs as "phylogenetically ancient, informationally encapsulated, reflexlike responses which seem to be insensitive to culture."[34] But disgust is clearly not insensitive to culture, even relative to other types of emotion. Therefore, this approach is limited in its capacity to account for the full range of disgust, including its puzzling aesthetic capacities.

If cognitivism overestimates the coordination of emotions with rational judgments, affect program theory locks them too intransigently into reaction patterns. Useful middle ground is offered by two other approaches that, in effect, revise the insights of each perspective and present overall pictures of emotions that better accommodate affective flexibility while at the same time retaining the embodied character of emotions, a pressing necessity in the case of disgust.

Affective Appraisals and Embodied Judgments

In this section of discussion I put together two approaches that are often construed as rivals: the noncognitivist theories of Jenefer Robinson and Jesse Prinz, and the cognitivist views of Robert Solomon and Martha Nussbaum. Without minimizing differences among their views, I think it fair to say that they come to many of the same insights from different directions.

Jenefer Robinson, whose work also derives substantial support from the evidence of psychological studies, argues that emotions are, at root, automatic affective appraisals. She maintains that the fundamental prerequisite for an emotion is a physiological change that marks its advent. Not all emotions require conscious cognition, but they all do require physiological disturbances. Therefore, one must make those changes foundational to an emotion theory.[35]

33. Jaak Panksepp, for example, believes that the neurobiology of animals is the key to understanding the more primitive human emotions, including disgust: "There are the very low-level emotive responses that are almost reflexive, such as startle, disgust, and the various hungers, that are time locked with precipitating conditions (though they may come to have metaphoric representations in higher cognitive sentiments, as in surprise and social contempt)." Panksepp, "The Basics of Basic Emotions," in Ekman and Davidson, eds., *The Nature of Emotion*, 23.

34. Griffiths, *What Emotions Really Are*, 16. By calling affect programs insensitive to cultural variation, Griffiths means that these emotions are constant across populations, that they have the same autonomic nervous system profiles, that their arousal displays the same musculoskeletal changes, that they arouse the same kinds of facial expressions, the same heart rate changes, and so on. He does not mean that exactly the same things arouse disgust for all people in all societies.

35. Jenefer Robinson, "Emotion: Biological Fact or Social Construction?" in Solomon, *Thinking about Feeling*, 28–43.

Robinson disconnects emotions from judgments about their objects, because one can arrive at the very same judgment in the absence of affect.[36] For example, I can note that someone is insulting me without feeling resentful or indignant. Moreover, one can experience an affect in the absence of a judgment, as when one is agitated over an event despite the fact that one judges it to be trivial. The independence of the advent of an emotion from conscious judgment is a feature of her theory that agrees with affect program analysis, though she also argues that emotions involve conscious assessment as they unfold.

Robinson proposes that emotions are processes with increasing levels of complexity. The necessary first stage consists of an affective, noncognitive appraisal that occurs very fast, even possibly below the threshold of awareness. This produces physiological changes of the sort already reviewed with affect program theory. But this is just an initial stage, for on the heels of noncognitive affective appraisal comes what she terms "cognitive monitoring."[37] Fully developed emotions result from a process that involves registering and monitoring their first stages and evaluating their significance in relation to information gained from other sources and from memories. With monitoring, emotional tenor can dissipate, focus, or alter. The latter stages afford the opportunity for culture to influence emotion, including by providing the concepts by which we categorize emotions and understand their significance.

Jesse Prinz formulates an emotion theory that similarly stresses the significance of bodily change, as is indicated by the title of his book: *Gut Reactions*. He refers to emotions as "embodied appraisals," perceptions of bodily changes that bear upon an organism's well-being. Cognitive evaluations also do this, but emotions do so not by deploying concepts but by responding somatically to the environment. "Our perceptions of the body tell us about our organs and limbs, but they also carry information about how we are faring," he states.[38] This means that emotions have meaning—have semantic content—that is delivered by the bodily changes that define them.

Accounts of emotions in terms of the significance of the physical changes they entail revive an older approach to emotion. In the late nineteenth century, William James (and independently the Danish psychologist Carl Lange) argued that an emotion is actually best understood as the perception of bodily changes. This proposal appeared outrageous at the time, since it would make the emotions the effect rather than the cause of their bodily symptoms, and it seems much more sensible to think that my fear causes me to tremble, rather than trembling causing me to fear. But James posed a telling rhetorical question:

---

36. Throughout this book I use "emotion" and "affect" interchangeably. These terms are sometimes separated and given distinct meanings, as with Susan Feagin, *Reading with Feeling: The Aesthetics of Appreciation* (Ithaca, NY: Cornell University Press, 1996).

37. Robinson, *Deeper Than Reason*, chap. 3.

38. Jesse Prinz, "Embodied Emotions," in Solomon, *Thinking about Feeling*, 57.

Can you imagine being afraid in the total absence of physical symptoms such as rapid pulse, trembling, or shallow breathing? Recent theories are more inclined to agree that some physical register is absolutely required for there to be an emotion, and the so-called James-Lange hypothesis is now regarded more kindly by those who emphasize the physiological changes correlated with mental states, including both Robinson and Prinz.[39]

Embodied appraisals that are cognitively monitored—to combine two terms from Prinz's and Robinson's accounts—can progress to a point where emotions act as reflective evaluations. This observation is the starting point for theories that argue that emotions themselves should be fundamentally understood not as physical responses but as judgments. Judgment theorists such as Robert Solomon and Martha Nussbaum maintain that emotions are the affective means by which we come to assess objects and events. This is an avowedly cognitivist approach, but unlike the brand of cognitivism discussed earlier, judgment theory does not construe propositional understanding as an invariably necessary component of emotions. Rather, it is the entire emotion itself, including the bodily changes that register the importance of an event or object, that constitutes the evaluative judgment. Part of the disagreement between embodied or affective appraisal theories and evaluative judgment theories refers to the degree to which emotions are located as bodily responses as opposed to mental assessments. While such judgments might be grounded in propositional understanding, they might also be the immediate recognition of patterns of value that form the basis for articulated reflective judgments. Solomon's "existentialist" perspective grants that emotions involve bodily responses, but their physiology does not capture what is important about emotions, which attach us to the world around us, inform us about what is going on, and supply instruments of evaluation. As he puts it, "Emotions are subjective engagements in the world."[40] Nussbaum, who maintains what she terms a "neo-Stoic" approach, endorses a cognitive-evaluative view, noting that emotions are "forms of evaluative judgment that ascribe to certain things and persons outside a person's own control great importance for the person's own flourishing."[41] These theories do not see emotions as merely "hot cognition," for they are more than beliefs-plus-feeling. Rather, they are distinct modes of apprehending value.

Both the embodied appraisal approach and the cognitive-evaluative theory place emphasis on the engagement of the body with emotions. The former lays more stress on automatic aspects of physiological reactions, while the latter

39. Also see Antonio Damasio, *The Feeling of What Happens: Body and Emotion in the Making of Consciousness* (San Diego: Harcourt, 1999), 287–89; Paul Redding, *The Logic of Affect* (Ithaca, NY: Cornell University Press, 1999) chaps. 1–2.

40. Solomon, "Emotions, Thoughts, and Feelings," in Solomon, *Thinking about Feeling*, 77.

41. Martha Nussbaum, *Upheavals of Thought: The Intelligence of Emotions* (Cambridge: Cambridge University Press, 2001), 22.

stress the evaluative meaning that physical changes register.[42] The manner in which Prinz articulates appraisals, in which it is the bodily feeling itself that possesses semantic content, indicates an especially useful way to understand aesthetic apprehensions involving disgust. Insights from both approaches need to be retained as we delve more deeply into the operation of disgust and the significance of its exemplary objects.

Disgusting Objects

Basic visceral disgust induces recoil from objects that are foul and polluting, such as putrifying organic matter, eviscerated bodies, and the swarms of devouring vermin that surge to finish what death, illness, or rot has initiated. Such objects trigger an affective state that is closely tied to involuntary physical responses such as the gag reflex, nausea, and even vomiting. The power and immediacy of this recoil qualify disgust as a reactive response built into our basic biology that functions as a somatic evaluation of its objects. Those objects include aspects of the human body that operate at its margins, such as its orifices and fluids—holes and leakages that appear to compromise the intact, self-contained, *clean* body. The intentional direction of this emotion is usually toward literal objects rather than propositions—a terrible taste or a foul odor, a lump of decomposing flesh, a squirming nest of maggots— though the intention easily spreads propositionally to the idea that the object may come too close and contaminate one. Because the proximity of the aversive object is requisite for its arousal, disgust is typically an occurrent emotion, an affective state that is interruptive and present to consciousness. One of the earliest psychologists to study disgust, stressing the need for proximity between subject and object, also notes "that the nucleus of the disgust reaction, the main threat against which disgust is directed, is the oral incorporation of certain substances."[43] This link between disgust and the sense of taste is endorsed by later researchers who believe that disgust originates in distaste but rapidly spreads to register noxious substances and even behaviors of all kinds.[44]

Unusual among emotions, disgust virtually requires sensory input, especially from the bodily senses of smell, touch, or taste, though vision can evoke

42. There may be less distance between these two approaches than at first appears. At the American Philosophical Association meeting in Chicago in April, 2007, at a memorial session honoring the late Robert Solomon, both Jenefer Robinson and Jesse Prinz remarked on the degree of agreement between their views and Solomon's.

43. Andras Angyal, "Disgust and Related Aversions," *Journal of Abnormal and Social Psychology* 36 (1941): 394.

44. Paul Rozin, Jonathan Haidt, Clark McCauley, and Sumio Imada, "Disgust: Preadaptation and the Cultural Evolution of a Food-Based Emotion," in *Food Preferences and Taste: Continuity and Change,* ed. Helen Macbeth (Providence, RI: Berghahn Books, 1997), 65–82.

disgust fairly easily by engaging the synaesthetic imagination. As William Ian Miller describes this feature,

> What the idiom of disgust demands is reference to the senses. It is about what it feels like to touch, see, taste, smell, even on occasion hear, certain things. Disgust cannot dispense with direct reference to the sensory processing of its elicitors. All emotions are launched by sense perception; only disgust makes that process of perceiving the core of the enterprise.[45]

Rather than taste, Miller finds smell and touch to be the core senses whose offense occasions disgust. Foul objects stink and nauseate; they are slithery, gooey, sticky, and oozing. These sensory properties signify the processes that produce them, as disgusting things fester and rot. The cycle of death to life is manifest in objects that disgust, for the decay of organic material invites microbes and vermin, which feed and reproduce with exorbitant fecundity. In the region of life and death, what seems at first to be a relatively primitive and simple affect becomes culturally sensitive. As Miller observes:

> Here we have the most embodied and visceral of emotions, and yet even when it is operating in and around the body, its orifices and excreta, a world of meaning explodes, coloring, vivifying, and contaminating political, social, and moral meanings. Disgust for all its visceralness turns out to be one of our more aggressive culture-creating passions.[46]

The role of disgust as a "culture-creating passion" will become especially evident in subsequent chapters when we consider its role in art, but even in its ordinary practical function, disgust possesses manifest social valence. For example, the lists of primary elicitors include menstrual blood, an aspect of womanhood that in many contexts identifies female bodies with the disgusting, an association that is evident in religious and social practices as well as art.[47] This example is one among many indicating that the link between disgust and cleanliness, while apparently universal, is by no means enacted uniformly.[48] Certain cultures such as those of Hindu India, for example, are more assiduous than others about protection from contamination.

The categories of objects (if not the specific objects) that are exemplary for disgust appear to be remarkably similar across history and societies.[49] Psychologist

45. William Ian Miller, *The Anatomy of Disgust* (Cambridge, MA: Harvard University Press, 1987), 36.

46. Miller, *Anatomy of Disgust*, xii.

47. Elizabeth Grosz, *Volatile Bodies: Towards a Corporeal Feminism* (Bloomington: Indiana University Press, 1994), 204–6.

48. The idea of boundary violation is central to anthropologist Mary Douglas's analysis of the notion of "purity" as well as the impurity that triggers disgust. See Douglas, *Purity and Danger: An Analysis of the Concepts of Pollution and Taboo* (London: Routledge and Kegan Paul, 1966). Her work has been influential for many who study the cultural uses of disgust, including Julia Kristeva's notion of the "abject," to be considered in chapter 5.

49. Curtis and Biran, "Dirt, Disgust, and Disease," stress this cross-cultural commonality. See also "Oh, Yuck!" *Discover*, December 2002, 32–34.

Paul Rozin and his colleagues identify the most basic sensory triggers for disgust as noxious tastes and smells. These arouse what they call core disgust, which is "revulsion at the prospect of (oral) incorporation of an offensive object. The offensive objects are contaminants, that is, if they even briefly contact an acceptable food, they tend to render that food unacceptable."[50] The mouth is an especially sensitive zone for the trigger of disgust, and indeed distaste may be the phylogenetic origin of disgust. Infants display typical facial expressions when given a bitter substance to taste, and bitterness is characteristic of many poisons. Not all disgust at food is innate, however, for most food preferences within social groups prescribe a far narrower scope of acceptability than the range of edible substances. North Americans rarely eat larvae, for example, and many consider them utterly disgusting; but they are both edible and nutritious. Even taste-based disgust has a strong learned component.

The root of disgust in distaste is just the beginning, for complex targets for the emotion issue from that point. Rozin, Jonathan Haidt, and Clark McCauley have identified six other categories of disgust elicitors. In addition to (1) contaminated foods, disgusting objects include (2) bodily products such as vomit, pus, mucus, sexual fluids, and excrement; (3) related violations of hygiene codes; (4) lower-order animals such as vermin; (5) violations of the bodily envelope such as wounds or evisceration; (6) perverse sexual activities; and—hovering over it all—(7) signs of death and decay.[51] As noted earlier, many of the substances singled out as disgusting are also disease carriers, such as decomposing bodies and excrement, so the idea that disgust is functionally protective is borne out with this list of elicitors. However, this explanation is clearly limited, for many violations of purity cannot be traced to avoidance of disease, as subsequent examples will indicate.

These categories range from very basic visceral reactions such as nausea to highly cognitive assessments such as moral recoil. Because of the expansion of disgust from sensory offense to other targets, these researchers stress the role of conceptual frameworks in identifying objects that disgust.[52] They are inclined to add to the list of elicitors (8) violations of the social-moral code. However, the categories of ethical violation do not test as consistently as the other elicitors of disgust, a fact that supports the suspicion I expressed in the introduction that what is called moral disgust is often a metaphorical extension of the language of this emotion.[53] On the other hand, there is good reason to

50. Paul Rozin and April E. Fallon, "A Perspective on Disgust," *Psychological Review* 94, no. 1 (1987): 23.

51. Jonathan Haidt, Clark McCauley, and Paul Rozin, "Individual Differences in Sensitivity to Disgust: A Scale Sampling Seven Domains of Disgust Elicitors," *Personality and Individual Differences* 16, no. 5 (1994): 701–13.

52. Rozin et al., "Disgust: Preadaptation," 67.

53. Haidt, McCauley, and Rozin attempted to include sociomoral gauges in their experiments with disgust responses but found no reliable correlations in their data—except for moral behaviors pertaining to sex ("Individual Differences in Sensitivity to Disgust," 703). For speculation that moral disgust actually evolved from oral distaste, see H. A. Chapman, D. A. Kim, J. M. Susskind, and A. K. Anderson, "In Bad Taste: Evidence for the Oral Origins of Moral Disgust," *Science* 323 (February 27, 2009): 1222–26.

expect an overlap between core and moral disgust on those occasions of injurious treatment when disgust is brought about by human agency with violent purpose. Miller puts this vividly:

> Disgust . . . operates in a kind of miasmic gloom, in the realm of horror, in regions of dark unbelievability, and never too far away from the body's and, by extension, the self's interiors. Disgust deals with harms that sicken us in the telling, things for which there could be no plausible claim of right: rape, child abuse, torture, genocide, predatory murder and maiming.[54]

A number of the brutalities that occupy the area where core disgust has marked moral valence have to do with sexual violence—rape, molestation, mutilation. Whether sex itself deserves an independent place on the roster of disgusting objects is a bit of a puzzle. It does not figure among the elicitors that have been demonstrated to have pancultural significance—at least not in general. Sexual fluids such as semen and menstrual blood are on the lists, but possibly because they are "unclean" emanations from the body that signal compromise of its boundaries. One might think that sexual intercourse would automatically disqualify as disgusting because it is the outcome of the very antithesis of disgust: attraction and desire. Indeed, in one philosopher's schematic organization of emotions, disgust is classified as the opposite of sexual desire.[55] Yet Miller, who employs aspects of Freud's analysis of sexuality and pleasure, maintains that desire itself depends upon a "prohibited domain of the disgusting."[56] Among other factors contributing to this assessment, there is the fact that since disgust signals the violation of the borders of the self, it must be overcome by love in order for sexual intimacy to be welcomed. Because the disgust response is palpably somatic, its propensity to record something in a particularly intimate way—literally as a gut feeling—is apparent, and this aspect of the emotion will figure repeatedly in my discussions of aesthetic encounters. At the same time, I suspect that the linkages posited between disgust and sex, desire, love, and hate have already entered zones where both cultural and theoretical perspectives exert especial influence over analysis. Variations on the themes of love, lust, revulsion, and allure will reappear from time to time throughout this study.

Disputes about how "natural" disgust is often refer to the fact that very young children do not seem to respond with disgust to objects that revolt adults. Babies, for example, do not appear to be bothered by full diapers. However, not all inborn traits appear in infancy. Language acquisition is a prime example of

---

54. Miller, *Anatomy of Disgust*, 36.
55. Aaron Ben Ze'ev, *The Subtlety of Emotions* (Cambridge, MA: MIT Press, 2000), 94.
56. Miller, *Anatomy of Disgust*, 137. See his chapter 6 for a fuller discussion of the connections between disgust and sexual attraction.

a human trait whose advent requires that a certain developmental stage be reached. If disgust is hardwired for objects such as feces, which is one of the constants on cross-cultural lists of disgust elicitors, then the affect appears only at a certain stage of development, which Rozin estimates to be between the ages of four and eight. And without doubt, disgust is enhanced through social interaction, and the emotion comes to act as an important means of socialization into community mores.[57]

Thus far I have by and large endorsed accounts of disgust that emphasize its qualifications as a basic emotion with visceral, reactive character—while at the same time reserving space for cultural inflection, an aspect of the artistic uses of disgust that will become increasingly important in this study. However, there is an important aspect of disgust that sets it apart from other so-called basic emotions. Whereas the emotions considered basic, including fear, anger, surprise, joy, and sadness, are assumed to be continuous with the affects of other animals, disgust seems to occur only in humans.[58] Rozin, Haidt, and McCauley claim that although "disgust has a precursor in nonhuman animals, it is the only one of the six or seven 'basic' emotions that has been completely transformed in the human condition, making it a uniquely human emotion along with such emotions as guilt, shame, and embarrassment."[59] Nonhuman animals exhibit distaste, and they become averse to substances that have made them sick. But they do not exhibit the traits of actual disgust. The uniquely human character of this emotion is perhaps surprising, and it indicates that culture is operating at the visceral level even as reactive mental states develop. To some, the distinctively human character of disgust suggests a diagnosis of the underlying meaning of this emotion, namely, that disgust recoils from indicators of our animal nature, thereby protecting the human "soul" from descent to a bestial condition and guarding our moral and spiritual being against degradation and pollution. Rozin asserts that "disgust is precisely the emotion that guards the sanctity of the soul as well as the purity of the body."[60] Thus this dramatically visceral emotion stands guard against compromise of both physical and spiritual integrity.

Miller, who is also inclined to view disgust as uniquely human, sums up the common denominator of this emotion with the phrase "life soup." Disgusting objects are those that endure the cycle of birth, growth, and death, after which they disintegrate and provide the material that generates and supports other life forms, especially those that are low and mindless:

57. Rozin, Haidt, and McCauley, "Disgust," 575.

58. Michael S. Gazzaniga, *Human: The Science behind What Makes Us Unique* (New York: HarperCollins, 2008), 137; Jonathan Haidt, Paul Rozin, Clark McCauley, and Sumio Imada, "Body, Psyche, and Culture: The Relationship of Disgust to Morality," *Psychology and Developing Societies* 9 (1997): 107–31.

59. Rozin, Haidt, and McCauley, "Disgust," 589.

60. Paul Rozin, "Food for Thought: Paul Rozin's Research and Teaching at Penn," *Penn Arts and Sciences*, Fall 1997, at http://www.sas.upenn.edu/sasalum/newsltr/fall97/rozin.html. Citing the same research, Gazzaniga states that "disgust is the emotion that protects purity" (*Human*, 137).

What disgusts, startlingly, is the capacity for life, and not just because life implies its correlative death and decay: for it is decay that seems to engender life. . . . Death thus horrifies and disgusts not just because it smells revoltingly bad, but because it is not an end to the process of living but part of a cycle of eternal recurrence. The having lived and the living unite to make up the organic world of generative rot—rank, smelling, and upsetting to the touch. The gooey mud, the scummy pond are life soup, fecundity itself: slimy, slippery, wiggling, teeming animal life generating spontaneously from putrefying vegetation.[61]

Life soup comes freighted with meanings. While Rozin, Haidt, and their colleagues surmise that disgust protects us from descending to the status of beasts, Miller speculates that the covert target of aversion is *us*. Disgust erects a protective barrier between subject and object, but the ultimate recoil is from our mortality and the recognition that, by being proximate to contamination, we lose our bodily integrity—die, decompose, and become the disgusting object itself.

Miller recognizes the magnetism that disgusting objects can possess, drawing on Freud to unmask the hidden appeal of the disgusting, especially in sexual encounters. He identifies two varieties of disgust. One he calls the "Freudian type," which is a reaction formation developed to serve as a barrier against our tendency to satisfy unconscious desires that violate the social order, for Freud surmised that disgust joins shame and morality to stave off excesses of the sexual instinct. This first ground for the allure of the disgusting emerges out of largely unconscious desire. Miller's second type of disgust results from the overindulgence of conscious desires and is most readily recognized in the phenomenon of overeating and surfeit. The two types of disgust cooperate to form protective barriers against dangerous or antisocial behaviors that nonetheless exert an allure. This line of speculation will be pursued in chapter 5, where I examine theories that offer accounts of the attraction of disgust and the complex mentality that underlies it. For now, however, let us turn to an earlier theorist who recognized the draw of the disgusting and located it in the very structure of the emotion itself. His work also introduces the first and most basic sense in which we can say that disgust has an *aesthetic* element.

In 1929 Aurel Kolnai published what is, as far as I know, the first extended philosophical investigation of disgust.[62] His ideas anticipate what are now staple elements in the analysis of this emotion, although his means of discovery

---

61. Miller, *Anatomy of Disgust*, 40–41.
62. Aurel Kolnai, "Der Ekel," *Jarbuch für Philosophie und phänomenologische Forschung* 10 (1929). This essay appears in English in Aurel Kolnai, *On Disgust*, ed. Barry Smith and Carolyn Korsmeyer (Chicago: Open Court, 2004). The above discussion of Kolnai's essay owes much to the editors' introduction to this volume, "Visceral Values: Aurel Kolnai on Disgust."

is quite different. Kolnai adopts a phenomenological method, which is marked by attentive investigation of the relation between the perceiving mind and the object of perception. Therefore, his ruminations squarely address the "feel" of this emotion, the elusive subjective qualia of disgust.

Phenomenology proceeds on the assumption that different sorts of intentional stances have different "structures" that are sensitive to qualities and patterns in their objects, and so analysis of the structure of emotions can disclose qualities of objects as well as properties of mental acts and states. For example, intense emotions such as fear, anger, and disgust fasten strongly onto their objects, which therefore command exclusive attention. In contrast, a weaker emotion such as annoyance may be only slightly distracted in the direction of its object.

The lists of disgusting objects that Kolnai identifies include but exceed the range proposed by Rozin and Miller. He also identifies two categories of disgust-inducing properties: things that are morally disgusting and those that are "materially" disgusting. The latter overlaps with Rozin's core disgust and the ingredients of Miller's life soup. Kolnai identifies nine typical traits of the materially disgusting, including putrefaction, excrement, bodily secretions, and dirt; lower forms of life such as insects, especially massed in swarms; foods in certain conditions; the unwelcome proximity of human bodies; exaggerated fecundity; disease and deformation. Objects of material disgust share the impression of life turning toward death, and of primitive and profuse regeneration of low life-forms generated out of the muck of decaying organic matter. Things that rot and putrefy become breeding grounds for maggots and bacteria. Swarming insects give the impression of mindless life in formless profusion. Like Miller, Kolnai notes that disgust is sensitive to the commerce between life and death. Disgust registers the transitory stages when an organism that had recently died begins to lose what once was its bodily integrity, decaying, disintegrating, and releasing foul odors. The disgusting is, as he puts it, "pregnant with death."[63]

Central to Kolnai's treatment of disgust is his perspective on the "aesthetic" character of this emotion. Although his observations will be useful in my later treatment of art, Kolnai's own use of this term does not refer to appreciation or works of art. Rather, he simply refers to the qualities of an object as they are presented to the senses. He identifies the primary sense that arouses disgust as smell, along with touch and vision, for these senses have a greater range of objects than does taste. All of the senses can act as conduits for disgust, though the role of hearing is relatively weak. The strong sensory qualities of disgusting things lead him to argue that the intentionality of disgust is directed to the *Sosein* of an object—its "so-being," that is, its presentational qualities—as

63. Kolnai, *On Disgust*, 74

opposed to the threat it poses to *Dasein*, that is, to the being-in-the-world of the perceiver.[64] When disgusted one is almost wholly occupied with the sensory presentation or appearance of the intentional object rather than with its existential status. The intentional structure of this emotion is directed so strongly toward the properties of the disgusting object that it rivets our attention, even at the same time that it repels. This aversion actually searches out its object. In Kolnai's vivid metaphor, the tip of the arrow of intentionality "penetrates the object," thus making this aversion paradoxically caressing and probing.[65] This may be the root of the attraction of disgust, for "there is already in its inner logic a possibility of a positive laying hold of the object, whether by touching, consuming, or embracing it."[66]

While in most respects Kolnai's analysis conforms to the majority view that sees disgust as a strong and socially important aversion, his analysis of disgust acknowledges the possibility that this emotion tends actually to dwell on the object of its aversion. Like psychoanalytic approaches, he recognizes a perverse magnetism, what he calls an "eroticism of disgust," in which aversion is superimposed "upon the shadow of a desire for union with the object."[67] Unlike psychoanalytic accounts, he discovers the origin of this magnetism not in the unconscious but in the subtle structure of the conscious emotion itself. His observations on this score are consonant with certain of the gauges of disgust that I have already noted, such as the fact that with disgust the heart rate slows, in marked contrast to fear, in which it increases, readying us for fight or flight. Perhaps the slower pulse marks a tendency for disgust to make us pause over its object, to savor it with loathing. It is not the most typical element of the disgust response, nor one that all would share; but Kolnai calls attention to the fact that something profoundly repulsive may also fascinate. While he only begins to indicate the depth to which this savor might be taken, his identification of a basic aesthetic trait possessed by disgust in its very structure opens a direction of thought that this study will probe in detail.

These various scientific and philosophical ruminations on disgust present us not only with a long list of the objects that trigger this emotion but also with a set of meanings that it can signify. Disgust has a semantic range that includes things that are low, base, foul—objects that are emphatically inferior to us the disgusted. But it also includes us in its embrace, for as it signals death and decay it includes any mortal being—not just its inevitable end but the point at

---

64. Kolnai's focus on *Sosein* interestingly contrasts with Jean-Paul Sartre's famous existential disgust at mindless facticity, analyzed in *Being and Nothingness* and dramatized in Roquentin's confrontation with the roots of a tree in Sartre's novel *Nausea*. See Korsmeyer and Smith, introduction to Kolnai, *On Disgust*.

65. Kolnai, *On Disgust*, 39.

66. Kolnai, *On Disgust*, 43.

67. Kolnai, *On Disgust*, 60, 46. Kolnai was interested in Freud in his early studies but then came to favor a phenomenological over a psychoanalytic approach to a study of mental phenomena.

which its life has ended and bodily integrity has begun to disperse. The immanent disintegration of our own borders lies in the shadows of this emotion. The attachment of the disgusting to aspects of the human body, to femininity, to illness, to sexuality, to inescapable indignities further disposes the emotion as a resource for social, cultural, and artistic deployment that produces the rich and disturbing dimensions of aesthetic disgust.

While the alluring, enthralling dimensions of disgust are not the most prominent properties of this affect, the fact that attraction is there at all is perplexing enough that it demands investigation and explanation. Disgust is not alone in being an aversion that simultaneously attracts, but it is the one that has posed the most recalcitrant puzzles, especially for philosophy of art and aesthetics. These puzzles are the subject of the next chapter.

2

Attractive Aversions

The survey of emotion theory in the previous chapter situates disgust as an aversion so intense that it occasions uncontrollable visceral recoil from its objects. At the same time, the peculiar attraction of the disgusting has not gone unnoticed. Kolnai even argues that the very structure of the emotion is prone to induce one to dwell upon loathsome sensory qualities. Certain artworks afford especially compelling examples of the allure he identifies, the most obvious cases—though neither the only nor the most interesting—coming from the genre of horror. Nonetheless, of all the emotions, disgust seems to present the greatest barriers to actual enjoyment, and thus it also raises some of the most recalcitrant problems for understanding an emotion in its aesthetic contexts.

There are three charges commonly leveled against disgust that appear to preclude its presence in aesthetically positive experiences. These charges received especially emphatic affirmation in the eighteenth century when modern theories of the aesthetic arose, but they have not altogether receded from contemporary thinking. First, as is apparent from ordinary experience and confirmed by the psychological studies reviewed in chapter 1, the objects of disgust are foul, polluting, lowly, and base. As such, they appear simply to be not worth extended attention in themselves. In effect, disgusting objects are aesthetically discountable. Second, this particular emotion achieves a direct and immediate arousal that penetrates the screen of mimesis or artistic rendition. That is, one recoils viscerally whether the object of disgust is aroused by art or by an object in life. To the extent that disgust functions in such an automatic, modular way, it offers little potential for artistic manipulation. Both these claims yield the third: on those occasions when artists do manage successfully to render objects that are disgusting in reality, the artwork commutes the disgusting properties of the object portrayed and achieves a more acceptable aesthetic emotive quality: tragic, grotesque, or comic, perhaps. The objects portrayed that would be disgusting in nature may be rendered so as to arouse pity, compassion, amusement, and so forth, but they lose their capacity to disgust. In the course of this study I hope to redirect all three claims away from their dismissive conclusion and toward recognition of the power and insight that aesthetic disgust can achieve. I shall reject the first and the third, but the second, I believe, turns out to be an aesthetic advantage rather than a disqualification.

The initial segments of this chapter review the patchy history of philosophical treatments of disgust, attending especially to the theories of the eighteenth century, when disgust was granted a consistent and unfavorable place in theories of the aesthetic. Along the way, this historical journey will suggest perspectives on some problems and paradoxes that have preoccupied contemporary aesthetics, and these constitute the subject of the final section. Two of those problems, the so-called paradox of fiction and the questionable status of emotions aroused by art, can be settled rather easily—or so I shall argue. The much larger paradox of aversion that queries how (or if) a "negative" emotion such as disgust can be transformed into a "positive" aesthetic experience will take somewhat longer to resolve, for it presents enigmas whose solutions vary depending on the particular objects of disgust and their artistic and aesthetic functions, as I shall seek to demonstrate in the rest of the book.

Disgust: Some History

The philosophical Ur-source for thinking about the peculiar and paradoxical allure of the disgusting is to be found, as with so many subjects, in Plato. Plato recognizes the magnetism of disgust but takes this apparently perverse attraction to be a symptom of a disunified mind at war with itself. In the *Republic* he identifies three competing parts of the soul: the heterogeneous appetites that power both sensuous desires and acquisitive impulses, the spirited part of the soul (or *thumos*) that is manifest in anger and provides energy for decision making and action, and the judicious rational element that is disposed to seek knowledge and goodness. When the rational soul governs the whole person, the more unruly elements fall into line and the energy of the spirited element allies with the intellect. Desire for anything that is not good disappears when the virtue of justice guides every aspect of personality. But this happy equilibrium is rare indeed.

Several sections of the *Republic* investigate the refractory power of the non-rational components of the soul. In Book IX Plato offers a vivid description of certain dreams that indulge in pleasures that are kept at bay when we are awake. Plato takes dreams as seriously as Freud, claiming that "in fact there exists in every one of us, even in some reputed most respectable, a terrible, fierce, and lawless brood of desires, which it seems are revealed in our sleep."[1] Socrates describes desires

> that are awakened in sleep when the rest of the soul, the rational, gentle and dominant part, slumbers, but the beastly and savage part, replete with food and wine, gambols and, repelling sleep, endeavors to sally forth and satisfy its own instincts. You are aware that in such case there is nothing it will not venture to undertake as being released from all sense of shame and all reason. It does not shrink from attempting to lie with a mother in fancy or with anyone else, man, god, or brute. It is ready for any foul deed of blood; it abstains from no food, and in a word, falls short of no extreme of folly and shamelessness.[2]

The desires disclosed in dreams describe an eclectic collection of wrongs chiefly having to do with gratifying the unfettered appetites, whether sexual or gustatory, both potent contributors to the emotion of disgust. Especially in the unguarded realm of dreams, the beastly portion of the soul carries on with voracity and lust, unchecked by conscience or any of the furtive secrecy with which it might operate in waking life.

Plato's most famous tale of desire for the disgusting occurs earlier in the dialogue when the tripartite soul is introduced. At this point in the discussion the separation between the intellect and the appetites has been established, and the question arises whether there is a third element, "the *thumos*, or principle of high spirit" with which we feel anger. There Socrates recounts the story of Leontius, whose experience is presented as a factual anecdote and not a dream image or allegory.

> I once heard a story which I believe, that Leontius the son of Aglaion, on his way up from the Piraeus under the outer side of the northern wall, becoming aware of dead bodies that lay at the place of public execution at the same time felt a desire to see them and a repugnance and aversion, and that for a time he resisted and veiled his head, but overpowered in despite of all by his desire, with wide staring eyes he rushed up to the corpses and cried, There, ye wretches, take your fill of the fine spectacle![3]

1. Plato, *Republic* IX, 572b, trans. Paul Shorey, in *The Collected Dialogues of Plato*, ed. Edith Hamilton and Huntington Cairns (Princeton, NJ: Princeton University Press, 1973), 799.
2. *Republic* IX, 571c–d, p. 798.
3. *Republic* IV, 439e–440a, p. 682.

Many unsettling aspects of desire, pleasure, aversion, and attraction are prompted by this vivid little tale. It is important to note that Leontius is not presented as a person of unusual disposition; he is just a man walking home. The discomfort of the divided soul filled with conflicting desires is a phenomenon Plato expects us to recognize readily from our own experiences. Second, this is a candidly seamy story. Plato might have ennobled it with the implication that Leontius was curious about mysterious profundities: life and death, man's inhumanity, or some other lofty interest. But what draws him to the corpses is just the grisly sight itself, and since the bodies are recently dead, one imagines that putrid smells and swarming vermin are also part of the disgusting allure that he failed to resist.[4] In other words, there is apparently no greater purpose that the sight of the bodies serves; Leontius is attracted to something that is just plain nasty. What is more, his own desires are in conflict. He wants and does not want to look upon the disgusting and is ashamed of the attraction he experiences. These opposing forces affect his very body—his eyes want to look away, and he virtually forces them open to satisfy the conflicting urge to see. Plato's little story thus illustrates that disgust can precipitate an unsettling dislike for one's own desires.

Plato's solution to the psychological dilemma faced by Leontius is to counsel training the soul under the guidance of the intellect, thereby to govern the appetites and the spirited element and to encourage perverse desires to wither away. This effectively removes disgust from among the emotions that can be aroused by mimesis to positive aesthetic ends, though this is no surprise given Plato's general mistrust of emotions altogether. He recommends suppression even of the great tragic poetry that expresses fear of death or pain, and he surmises that the arousal of pleasure in anything but Truth and Goodness leads to disunity in the soul. One would not seek in Plato's philosophy exoneration of aesthetically alluring disgust, therefore, for he outlines one of the strongest cases against the artistic exercise of all negative emotions, apt as they are to interfere with the journey of the intellect toward wisdom.

Perhaps he is right that the allure of the disgusting panders to an underside of human nature that ought to be quashed rather than cultivated. It can be tempting to pick at a scab, after all, but it is not advisable. Giving in to the fascination of disgust—or allure, attraction, pleasure, curiosity, magnetism (it is not clear at this point just which terms are most apt)—may be just a perversity that both we and art would be better off without. Even if this were the case, however, it is doubtful that disgust will disappear from the affective palette of our aesthetic lives. The lure of the disgusting persists in spite of ourselves both in nature, as Kolnai observes, and in art. So the question remains: Can disgust,

---

4. C. D. C. Reeve remarks in a footnote to this passage that "Leontius' desire to look at the corpses is sexual in nature, for a fragment of contemporary comedy tells us that Leontius was known for his love of boys as pale as corpses" (*Republic*, trans. G. M. A. Grube, revised C. D. C. Reeve [Indianapolis, IN: Hackett, 1992], 115). Even so, the struggle between appetite and reason captures the magnetism of the disgusting for its own sake as well.

like other aversions such as fear and dread, actually be transformed by art into some powerful, positive aesthetic quality? When put to use in art, does it always retain the immediately sickening recoil of nature?

Many theorists have been intrigued by the difficult emotions that are valued and even savored when they are aroused in artistic contexts. Fear is the chief "painful" emotion that has come in for examination because of its importance in appreciating the plots of tragedy and experiencing the thrill of the sublime. Pity, grief, and the like also have a presence in art of the highest order, despite the fact that they are generally speaking "negative" emotions. It is less often granted that disgust has its own potential for artistic transformation, although Aristotle suggests that it might when he observes that the power of mimesis can make even corpses pleasurable to behold: "We take pleasure in contemplating the most precise images of things whose sight in itself causes us pain—such as the appearance of the basest animals, or of corpses. Here too the explanation lies in the fact that great pleasure is derived from exercising the understanding."[5]

Aristotle's perspective on this subject is grounded in his conviction that the pursuit of knowledge is one of the fundamental dynamics of human personality. All men by nature desire to know, as he asserts at the start of the *Metaphysics*. In the *Poetics* he adds to this innate cognitive desire a parallel tendency to imitate: to mimic behavior, repeat stories, and copy images until they become thoroughly understood, even incorporated into personality (for the mimetic tendency is a potent influence on character, as he asserts in the *Nicomachean Ethics*). The very imitation of objects—whether actions copied or images studied—enlivens the mind and expands its fund of knowledge, and so the imitation even of a disgusting object can become a source of pleasure.

Aristotle's analysis of negative emotions in art—especially the tragic emotions of pity and terror—has had enduring influence. Two elements of his theory are points of perennial controversy: his claim that the nature of the pleasure in difficult art is essentially cognitive, an expansion of understanding; and his assumption that the negative object (the target of fear, pity, disgust) becomes an object of pleasure by means of the transformation wrought by mimesis. Both of these issues continue to be disputed in the centuries that follow him. We shall not revisit the first until chapter 5, which reviews several general theories of the magnetism of disgust. The role of mimesis in rendering difficult emotions is of immediate relevance.

Although many difficult emotions are granted aesthetic importance, historically the majority opinion firmly excludes disgust from the emotions deployed to positive artistic effect. The Enlightenment philosophies that give rise to much of the conceptual framework for contemporary aesthetic thinking

5. Aristotle, *Poetics*. Excerpts from *The Poetics of Aristotle*, trans. Stephen Halliwell, in *Aesthetics: The Big Questions*, ed. Carolyn Korsmeyer (Malden, MA: Blackwell, 1998), 231.

explicitly take exception to Aristotle's claim, for they are virtually unanimous that disgust is uniquely disqualified from the lists of aesthetically enjoyable emotions.

Disgust versus Aesthetic Pleasure

Of all the emotions that art can inspire, disgust is the most difficult to incorporate into positive aesthetic response, especially when that response is cast in the standard terminology of "aesthetic pleasure," language that became systematized in the eighteenth century and remains current to this day.[6] While later I shall challenge the adequacy of pleasure to explain aesthetic apprehension, its philosophical dominance cannot be gainsaid and must be examined to account for the peculiar position of disgust in aesthetic theory. The theoretical centrality of pleasure—of a carefully delimited aesthetic sort—within Enlightenment theories brought into special prominence what can be called generally the "paradox of aversion." If beauty (later generalized as "aesthetic experience") is a pleasure, how can we account for the fact that many objects of aesthetic pleasure—both in nature and in works of art—contain subjects that in life are so painful that they are strenuously avoided? Moses Mendelssohn posed the perplexing transport of terrible images this way:

> Human beings are so peculiar in their delights that often they take pleasure in what ought to arouse their sorrow; indeed, even in the very instant that it arouses their sorrow.
>
> That rocky cliff which juts outward above the river rushing by presents a grisly sight. The vertigo-inducing heights, the deceptive fear of falling, and the plunge to the depths below that those pieces of rock hanging over the edge appear to threaten—all this often forces us to avert our agitated gaze from it. Yet, after a quick recovery, we direct our eyes again to this fearful object. The grisly sight pleases. Whence this peculiar satisfaction?[7]

Whence indeed? The many thinkers who addressed this puzzle proposed a number of means by which the aversion of fear transforms into the thrill of the sublime, as a rule invoking the awe or even worship that objects of overwhelming power and danger inspire. But disgust rarely inspires awe or respect,

6. Winfried Menninghaus states that the first wholesale exclusion of disgust from artistic transformation comes from Johann Adolf Schlegel in a footnote to his 1751 translation of Charles Batteux's *Les beaux arts réduits en un même principe*. Menninghaus, *Disgust: Theory and History of a Strong Sensation*, trans. Howard Eiland and Joel Golb (Albany: State University of New York Press, 2003), 25.

7. Moses Mendelssohn, "On Sentiments," (1761) in *Philosophical Writings*, trans. Daniel O. Dahlstrom (Cambridge: Cambridge University Press, 1997), 36.

and this is one reason it is either neglected or rejected from theories about the conversion of painful emotion to aesthetic pleasure. As Kant emphatically states: "There is only one kind of ugliness that cannot be presented in conformity with nature without obliterating all aesthetic liking and hence artistic beauty: that ugliness which arouses *disgust*."[8] Edmund Burke, whose iconoclastic ideas on the terror of the sublime admit a natural fascination with pain and death, contrasts the terrible with the "merely odious." He dismisses disgust (or at least the loathsome, which is very like the disgusting in this context) in one sentence in the midst of his lengthy ruminations on the sublime and beautiful. He says, "Things which are terrible are always great; but when things possess disagreeable qualities, or such as have indeed some degree of danger, but of a danger easily overcome, they are merely *odious*, as toads and spiders."[9] In his ruminations about tragedy, Hume managed to reconcile beauty with the arousal of sorrow, terror, and anxiety, but he too drew the line at the depiction of "mingled brains and gore" on stage.[10]

In other words, uncomfortable as it is, terror is an appropriate response to confrontation with something that has might and power and is therefore worthy of our attention, perhaps even of our awe and respect. There is a reward for encountering terror if it results in the sublime, which is a transcendent experience well worth the pain of its achievement. But encounters with disgust do not seem to pay this kind of dividend, as its objects are base and foul—unworthy of our regard. It is hard therefore to defend the idea that disgust is the vehicle for any aesthetic uplift equivalent to sublimity.

The context for Kant's dismissal of disgust is his exploration of the nature of artistic genius, by which term he refers to artists of exceptional talent who are so original that they set standards for their genres. In keeping with the long tradition initiated by Aristotle, he observes that the artist of genius is by and large able to render beautiful and admirable that which in nature is disagreeable, ugly, or painful—except for that one exception: the disgusting cannot be transformed by art, either by context or narrative drama or stylistic rendering, into anything approaching a valuable aesthetic quality. Even in art, disgusting objects present themselves to the imagination with an inescapable immediacy that prevents the conversion of the disgusting into something discernibly artistic and aesthetically valuable. Here is the fuller context of the remark quoted earlier:

Fine art shows its superiority precisely in this, that it describes things beautifully that in nature we would dislike or find ugly. The Furies,

8. Immanuel Kant, *Critique of Judgment* (1790), trans. Werner S. Pluhar (Indianapolis IN: Hackett, 1987), §48, p. 180.

9. Edmund Burke, *A Philosophical Enquiry into the Origin of Our Ideas of the Sublime and Beautiful* (1757), ed. James T. Boulton (Notre Dame, IN: University of Notre Dame Press, 1968), 86.

10. David Hume, "Of Tragedy," in *Essays Moral, Political, and Literary*, vol. 1 (1882), ed. T. H. Greene and T. H. Grose (Darmstadt: Scientia Verlag Aalen, 1964), 265. I shall return to both Burke and Hume in later chapters.

diseases, devastations of war, and so on are all harmful; and yet they can be described, or even presented in a painting, very beautifully. There is only one kind of ugliness that cannot be presented in conformity with nature without obliterating all aesthetic liking and hence artistic beauty; that ugliness which arouses *disgust*. For in that strange sensation, which rests on nothing but imagination, the object is presented as if it insisted, as it were, on our enjoying it even though that is just what we are forcefully resisting; and hence the artistic presentation of the object is no longer distinguished in our sensation from the nature of this object itself, so that it cannot possibly be considered beautiful.[11]

Kant observes that when it appears in artworks, the disgusting seeks to sneak into our aesthetic approval by associating with other elements of the artwork that merit our liking, sidling in alongside things that are noble and beautifully formed, including those that are otherwise painful. Subjects that are noble and awesome in art may be representations of things that in nature are truly terrible, but in their artistic representation they are rendered with a significance that both mimics their appearance in nature and transforms them into objects of sublimity or beauty. This does not seem to work with disgusting objects.

This very point is made more explicitly in the earlier work of Mendelssohn and of Gotthold Ephraim Lessing. In his essay *Laocoön* (1766), Lessing quotes Mendelssohn on the essential unrepresentability of the disgusting:

> But do not even unpleasant feelings become pleasing in imitation? No, not at all. A perceptive critic [Mendelssohn] has already noted this fact about disgust. "Representations of fear," he says, "of melancholy, terror, compassion, etc., can arouse our dislike only insofar as we believe the evil to be real. Hence, these feelings can be transformed into pleasant ones by recalling that it is an artificial illusion. But whether or not we believe the object to be real, the disagreeable sensation of disgust results, by virtue of the law of our imagination, from the mere mental image. Is the fact that the artistic imitation is ever so recognizable sufficient to reconcile the offended sensibilities? Our dislike did not arise from the supposition that the evil was real, but from the mere mental image of it, which is indeed real. Feelings of disgust are therefore always real and never imitations."[12]

11. Kant, *Critique of Judgment*, 180.

12. Gotthold Ephraim Lessing, *Laocoön: An Essay on the Limits of Painting and Poetry* (1766), trans. Edward Allen McCormick (Indianapolis, IN: Bobbs-Merrill, 1962), 126. The internal quote is from Moses Mendelssohn, *Briefe, die neueste Littertur betreffend*, Vol, 102. For discussion of Lessing's remarks on disgust, see Carol Jacobs, "The Critical Performance of Lessing's Laokoon," *Modern Language Notes* 102, no. 3 (1987), 483–521. Also Carole Talon-Hugon, *Goût et Dégoût: L'art peut-il montrer tout?* (Nîmes: Éditions Jacqueline Chambon, 2003), chap. 6.

Lessing goes on to cast doubt on Aristotle's claim that even the ugly is enjoyed in art because of the learning it imparts. Curiosity is soon satisfied, he asserts, and what is left is the discomfort of exposure to something unsightly with no redeeming artistic features. Though it can participate in comedy and the grotesque, disgust is not easily mixed with more uplifting emotions. Fear may be combined with hope, sorrow with fond memories. Disgust does not have many happier companions. At best it mingles with terror or pity to produce the tragic, as in the case of Sophocles' hero Philoctetes, whose stinking infected foot so revolted his companions that it drove them from his company. (In such cases, Lessing noted, literary forms permit descriptions that would be too revolting for imitation by means of visual art.)

These various comments sort out into the three distinct strikes against disgust previewed at the beginning of this chapter. First, the triggering objects that arouse the emotion are too base to afford positive aesthetic functions; they are especially inappropriate for an experience that approaches beauty. Disgusting objects are unworthy of extended attention—more or less Plato's point. Disgusting objects are contaminating and foul; they repel and nauseate. Therefore they are, in Burke's words, merely odious and as such aesthetically discountable. Second, unlike other emotions, disgust is aroused immediately by art just as it is by ordinary objects—a thesis that isolates disgust from the artistic representation of all other emotions. More than any other emotion, disgust seems to escape the shield of representation and arouse immediate repulsion, making it impossible to convert into "aesthetic liking," especially beauty. Mendelssohn, Lessing, and Kant all note the failure of the screen of mimesis to distinguish between reality and representation with disgusting objects. The "strange sensation" of disgust "rests on nothing but imagination," as Kant put it (i.e., the mental ability to form images). The artistic depiction of disgust arouses the emotion as if the artwork were a real existing object—with all the attendant unpleasant recoil and aversion.

This *transparency* of disgust, so to speak, is a signal of the strong sensory grounding of the emotion and the way it commands attention to the presentation to the senses, regardless of its mode of existence. This claim resonates with Kolnai's observation that disgust rivets attention on the *Sosein* of the thing—its "so-being" or presentation to the senses—rather than on its *Dasein*, the fact that it exists. The artwork is not a filter through which the disgusting thing can be rendered differently from the way it would naturally appear— unless it is rendered not as disgusting but as grotesque or ugly. Hence the third count against disgust follows from the second: when objects that would be disgusting in nature are *successfully* rendered in art, they take on a different affective quality altogether, becoming grotesque, ridiculous, tragic, but no longer actually disgusting. All three points are connected, though the first and third are particularly linked. If the third can be proved false and we can show how disgust can indeed transform into an aesthetically important affect, then the first worry about the unworthiness of disgusting objects disappears. Transparency is harder to dispute. In fact, it is a useful observation about the uniquely sensory character of disgust.[13]

The sensory nature of its triggers means that even in artistic contexts disgust retains its signature physical arousal. Moreover, the bodily disturbance of the emotion further contributes to its traditional aesthetic disqualification. In the course of delimiting the nature of aesthetic pleasure from other kinds of enjoyment, modern philosophical theories insisted with more or less vigor on a distinction between *aesthetic* and *bodily* pleasures. The senses of vision and hearing had long been categorized as the only ones that could apprehend beauty, whereas sensations of taste, touch, and smell could deliver at best sensuous pleasures.[14] A particularly emphatic version of this common tenet is articulated by Schopenhauer, who identifies the disgusting in art as the obverse of appeals to bodily and erotic pleasures. He intensifies the distinction between sensuous pleasure and aesthetic pleasure, and when he addresses disgust he also excoriates painted images that render the human body so alluringly that they inspire an opposite of disgust—lust, a clear signal of physical rather than aesthetic anticipation. According to Schopenhauer, anything that stimulates the bodily senses interferes with the suspension of the will, which also interrupts the serene, will-less aesthetic experience. He identifies art that exploits disgust as the counterpart of art that renders the human body physically appealing or "charming." As he draws the comparison:

> There is also a negatively charming, even more objectionable than the positively charming . . . and that is the disgusting or offensive. Just like the charming in the proper sense, it rouses the will of the beholder, and therefore disturbs purely aesthetic contemplation. But it is a violent non-willing, a repugnance, that it excites; it rouses the will by holding before it objects that are abhorrent. It has therefore always been recognized as absolutely inadmissable in art, where even the ugly can be tolerated in its proper place so long as it is not disgusting.[15]

This rejection of the disgusting alongside the charming links disgust in foods and in art, for the other prime examples of charming art that he considers aesthetically unworthy are still life paintings of foods that render their subjects with such delectable appearance that the paintings inspire a sensory anticipation of taste pleasures rather than pure aesthetic contemplation. The

13. I believe that Robert Rawdon Wilson overlooks this point when he asserts too easily that "imagination can appropriate in-the-world disgust and transform it." Wilson, *The Hydra's Tale: Imagining Disgust* (Edmonton: University of Alberta Press, 2002), xxv; also chap. 3 passim.

14. Carolyn Korsmeyer, *Making Sense of Taste: Food and Philosophy* (Ithaca, NY: Cornell University Press, 1999), chap. 2.

15. Arthur Schopenhauer, *The World as Will and Representation*, vol. 1 (1859), trans. E. F. J. Payne (New York: Dover, 1969), 208.

two categories of the charming unite gustatory with sexual appetite, and the satisfaction of either is a purely sensuous as opposed to aesthetic pleasure. In counterpart, its physicality traps disgust in the same category of response. Schopenhauer's resounding refusal of disgust as an aesthetic emotion recognizes that disgust is an affect that profoundly engages the body and its senses. The experience delivered is incompatible with the apprehension of beauty, for to his mind true aesthetic attention draws attention away from the body and its mundane circumstances to an ideal world of pure contemplation.

In short, disgust has such sensuous immediacy that imitation in art fails to cushion or distance the emotion to any appreciable degree. Therefore, there does not seem to be room for its adjustment to something aesthetically pleasing. Compare the artistic rendering of something fearsome: an image of Medusa, say, or the Furies. They might be presented as appropriately terrible and fearsome, but they could also be depicted as awe-inspiring, presenting qualities that might make us admire them even as we quail. But something disgusting cannot so readily be adjusted without *losing* its disgusting qualities and becoming another affect altogether. In short: the founders of our traditions of aesthetic theory are more or less unanimous in their judgment that disgust is an emotion that is uniquely disqualified from positive artistic rendering. Its arousal by art is always an aesthetic defect.

Disgust's Hidden Role

From the preceding review of the philosophical history of disgust it might appear as if the founding fathers of aesthetic theory rejected disgust outright, simply jettisoning it from their deliberations as an inconsequential emotion for artistic consideration. However, this proves a superficial reading. According to Winfried Menninghaus, who has investigated the trajectory of ideas about disgust in the German tradition where it has figured most prominently, disgust plays an indispensable, central role, albeit implicit and sometimes hidden, in theories of beauty and the aesthetic. As he interprets these texts, disgust is not merely a repellent emotion unworthy of aesthetic attention. Rather, it represents the containment of the beautiful, that which keeps beauty itself from overreaching its own value and revolting us with a surfeit of pleasure. (Kolnai has a somewhat ironic comment along these lines as well: he remarks that disgust keeps us from "drowning in pleasure.")[16] Menninghaus asserts that the numerous comments in the burgeoning German aesthetic tradition of the eighteenth century that reject disgust from aesthetic receptivity in effect assign that emotion a uniquely defining role: the affective condition that in principle cannot tender aesthetic pleasure and defines pro tanto the limits of beauty.

16. Aurel Kolnai, *On Disgust* (1929), ed. Barry Smith and Carolyn Korsmeyer (Chicago: Open Court, 2004), 63.

The type of elicitor for disgust that Menninghaus emphasizes is *surfeit*, the overindulgence in sensation singled out by Miller and Kolnai as well. This inclines Menninghaus to focus on taste as the sensory foundation for the emotion, for surfeit is paradigmatically a result of too much sweetness. Indeed, the importance of surfeit as an elicitor of disgust leads Menninghaus to refer to "the dietetics of the beautiful."[17] Just as sweet is an immediate pleasure that can pass satisfaction, reach surfeit, and turn to nausea, so beautiful can be so very pleasurable that it too exceeds itself and becomes disgusting. Disgust is therefore not just an opposite of beauty, for other opposites include the ugly, grotesque, terrible, even sublime. It is an antithesis that also provides the implicit background constituent of the very possibility of beauty, a defining phenomenon that marks the extreme boundaries of aesthetic pleasure.[18]

By this analysis disgust is not merely excluded from aesthetic theorizing because it is a low and unworthy emotion (though it is that as well), but also of necessity it must be excluded from the explicit realm of aesthetic experience because it sustains the possibility of that experience by constituting its negation. In this respect it is unlike other "painful" emotions such as fear, pity, grief, or sorrow, or qualities such as the ugly and grotesque. These latter are all affective qualities that theorists welcomed into the aesthetic realm for their profundity and weight, as well as for the complexities they afford the easier forms of beauty, their appearance preventing aesthetic pleasure from becoming facile or saccharine.[19] The potential of surfeit from the beautiful keeps disgust patrolling the boundaries of beauty as an indicator that aesthetic pleasure has reached a point of excess and transformed into its antithesis. As he puts it:

> The different theories centered on the aesthetic amenities of fear, horror, terror, and pity . . . were here recapitulated as a pretext, from which *one* single "unpleasant passion" stands apart, as the scandal that *cannot* be incorporated into the field of aesthetic pleasure. Or to repeat the words of J. A. Schlegel: it is *"disgust alone"* that "is excluded from those unpleasant sensations whose nature can be altered through imitation."[20]

Here again we are presented with the observation that disgust is essentially inimitable, but now we have a different stress on why disgust remains outside the aesthetic. It is not just that, as Lessing, Kant, and Mendelssohn assert, once objects that are disgusting are portrayed in art, they either compromise aesthetic quality or are tamed into something like the grotesque or the merely ugly. In addition, pure disgust, understood as a fundamental recoil, a radical *no*,

17. Menninghaus, *Disgust*, 37.
18. Menninghaus, *Disgust*, 29–31.
19. This point is examined further in chapter 7. See also Bernard Bosanquet on "easy" and "difficult" beauty; *Three Lectures on Aesthetic* (1915) (Indianapolis, IN: Bobbs-Merrill, 1963), lecture 3.
20. Menninghaus, *Disgust*, 35.

remains outside the containment of art in any form whatsoever: "As the aesthetic's entirely other, it remains basically unrepresentable, invisible, unidentifiable for the field that it limits: an empty cipher for that which the world of beautiful forms cannot appropriate or integrate."[21]

Moreover, Menninghaus maintains, the characteristic reactive recoil of disgust bestows upon this emotion a peculiarly "unreflective" quality. Reflection occasions a pause in experience that permits the subject to dwell on the significance of an object, enhancing aesthetic pleasure and extending it beyond the moment of arousal. Only objects of the so-called higher senses of hearing and vision invite such reflection, for the bodily senses of touch, taste, and smell are not only immediate and fleeting, they are direct and reactive, insensitive to whether their objects are real or imitations—in effect making imitation an impossibility for disgust. Thus the division between "aesthetic" and "nonaesthetic" senses, which is prominent in modern aesthetic theory, is also significant for the exclusion of disgust from among the aesthetic emotions. As Menninghaus puts it:

> The functional circle of disgust is short and quick. It allows no reflective shock-defense: there are no mediating links between a disgusting stench and the sensation of disgust, and hardly any possibility for conditioning and intervention. True, over large expanses of time, disgust reactions can be either learned or unlearned—they constitute no timeless natural occurrence. But the role of intellectual processing is far less important than with fear, horror, grief, or pity, and the relative distancing is thus far smaller: a further reason why these emotions are fit for "aesthetic" representation, while disgust is not. The absence of longer intellectually reflective sequences in disgust's regulatory circle is the source of this sensation's violence. . . . An irreconcilability with the temporality of reflection reveals itself as the decisive aesthetic defect of disgust. Being a violent response to an intrusion into our organs, the sensation simply leaves no room for reflection.[22]

In order to substantiate this claim, Menninghaus singles out the characteristics of disgust that are also emphasized by affect program analyses, which stress the degree to which disgust is simply reactive recoil, rapid and hard to control. As such, it does not invite rumination, and thereby it may be seen as "unreflective" because of its immediacy and speed. A second dimension to this claim is located in the philosophical tradition under study, for according to Kant, aesthetic judgments are categorized as reflective judgments in which the

21. Menninghaus, *Disgust*, 48. See also Jacques Derrida, "Economimesis," *Diacritics* 11, no. 2 (1981): 3–25; Sianne Ngai, "Afterword: On Disgust," in *Ugly Feelings* (Cambridge, MA: Harvard University Press, 2004).
22. Menninghaus, *Disgust*, 43.

understanding of the subject partly constitutes the object of the judgment of taste. For judgments of pure beauty, it is the free play of the understanding that comprises the Third Moment of beauty, the experience of "purposiveness without purpose" in which a beautiful object appears to have a purpose free from the application of any determinate concept of that object. Even more to the point is the experience of the sublime, which for Kant is a "negative pleasure" whose proper object is the mind itself. In experiencing the overwhelming power and vastness characterizing the sublime, the subject also becomes aware of his independence from that power and the fact that his mentality can grasp its own limits—thus putting human rationality outside the laws of nature. The complex mentality that turns terror to sublimity would be impossible without the occasion for the mind to reflect on its own activity.

The speed of the disgust response underwrites Menninghaus's generalization. Disgust occurs with the immediacy of a sensation, provoking aversion with no interval in which the subject might reconsider its reactive recoil. But is this in fact substantiated by experience? On the contrary, there is little reason to conclude that the speed and force of a reaction preclude reflection on that response. Even an immediate reaction can be assessed and subject to what Jenefer Robinson calls "cognitive monitoring," by which the first stage of an affective response can be assessed and either revised or continued. Even more, one can readily reflect upon the fact of a response, assessing its appropriateness and its meaning. In short, there is no reason to conclude from the rapidity of the disgust response that this emotion alone among all affects is incapable of prompting "reflection" in any meaningful sense. To insist upon this as a feature of disgust would be to make the exclusion of this emotion from contributions to positive aesthetic encounters analytically true. Although its force and rapidity cannot be gainsaid, disgust permits reflection as much as any emotion.

Despite this shortcoming, Menninghaus's interpretation of disgust in this generative period of theoretical formation provides an exceptionally probing analysis of the exclusion of disgust from the aesthetic and from the emotions that can be aroused by art within the purview of beauty or sublimity. (He also calls attention to the gendered implications of disgust, which are important for understanding not only Enlightenment theories but also contemporary uses of disgust in art, a subject to be discussed in chapter 4.) Absent the sort of systematic understanding that he outlines, it would be all too tempting to regard the various comments precluding disgust's aesthetic potential as simply an outcome of narrow eighteenth-century taste. But disgust is more than a merely unseemly emotion that represents an unpalatable experience and violates canons of good taste. In the course of his deconstruction of the texts that exclude it from aesthetic pleasure, Menninghaus deepens understanding of how disgust is an anomaly in the aesthetic catalog of emotions.

Partly for this reason, his account also runs the risk of mystifying disgust, simultaneously making it the kind of automatic response that aligns it with mere reactions rather than sophisticated emotions and elevating it to a response so recondite and mysterious that it reaches an utterly inexpressible realm. The latter is partly a consequence of a Lacanian inflection bestowed upon the "real" experience that disgust in its transparency always signifies—an encounter that in principle exceeds understanding.[23] Therefore, the unique status of disgust is both perpetuated and intensified by his treatment. Moreover, Menninghaus emphasizes just one type of disgust elicitor—surfeit, extending the application of surfeit and its relation to the too-beautiful or the too-sweet to all other elicitors of disgust as well. Most important, as a result of the function he assigns disgust as that which always resides outside the aesthetic, Menninghaus leaves little room for establishing the subtle but potent role of disgust in the generation of the most profound and beautiful experiences of art.

However, disgust can indeed provide us with its own foundation for difficult aesthetic apprehensions—those in which the traces of disgust are not artistically transformed into other affects but remain in all their immediacy and power. In this role, the transparency of disgust turns out to be an aesthetic virtue.

Transparency and the Paradox of Fiction

Although I reject the exclusion of disgust from among the emotions that can be transformed in art into what Kant calls "aesthetic liking," I endorse the claim that it is a relatively transparent emotion. That is, when it is rendered artistically, that which is disgusting in nature remains disgusting in art, and for much the same reasons that occasioned censure on the part of the Enlightenment philosophers who were so agitated by the arousal of this emotion. Mimesis *transfers* but does not *transform* the disgusting image in art. While this feature of disgust makes it doubly difficult to explain its objects in terms of positive aesthetic experience, it actually averts one of the standard philosophical problems regarding the nature of emotions aroused in aesthetic contexts. With disgust, what is known as the "paradox of fiction" is easily resolved.

The paradox of fiction refers to a puzzle about the very phenomenon of emotional arousal by works of art. As we saw in the previous chapter, emotions are sensitive to events of particular importance to the subject. Fear signals the presence of danger; grief registers the profundity of loss; embarrassment recognizes that one has publicly done something stupid; and so forth. But if we know that we are confronting something imaginary, as is the case with art or with fictions of any kind, we also know that it poses no real concern to us. So

---

23. Menninghaus, *Disgust*, 48–49.

how can emotions, at least genuine, full-bodied emotions, be aroused by art in the first place? The paradox of fiction is most acute for a strong cognitivist theory of emotion that maintains a belief requirement for the arousal of a genuine emotion, because it is precisely belief in the existence of fictional objects that is missing when art arouses emotions. But even without commitment to cognitivism, emotional engagement with fictions (or falsehoods, as Plato would have it) may seem puzzling.

Part of the complication of dealing with the emotions that art occasions is that different emotions are aroused by different means and with different aesthetic effects.[24] Some do indeed require a propositional component, even a belief. When emotions such as these—grief is a good example—are aroused by fictions, then one has a particularly convincing example of the paradox of fiction: How can an object in which one does not believe give rise to an emotion that requires belief in order to come into being? Although the wane of strong cognitivism in emotion theory has made the paradox of fiction less urgent than it once was, the discrepancy between emotions and beliefs is puzzling nonetheless. How can emotional responses to art override what we rationally believe to be the case? Even at times override the values we hold dear?[25] Why do audiences cringe in fear at the appearance on-screen of a ghostly presence, when they believe neither in ghosts nor in the reality of the fictional presentation before them? Why is an audience of children and adults alike elated when Dumbo first spreads his ears and takes flight, when even the youngest child present is unlikely to believe that elephants can fly? Or to use an example from the master of Truth himself, why does a reader who subscribes neither to the theory of Forms nor to the immortality of the soul, nor perhaps even to a shred of Plato's philosophy, still feel a swelling heart at Socrates's serene death at the end of the *Phaedo*, weeping with his followers at the loss of their noblest companion? This is not a fictional example, at least not completely so, but the incompatibility between beliefs held and emotions aroused is similar to the situation with fictional artworks. Those who respond emotively to a story need believe neither in the existence of the intentional object of their emotions (Dumbo), nor in the state of affairs depicted (a flying elephant), nor possibly even in the background beliefs sustained by a story (that good triumphs over evil). No belief ought to result in no emotion. But it does not.

Within the field of philosophical aesthetics, there is a fairly large literature on the paradox of fiction, the puzzle of why and how things we know are not

24. Susan Feagin, *Reading with Feeling: The Aesthetics of Appreciation* (Ithaca, NY: Cornell University Press, 1996), contains a particularly detailed analysis of the different ways that fictions generate emotions; see especially her chapters 4 and 5. See also Alex Neill, "Fiction and the Emotions," *American Philosophical Quarterly* 30 (1993): 1–13; Stephen Davies, "Responding Emotionally to Fiction," *Journal of Aesthetics and Art Criticism* 67, no. 3 (2009): 269–84.

25. Kendall Walton, *Mimesis as Make-Believe: On the Foundations of the Representational Arts* (Cambridge, MA: Harvard University Press, 1990); Berys Gaut, *Art, Emotion, and Ethics* (Oxford: Oxford University Press, 2007).

real apparently prompt responses as if we believed them to be actual.[26] There are several ways to cope with the problem. (1) One can deny that emotions entail full beliefs, especially existential beliefs about their objects. Perhaps entertaining a possibility without holding a full belief is sufficient to supply the propositional content for an emotion. (2) One even can deny fictional entities do not exist, although this position raises ontological problems that demand their own solution.[27] (3) Or one can deny that the responses aroused by art are genuine instances of emotions. Certain of the emotions aroused by fictions, including strong emotions such as grief, have a duration in practical life that extends in directions that have no equivalent to their arousal in aesthetic form. Does a reader truly experience grief at the death of Anna Karenina under the wheels of a train? The reader of the novel closes the book, blows his nose, and goes about his daily tasks. It felt a bit like grief for a while, perhaps, but the fictionality of the object shields the reader from the aftereffects of the emotion to such a degree that one suspects the aesthetic affect to be not quite the same as the emotion experienced in nonfictional circumstances.

Different emotions require different solutions to the paradox, but the need to choose among these alternatives is avoided altogether by the transparency of disgust. Transparency renders the first and second options needless, for it is already established that disgust can be aroused by an image that is not taken to be real. It can be induced by the presentation of qualities alone, regardless of whether one believes in the existence of the object possessing those qualities. The third option, which would dilute fictional emotions or classify them as somehow weaker than real affects, is thus also avoided. This element of transparency was decried by Kant and company, but it provides a neat bypass of one of the less appealing solutions to the paradox of fiction.[28]

It should be noted that disgust is not alone in having sensory triggers; other emotions share this quality, including some varieties of fear. Fear is an especially complex emotion to consider, partly because it comes in so many forms.[29] Like disgust, fear has reflex components, including the startle response often exploited by horror and suspense dramas. Startle is an uncontrollable reaction, and when one is already tense from being absorbed in a plot involving danger and mystery, being startled by something scary on-screen can leave one

---

26. See essays in Mette Hjort and Sue Laver, eds., *Emotion and the Arts* (New York: Oxford University Press, 1997), for a review of these problems, especially Jerrold Levinson, "Emotion in Response to Art: A Survey of the Terrain," 20–34.

27. For a review of the metaphysics of fiction and a sound solution to its ontological questions, see Amie L. Thomasson, *Fiction and Metaphysics* (Cambridge: Cambridge University Press, 1999).

28. This account of the arousal of disgust by art is supported by Jenefer Robinson's treatment of the triggers for emotions, whether real or fictional, in *Deeper Than Reason: Emotion and Its Role in Literature, Music, and Art* (Oxford: Oxford University Press, 2005). She argues for an even wider range of emotions that are aroused absent any propositional attitude or judgment.

29. Just as fear is the most-studied emotion among scientists, it has received the preponderance of treatment in philosophies of art, partly because it has long been recognized as a foundation for the experience of both tragedy and sublimity. Moreover, it is an especially strong affect that can be aroused in the face of contrary beliefs.

trembling and with a racing pulse, which only makes one more sensitive to the next scary scene. The skillful use of startle arouses affects in an audience that are quite clearly genuine—not imitative, fictional, or pretend. The object of startle is the event in the film itself, so like disgust its intentional object is immediately present as a component of the artwork.

But there are other elements of fear that complicate the question of whether one is actually afraid in the fullest sense of the term. Fictions arouse fear, but we know we are safe when reading a book or watching a movie. Therefore, there is a gap between this recognition and the emotion that requires explanation. One may fear for a character, at the same time that one realizes that character is not real. One starts and flinches at a movie, but real full-blown fear would make one leave the theater. Disgust, in contrast, is simpler to explain. We are really disgusted even when we know the intentional object of disgust is a fiction. There is little gap between belief and emotion, because it is what is presented by the artwork itself that is the object of disgust. Again, Kolnai makes this point when he observes that disgust focuses on the *Sosein* of an object, its presentational qualities, while fear is also occupied with its *Dasein*, the fact of its existence. Even with the full knowledge that the image is not of something really existing—say, a body opened for autopsy in a forensic TV drama—the disgust is still prompted by the image. No matter that we know it is not real; it is disgusting whether or not a real-life equivalent stands before one.

In short, like the contributions of startle to fear, disgust is triggered immediately by elicitors that may be supplied equally well by reality or fiction. It may be significant as well that the avoidance behavior that disgust prompts is far less dramatic than with the case of fear. Recoil occurs with that characteristic pause; no flight or fight reaction is necessary as a follow-up. As a result, aesthetic disgust is an unambiguously and completely real case of the emotion, and its target object is the work of art. While Mendelssohn, Lessing, and Kant considered this an aesthetic disadvantage because it transfers the immediate aversion of disgust to the work of art, there is a philosophical advantage. So dependent is disgust on its sensory elicitors that it is easily triggered, bypassing the paradox of fiction and confounding no contrary beliefs. This fact, I believe, gives its palpable qualia a special aesthetic force.

Sense Experience and Disgust

The ability of the imagination to summon the sensory triggers of disgust permits that emotion to be aroused in all its repulsiveness. The most dramatic physical responses to disgust are nausea and vomiting, the actual expulsion of a disgusting substance from the body—a most unpleasant bodily experience. Art rarely triggers such visceral responses, but the calmer tenor of aesthetic disgust is readily and rapidly aroused by art, especially movies, visual art, and literature. This distinction points to the fact that disgust in art usually has its own mitigation—if not mediation—because its *primary* sensory triggers are rarely present in art at all.

The chief senses for disgust are taste and smell; touch is a candidate; hearing may have a small role; and vision has a very large capacity to be disgusted. With a few exceptions artworks, whether graphic presentations or vivid narratives, do not directly stimulate the senses of taste and smell or even touch.[30] Partly this has to do with museum and gallery regulations that prohibit touching exhibits; partly it has to do with safety, for disgusting tastes and smells can be dangerous. And partly it has to do with the history of art and aesthetic conventions, for only vision and hearing are traditionally considered aesthetic senses. Mostly it has to do with the difficulty of stimulating taste and smell directly in ways that at once arouse disgust, are aesthetically compelling, and are physically tolerable. Limits of physical tolerance advise that extreme visceral disgust in art is best aroused by means of the imagination.

In place of direct stimulation of the primary disgust senses, vision and imaginative description vividly conjure disgusting images. They are still disgusting—fully so. Recall that Kolnai actually considers vision to be one of the chief senses for disgust. But they have less potent effects on the viscera, and consequently disgusting things can be experienced in art that would be intolerable in reality. Taste and smell and touch are aroused only synaesthetically as a rule; vision and imagination conjured by description provide disgust. Hearing can have a role as well, but it is uncommon—the sound of someone retching, perhaps. Thus while there are plenty of disgusting narrative passages in literature, plenty of disgusting scenes in television and film, and lots of disgusting graphic art, sculpture, installations, and performance, and disgusting song lyrics, there is little to no pure music that arouses disgust.[31]

However, the role of sense stimulation with this emotion is not straightforward, and the strongly sensory aspect of disgust cannot alone explain its vivacity in art. There are many emotions other than disgust that are easily aroused by art, such as sadness or elation, for which there is no sensory stimulus. Conversely, there are sensations that can be vividly depicted or described that never are aroused by art. The scope of sensory stimulation by means of art is interestingly limited, and the limitations and scope are different with different genres. Theorists such as Lessing, of course, recognized this. In

30. See also Lessing, *Laocoön*, chap. 25; Talon-Hugon, *Goût et dégoût*, 112–14. From the preceding comment it is evident that I am thinking of the standard fine arts and their heirs, such as film and television, but I am not including consideration of the "arts" of perfumery or cooking. The latter is the subject for chapter 3. Some contemporary artists do attempt to incorporate stimulation of bodily senses in their work. Their place in the world of art that arouses disgust will be discussed further in chapter 4.

31. The end of the third movement of Mahler's Second Symphony contains a section he describes as a "cry of disgust." It is an expression of a kind of existential meaninglessness, perhaps like Sartre's *nausée*. It does not, however, arouse visceral disgust in the listener. Martha C. Nussbaum analyzes this passage in *Upheavals of Thought: The Intelligence of Emotions* (Cambridge: Cambridge University Press, 2001), chap. 14.

Laocoón he compared the relative abilities of poetry and painting or sculpture to portray pain and distress within the parameters of beauty. What can be described easily in narrative or verse may resist visual representation and vice versa. The absence of primary sensory stimuli permits the (sometimes barely) tolerable arousal of disgust. In contrast, the experience of physical pain, a sensation par excellence, cannot be aroused by art at all, although vivid descriptions of pain are important parts of many narratives. Reading passages where a character inflicts or suffers pain may arouse responses of pity, anger, horror, or gloating satisfaction—but it is incapable of arousing pain in the reader. Unlike the emotive varieties of aversions, physical pain is not mirrored in aesthetic responses. We might cringe in sympathy, but the arousal of the actual pain does not occur even slightly.[32] Obviously, this has something to do with the nature of sensation, though it is not entirely clear precisely what prevents the imagination from supplying a substitute mental image, as it does with disgust. The simple absence of touch cannot supply the whole answer, for sexual arousal is easily produced by mere images or descriptions.

This chapter has argued that aesthetic disgust is a genuine instance of the emotion and that part of its elicitation by art occurs through conjuring up the sensory triggers that provoke disgust. The immediacy of the arousal of disgust by art converts one of the characteristics of this emotion traditionally considered an aesthetic deficiency to a small advantage: there is no paradox of fiction that arises with disgust.

But the directness and transparency of disgust heightens the more perplexing paradox of aversion: How does this genuine aversion ever become the occasion for appreciation or enjoyment? There is no single answer to this question, for when disgust does become a mode of appreciation, its aesthetic operation varies hugely according to circumstances. Sometimes that which is disgusting actually converts to positive savor and pleasure; oddly enough, this happens with some kinds of food, as I shall argue in the next chapter. In this case what was once disgusting is no longer so; the aversion has actually altered to a positive pleasure. But often with art, the disgusting remains disgusting but also attains aesthetic virtues, becoming interesting, comic, curious, dreadful, titillating, tragic, uncanny. Some of these appreciative experiences are exceedingly difficult to tolerate. Others achieve a weird poignance and even beauty.

Theoretical speculation about the immense variety of aesthetic disgust is the subject for chapters 4 and 5, where additional examples of art that

---

32. Elaine Scarry, *Resisting Representation* (New York: Oxford University Press, 1994); Scarry, *The Body in Pain: The Making and Unmaking of the World* (New York: Oxford University Press, 1985).

arouses appreciative disgust are considered. In the meantime, I turn to a subject that has been submerged for a while: disgust in foods. Since I argued earlier that it is the absence of the primary disgust senses that permits the enjoyment of this emotion in art, one might conclude that disgust from the sense of taste is barred from becoming an occasion for enjoyment. But as we shall now see, disgust has a hidden aesthetic resonance in food—even in the finest cuisine.

3

Delightful, Delicious, Disgusting

The objects typically advanced to demonstrate the magnetism of disgust are usually apprehended visually or by means of imaginative description. It was his eyes that Leontius admonished for their unseemly desire for the terrible sight of corpses. However, the primary senses in play when visceral disgust is aroused are the bodily senses of taste, smell, and touch. As we have seen, one of the most basic functions of disgust is to inhibit dangerous ingesting, and it would seem that the protective role of disgust should keep that emotion steadfastly aversive when it comes to physical contact with noxious substances. Merely observing the foul and the loathsome is repugnant to the imagination but leaves the body unscathed. It would be sensible of nature to have provided us with modular responses that remain stalwart sentinels against disgusting invasions of our bodies, permitting leeway to seek out and explore the objects of this powerful aversion only when commerce with disgusting objects involves the safe distance provided by vision.

Nature, however, does not seem to have been so prudent. Exploration and cultivation of disgusting objects occurs even with the dangerously intimate contact senses. Surprisingly, there are numerous examples of foods that begin as objects of disgust and migrate over into the category of the edible. Some of them even rise to the level of gourmet delight—at which point their disgusting origins are mere shadows. This chapter explores the malleability of sensation and enjoyment, as well as the unexpected route that tastes traverse from the disgusting to the delicious.

Difficult Eating

Encountering an artichoke, one might wonder how the first person to eat that vegetable ever got past the exterior spines and the interior core of throat-raking needles to discover the sweet heart hidden within. Many foodstuffs present similar mysteries, such as rhubarb, whose poison parts surround succulent stems, or vegetables and meats whose toxins require careful flushing before they relinquish edible substances. The vast family of peppers can painfully burn the tissues of the mouth, eyes, and nose, yet they also have become immensely popular in the diet of many peoples. None of these examples represents bounties of the earth immediately inviting to the palate, and given the sheer difficulty of finding the nutriments to be had from fierce, dangerous, or toxic substances, we might well wonder that human beings ever learned to eat anything beyond the first fruits of the Garden of Eden. The ultimate origin of our diets is lost in the shadows of prehistory and evolution, though one suspects that sheer necessity often prompted discovery of food from forbidding sources. The remarkable thing is not just that we managed to eat but that we managed and continue to manage to take considerable *pleasure* in foods that present us with challenges both to our senses and to our sensibilities. It is the perplexing and elusive nature of this pleasure that will occupy me here.

One might think that we can distinguish that which tastes good by looking for the opposite of that which disgusts. A link of this sort is embedded in languages derived from Latin such as English and French that employ a root meaning "taste" in their words for disgust.[1] As we saw in chapter 1, this emotion is often interpreted as a basic aversion reaction to that which is foul and toxic, thereby protecting the organism by inducing recoil and revulsion. Conversely, the natural disposition to like sweet substances is considered to have its functional roots in the healthful, nourishing properties of ripe fruits. When it comes to cuisine, however, the disgusting and the delicious do not always function as opposites. A good deal of recondite and sophisticated eating actually seems to be built upon (or even to be a variation of) that which disgusts, endangers, or repels. Indeed, much of the haute cuisine of a culture retains an element that some people—both inside and outside that culture—find revolting. It would be no surprise to find that people are easily disgusted by foods produced according to unfamiliar dietary cultures, but that they cultivate disgust at home is unexpected. Here revulsion appears to be deliberately approached and overcome—not as a matter of necessity (as might be understandable in times of scarcity) but apparently as a way to increase the potency of taste experience.

---

1. Although William Ian Miller argues that this linguistic link is deceptive and skews theoretical attention to taste. Miller, *The Anatomy of Disgust* (Cambridge, MA: Harvard University Press, 1997), 1–2.

No one can stand outside culture and proclaim a neutral list of disgusting foods, and the following does not pretend to be one. With that caveat, I offer a provisional list of disgusting things to eat. These are culinary varieties of the prototypical disgusting objects identified by the theorists discussed in the first chapter. I have six categories that fall into two groups: one that singles out the taste experience itself, and the other that considers the nature of the object being eaten.

1. First of all, there are objects with initially repellent tastes, such as, perhaps, peppers, coffee, parsnips, or cod-liver oil. This category includes objects that retain a residue of a substance that is disgusting, such as the decay present in aged meat.

2. There are also a number of foods that are tasty in small quantities but cloy when one eats too much and reaches surfeit. This phenomenon is especially present with the relatively easy enjoyment of sweet things, such as cheesecake or candy. (And as we have seen, the phenomenon of disgust through excess affords tempting theoretical territory.)

Objects in these two initial categories disgust because of their sensory qualities, but there is a longer list of repellant foodstuffs that refers to the nature of what is eaten, thus engaging the concepts that Rozin and other researchers find indispensable for the arousal of disgust. This list includes two pairs of apparent opposites:

3. Objects that are too alien from ourselves and that we recoil from when we encounter them in nature, such as spiders or snakes. Something repellent to touch is doubly repulsive to touch with the tongue.

4. Objects that are too close to us, not alien enough. The prime example of this would be another human being.

5. Objects that are insufficiently removed from their natural form—that declare their identity and perhaps even appear to be still alive and resisting. Therefore, we prepare our foods, remove meats from their skin, and so on.

6. Objects that have been dead too long and have started to decompose. Because decay produces foul odors, this category bends back toward the first.

I am sure that this initial catalog of disgusting foods will be controversial, as it should be. Quite apart from the cultural bias that any such list inevitably manifests, these are also categories where one can discover instances in which taste is deliberately cultivated. Such cases disclose circumstances when disgust or revulsion is transformed, and what was at first disgusting becomes delicious.

Disgust and Sensation: From Revolt to Savor

The emotion of disgust can be quite hard to separate from its triggering sensations. Imagine accidentally swallowing milk that has spoiled. How easy is it to distinguish between the nauseous yuck sensation and the emotion that is disgust? Although the emotion is far more than a reaction of distaste or nausea, in experience the two blend seamlessly. Moreover, disgust is so immediate that it acts rather like the startle response, a comparison discussed in the last chapter. Since it has been proved that the startle reaction is uncontrollable and universal, from humans down to fish, the idea of cultural molding of such sensory affects might seem precluded. Disgust is more complicated, however, even if we begin with its most immediate and reactive versions.

Some foods disgust with their immediate taste or smell, and others disgust when they are presented in excess or surfeit. Too much rich, sweet cheesecake, for example, begins to cloy and then to revolt. Of the basic flavor categories—sweet, sour, bitter, and salt—sweet substances are especially prone to switch over to the disgusting when consumed to excess, as both Miller and Kolnai note. Perhaps this is due to the fact that humans have a natural liking for sweetness, so bitter and sour are more sophisticated and acquired sensory enjoyments that are less tempting to overindulge. Salt in limited quantities is needed to sustain the body's chemical balance, though it is also easy to consume salty substances in excess, and a strong salt solution is an emetic. Still it would seem that sweetness is the readiest flavor for overdose to the point of disgust. In any event, surfeit is one familiar means by which taste attraction becomes aversion. It is perhaps less often noticed that gustatory responses can also travel in the opposite direction. But indeed they can, and here we find the sensory beginnings where disgust may be cultivated and transformed into something pleasurable.

A familiar example that illustrates this is cheese. Cheese is a common food that many people enjoy. It is made by fermenting dairy products and permitting appropriate invasion of bacteria and mold spores. The process of becoming-cheese releases bad smells, some of them resembling bile, vomit, urine, or even feces—all exemplars of the disgusting. Moreover, this is not just an unpleasant stage in the process, the traces of which disappear. The finished product often retains residues of those smells and tastes in all their mordant immediacy. The result—a wheel of fine Stilton. The runny apex of aged Camembert hovers on the thin edge between pungent delicacy and the ammoniac reek of old diapers. Roquefort and Limburger are also examples of highly valued cheeses that skirt the edge of the revolting. In such cases, sensory properties that are the very paradigm of the disgusting have been transformed into the delicious, the savorable.

While some dubious sensory properties linger in these examples, they no longer disgust. (They may remain disgusting to one who simply does not like cheese, but that is another issue.) Rather, for items occupying this first category of the cultivation of disgust, the properties have altered and become delectable, although it may take some practice and maturity to find them so. One might object that the difficult properties that enter into cheese flavor are no longer the same as the disgusting ones at all, that the cheese's odor and taste have been annexed to a sensory realm that is altogether new. But this is doubtful: there is still sufficient likeness between Roquefort and vomit that the innocent person opening the fridge in search of a glass of milk might recoil at the impression that something has badly spoiled. Only identifying the cheese restores the sensory world to trustworthy order such that milk can be poured with confidence. Even so, one must quarantine Roquefort (or, even more, Limburger) from its neighbors, for what is savored in cheese is still pretty obnoxious in its cousin the glass of milk. In short, cheeses and more abhorrent substances bear a sensory family resemblance. Although there is a change of affect from recoil to savor, the shadow of the former lingers; indeed, it is in that shadow that the sophisticated depth of flavor resides. On the other hand, though the sensation has shifted only a little, the affective response has radically altered, having switched from recoil to appetite. Disgust has been replaced by savoring.[2]

Sometimes observations like the preceding are taken to have a different message: that disgust even at sensory experiences is learned rather than natural. That is, the fact that we may waver over the acceptability of a flavor before knowing the identity of the substance we are tasting might indicate that it is the knowledge of the substance rather than the flavor itself (the sensory property) that is the deciding factor in disgust. Rozin and Fallon note that when presented with ambiguous smells that could be cheese or feces, subjects hesitate over their disgust response until they learn the identity of the substance they are presented with. This leads them to conclude, "It is the subject's conception of the object, rather than the sensory properties of the object, that primarily determines the hedonic value."[3] I think that the lesson to be learned from this ambiguity is not so straightforward, however, for this diagnosis assumes that sensory properties are severable from properties *of* something, that is, that there is such a thing as full and complete sensory properties *tout court*. Granted, a mere whiff may be irresolvably ambiguous, but no full and complete taste sensation—which of course requires the use not only of taste but also smell and touch—is ever free from an awareness of its object.[4] That is, there is no coherent sensation without cognition—that is, without taking the object of sensation to be something or other. Different interpretations of the object of taste or smell yield different sense experiences. This is not the claim that one has a sensation that is then interpreted and categorized, but rather that without a category the sensation itself is inchoate and indistinct, even though very strong smells and tastes may provoke powerful physical responses.

2. For a vivid description of the repellent/delicious taste of *koumiss*, fermented mare's milk enjoyed in traditional Kazakhstan, see Alan K. Outram, "Hunter-Gatherers and the First Farmers," in *Food: The History of Taste*, ed. Paul Freedman (Berkeley and Los Angeles: University of California Press, 2007), 42.

3. Paul Rozin and April Fallon, "A Perspective on Disgust," *Psychological Review* 94, no. 1 (1987): 24 n. 1.

4. "Taste" can have narrow or wider referents. When a scientist is interested in identifying the receptors for taste sensation, he or she must distinguish them from the contributions to experience provided by smell or touch or vision. So isolated, taste is only the sensation provided from the tongue. But it does not match taste experience in eating or drinking, which is the target of my argument here.

To return to the cheese example: certain blue cheeses have a sharp smell that is often described approvingly as "piquant." This quality when added to salad or fruit enlivens a dish and increases its tastiness. Yet because the odor of blue cheese is rather similar to the smell of vomit, unless one is prepared to encounter cheese, the wafting vapors alone will not register as pleasant at all. Only once identified can the sensation come into focus and take on its aesthetic properties. In short, recognition and identification of a substance enter into the pleasure-displeasure valence of taste, but not as an addition to the sensation. Foods have meanings, as do objects of the other senses; part of their meaning is just what sort of substance they are. And meaning always enters into the full and complete experience of properties of an object.

Philosophers are used to an argument of this sort in the case of vision. It is common to observe that one does not see visual properties free from interpretation of what they are; visual sense data are not the bare bones of visual experience that builds upon that foundation. Rather, seeing without recognition is a partial, ambiguous, shifting, and even inchoate experience not typical of full seeing at all. As some put it, seeing is always "seeing as" something or other. One often experiences visual illusions, such that a patch of sunlight on a carpet may look like dropped scarf, but the visual properties subtly shift when the sun is rightly identified as a pattern of light. (The apparent volume of what one sees alters, for example.) It is not the case that one sees a light patch that is then overlaid with the interpretation: scarf or sun. The experience of seeing is an experience of seeing as: the veridical seeing as sunlight or the illusory seeing as scarf. I am making a similar case for taste, a case that is readily made but often overlooked because taste (and smell, and sometimes touch) is a sense whose epistemic role is frequently ignored.[5] But virtually all sense experience has epistemic weight, and the identity of the substance tasted is part of the meaning that flavor attains.

Decomposing flesh is another exemplar of the disgusting, producing among the most revolting odors one can encounter. But sometimes we eat it willingly if it has not progressed to a completely unusable stage. This culinary fashion waxes and wanes, but many older books of household management instruct one to hang game until it has started to "turn" in order to bring out the deeper aspects of its flavor. This may even involve washing away maggots or mold before cooking, indicating the degree to which the meat has decayed. Good steak is aged just like good cheese and wine, and since the aging process begins at death, the more time that goes by, the more rotten the meat. We call this "high" meat; in French it has achieved *haut goût*, and it is an irony of metaphor that the closer the substance comes to sinking back to original clay the more elevation its flavor achieves.

---

5. See my arguments in chapter 1 of *Making Sense of Taste: Food and Philosophy* (Ithaca, NY: Cornell University Press, 1999).

Aurel Kolnai, who recognizes a furtive allure in objects that disgust, also ponders how a substance that skirts the edge of the revolting may be thereby rendered, not marginally acceptable, but actually better than the fresh variety would be: "A slight putrefaction still does not suppress the specific smell and taste of the material in question, but indeed accentuates them to an extent which makes them even more characteristic—the phenomenon of *haut goût*."[6] Kolnai surmises that decay induces an intensification of taste that can enhance the flavor of meat beyond its fresher version. The flavor thus achieved records the passage of time, thickening and deepening in quality. The father of gastronomy, Jean-Anthelme Brillat-Savarin, agrees. He writes repeatedly of the preparation of game birds that must decompose a fair amount before they reach their peak flavor. Of the pheasant, he remarks:

> This last-mentioned bird, when eaten within three days of its death, has nothing distinguishing about it. . . . At its peak of ripeness, however, its flesh is tender, highly-flavored, and sublime, at once like domestic fowl and like wild game. This peak is reached when the pheasant begins to decompose. . . . The exact moment of perfection reveals itself to the uninitiate by a slight smell, and by the difference in color of the bird's belly; but the inner circle guesses it by a sort of instinct.[7]

This phenomenon can occur with smell alone. We can see a similar deepening effect with the perfume of a rose, which achieves its richest aroma when the fully opened blossom just begins to wither.

However, there is more than just sensory enhancement in the cultivation of tastes that suggest the beginning of decay. Again, such flavors can signal that foods have certain meanings, meanings that accrue to the tastes themselves. The historian of food T. Sarah Peterson recounts how during the sixteenth century Europeans, desiring to emphasize the continuity of their own culture with that of classical antiquity, diligently altered their customary food habits because of scholarly discoveries about what peoples of ancient Greece and Rome had eaten. This required consuming vast quantities of animal flesh and parts of animals hitherto not commonly eaten, and preparing high or gamy meat very rare.

> Fashion setters crunched on ears; blood from meat nearly oozed from the mouth; livers silken with fat melted on the tongue; and the taste for pronouncedly high meat, decomposed to the fine point just this side of maggoty . . . was cultivated in France. . . . By at least the eigh-

6. Aurel Kolnai, "Disgust" (1929), in *On Disgust*, ed. Barry Smith and Carolyn Korsmeyer (Chicago: Open Court, 2004), 71–72.

7. Jean-Anthelme Brillat-Savarin, *The Physiology of Taste* (1825), trans. M. F. K. Fisher (New York: Heritage Press, 1949), 401.

teenth century the stylish English were more than partial to them too. Although he considered himself to be in the new French fashion, Richard Bradley, the Cambridge botanist, was aghast at the high meat he was now served. "In many places I have sat down to a Dinner which has sent me out of the Room by the very smell of it."[8]

This trend was a deliberate cultivation of taste because of the cultural meanings of the foods consumed, but it became internalized quite literally as people's liking for the new tastes grew. Note the moldability of pleasure out of disgust in these heroic attempts to eat what is initially repulsive (although the case of Bradley demonstrates that not everyone was persuaded to relish the new fashions in taste).

These brief examples indicate a perplexing complication regarding the sensory grounds for disgust. Despite the power of this aversion, within a certain range what are presented to the nose and tongue as disgusting sensory qualities may be cultivated and converted into sensations that are the same or very similar, except for the important fact that they have become pleasurable. The transformation of a disgusting sensory quality into something delicious and savorable signals the enigma of disgust, which despite the power of its aversive recoil often contains elements of attraction even at the sensory level. That "level" is difficult to isolate in practice, however, for it is penetrated with meanings that abet the transformation of disgust to savor.

Disgusting Food and Aesthetic Cognition

The pleasures to be had from food and drink are, as a rule, considered relatively low forms of enjoyment, satisfying only the body and its desires. Since classical antiquity, the Western philosophical tradition has ranked two senses above the others, elevating sight in particular to the top of the list because of its cooperation with intellect in the development of knowledge. Sight is the chief sensory means by which we make discoveries about the world, assess practical decisions, and achieve aesthetic insights. Vision and its companion hearing are philosophically, scientifically, and in common parlance considered the "higher" senses, while touch, taste, and smell are "bodily" senses, and by the long tradition that ranks mind over body, they are also considered "lower" senses. While sight and hearing operate at a distance from their objects, food and drink are taken into the body, providing it life-sustaining nutrition. (The long-standing association of taste and smell with our animal bodies doubtless

---

8. T. Sarah Peterson, *Acquired Taste: The French Origins of Modern Cooking* (Ithaca, N.Y.: Cornell University Press, 1994), 96.

contributes to the tendency of many emotion theorists to brand disgust as a relatively primitive emotion whose job is merely to protect the body from inappropriate ingestion and contact.)

All of the senses can give us pleasure, but again we find a crucial distinction drawn between the "intellectual" pleasures of sight and hearing and the "bodily" pleasures of touch, smell, and taste. Enjoyment of objects of the eyes and ears—beautiful scenes, sounds, works of art—directs attention outward to the world around. The "objective" intentional direction of vision and hearing aids our knowledge of the world and gives us aesthetic pleasure. By contrast, the pleasures of touch, smell, and taste supposedly direct our attention inward to the state of our own bodies. These senses are traditionally considered cognitively dull, and pursuit of their pleasures supposedly leads to self-indulgence, laziness, gluttony, and overall moral laxity.

The complicated philosophical history of pleasure has posed some obdurate difficulties for those few theorists who have attempted to argue on behalf of the aesthetic dimension of taste. Fine cuisine certainly is to be admired for, among other qualities, the subtle pleasures it delivers, and this has been the chief grounds for defense of the artistry of food and the delicacies of taste.[9] A discriminating palate is a result of sophisticated learning and experience, and the artistry of the great chef or vintner yields subtle qualities in their products that are fully as difficult to discern as are the aesthetic properties of music or painting.[10] While at first this approach seems to put art and food on common ground, it inadvertently truncates the comparison because gustatory pleasures appear insignificant compared with "genuine" aesthetic pleasures. The crux of the matter is that the meanings that works of art convey and the insight and understanding they deliver are hardly captured at all in the standard concepts of bodily, sensuous pleasure.

Yet food and works of art share significant features that are often overlooked if one focuses only on sensuous taste pleasure. The more important similarities lie in the meanings that they capture and convey to the mind as well as the senses. This approach to food does not simply ignore pleasure, however. Rather, our pleasure responses to tastes themselves can be complex cognitive responses that sometimes involve highly compressed symbolic recognition. The upshot of this recognition may not result in classifying cuisine as art, but it deepens the significance of foods in their own right. What is more, it offers clues about the meaning of culinary disgust.

9. David Prall, *Aesthetic Judgment* (New York: Crowell, 1929); Kevin Sweeney, "Alice's Discriminating Palate," *Philosophy and Literature* 23, no. 1 (April 1999): 17–31.; Elizabeth Telfer, *Food for Thought: Philosophy and Food* (London: Routledge, 1996); Dave Monroe, "Can Food Be Art?" and Glenn Kuehn, "Food Fetishes and Sin-Aesthetics," both in *Food and Philosophy: Eat, Think, and Be Merry*, ed. Fritz Allhoff and Dave Monroe (Malden, MA: Blackwell, 2007), 133–44 and 162–74.

10. On the nature of taste properties, see Barry C. Smith, "The Objectivity of Tastes and Tasting," in *Questions of Taste: The Philosophy of Wine*, ed. Barry C. Smith (Oxford: Signal Books, 2007), 41–77.

Eating Representations

As a rule we see what we eat, and because foods are malleable substances they may be prepared in eye-catching, decorative designs. A large number of things we eat are crafted to look like something else. Although most of these "pictorial" foods are whimsical or decorative, they are a convenient entry point to pursue the meanings of foods beyond the flavors they exemplify, which will help us further to understand the difficult meanings that disgust can manifest.[11] Darwin noted "the strong association in our minds between the sight of food, however circumstanced, and the idea of eating it."[12] Pictorial foods confirm his observations.

Pictorial foods can achieve elaborate form, such as the famous *pièces montées* of the revolutionary nineteenth-century chef Marie-Antoine Carême. These extraordinary decorative showpieces were several feet high and were made from sugar, marzipan, flour, and, when necessary, nonfood armatures. Usually these confections were purely decorative, but the decorative and the edible combine in the presentation of ornately prepared foods, including items familiar to us today such as birthday and wedding cakes and fancy molded candies. Whether exotic or quotidian, foods can be crafted to *look* certain ways above and beyond what their food substances themselves look like. Pictorial foods can challenge, tease, amuse—or revolt. Indeed, revulsion is sometimes the purpose of amusing foods. At the Jell-O Gallery in Le Roy, New York, one can buy a mold the shape and size of a human brain, and with the addition of condensed milk to strawberry Jell-O, which produces appropriate opacity, the result is a nice, plump brain on a plate (figure 3.1). A popular restaurant called Modern Toilet in Taiwan serves curries with names like "green dysentery." Numerous recipes for Halloween snacks feature ghastly treats, including little kitty-poop cakes served in a litter box.[13]

The familiar and popular world of chocolate supplies numerous examples of pictorial foods, some of which approach the border of the disgusting. In addition to the kinds of shapes one would expect to find in chocolate, such as animals, flowers, holiday icons, and toys, one finds chocolate shoes, chocolate tool sets, chocolate hair dryers, keyboards, televisions, calculators, cell phones, ears, noses, lips, hairbrushes, paintbrushes, pool tables, lacrosse sticks, space shuttles, crosses, flags, umbrellas, baseballs, birdcages, and birth

11. See my *Making Sense of Taste*, chap. 4, for a fuller discussion of representation and meanings in foods.
12. Darwin quoted in Miller, *Anatomy of Disgust*, 1.
13. Natalie Tso, "Edible Excretions: Taiwan's Toilet Restaurant," *Time*, March 2, 2009, http://www.time.com/time/arts/article/0,8599,1882569,00.html (accessed February 20, 2010). And http://allrecipes.com/Recipe/Kitty-Litter-Cake/Detail.aspx (accessed February 20, 2010). Phil Alperson and Cynthia Freeland provided these two examples.

FIGURE 3.1.   Jell-O mold in the shape of a brain.

announcements. There are "adults only" chocolate sexual organs sold covertly from bins not on display. One can find chocolate works of art (sculpture and architecture such as the Statue of Liberty and the Eiffel Tower and the Sydney Opera House) and even paintings, including *The Scream* and—an Easter specialty—*The Last Supper*. (And these are only items sold in candy stores; I omit consideration of Janine Antoni's mammoth chocolate sculptures.)

All these candy pieces have similar chemical properties, and thus they all taste the same in the bare sense of basic, uninterpreted sensation. However, some representations are harder than others to put in the mouth. One wonders fleetingly how clean it is before taking a bite of a chocolate hairbrush, for example. Eating a chocolate tarantula presents a momentary challenge. Indeed, probably there are some shapes that are untastable. Note the mixture of sensory categories in that sentence: some *shapes* are *untastable*. Sometimes we find we cannot come near something that appears repellent, even if we "know" that it is perfectly safe or even nutritious, as Rozin's experiments reported in chapter 1 indicate. As food historian Jean-François Revel puts it, "Food is inseparable from imagination."[14] We seem to have here a culinary version of the paradox of fiction: one responds in contrary ways, both taking the object to be real and recognizing that it is not. The referential potential of pictorial foods widens the experience of eating considerably beyond flavor. It underscores the role of vision, cognition, and recognition in experiences of eating, drawing attention to additional aspects of foods that challenge both sense and sensibility.

14. Jean-François Revel, *Culture and Cuisine: A Journey through the History of Food*, trans. Helen R. Lane (New York: Da Capo Press, 1984), 8.

Eating Sublime and Terrible

We have already examined several cases of foods that are valued for their sophistication and the depth of flavor supplied by the presence of substances that are in raw or pure form disgusting. This has taken us through the first two categories of disgusting things to eat: those whose sensory properties are immediately aversive. In addition, pictorial foods provide what might seem aberrant instances of substances crafted into shapes that challenge us, because in their real form they too would be disgusting to eat. However, many of these examples, such as the Jell-O brain and strange chocolates, are so fanciful that they may not seem to represent a serious category of eating. This final section situates representational foods in contexts with greater moral and social significance.

If it is the case that some of the most important types of cuisine and the cultivation of sophisticated taste arise out of substances that have a disgust quotient, this is not unique among aesthetic phenomena. Philosophy of art and aesthetics are peppered with examples of the paradox of aversion: the attraction to an object that both inspires fear or revulsion and is transformed into something profoundly beautiful, an experience that philosophers from ancient times to the present have analyzed as a type of pleasure. There are three standardly recognized categories where aversions can convert into positive aesthetic experiences. The first and most ancient concerns tragedy. Aristotle discussed the enjoyment to be found in this poetic form, where the evocation of the painful tragic emotions of pity and terror is the foundation for both catharsis and the aesthetic understanding that he interprets as a pleasure in learning. Second, there is the powerful experience of the sublime, which was widely analyzed in modern philosophy in terms of the conversion of fear into thrilling delight. And more recently theories of horror have tried to comprehend how the disturbing spectacles that mark that genre manage to deliver aesthetic pleasure. I am proposing a fourth category: the conversion of the disgusting into the delicious. Certain encounters with what we might consider particularly profound eating transform an initially aversive experience into something significant and savorable. I believe there are especially illuminating parallels between terrible eating and the experience of the sublime.

In his *Philosophical Enquiry into the Origin of Our Ideas of the Sublime and Beautiful* (1757), Edmund Burke observes that there are three basic feeling states: pleasure, pain, and an in-between state of indifference. Beauty is a particular species of pleasure, but what he calls the "delight" of the sublime is built upon intense emotional pain, namely, terror: "Whatever is fitted in any sort to excite the ideas of pain, and danger, that is to say, whatever is in any sort terrible, or is conversant about terrible objects, or operates in a manner analogous to terror, is a source of the *sublime*; that is, it is productive of the strongest emotion which the mind is capable of feeling."[15]

As we saw in the previous chapter, some theorists seeking to resolve the paradoxes of aversion have appealed to the safety of representation to account for the enjoyment in art of subjects, emotions, and situations that in reality are too dreadful to afford any pleasure. It is the *mimesis* of tragedy that Aristotle believed permits us to enjoy that difficult theatrical form, for example. But Burke stands out for boldly stating that we need no shield of representation in order to delight in pain, for indeed we are equally fascinated by pains, terrors, and horrors in reality, so long as they do not press too closely. (He offers the shocking speculation that a theater audience would readily forgo the pleasures of the best tragedy in order to attend a public execution.) At a sufficient degree of remove that permits safety, human beings are simply fascinated by—and therefore take delight in—all manner of things that terrify, for either their size or might or ferocity or power.

Burke suggests that objects that inspire terror may trigger the ecstatic delight of the sublime because a state of emotional contentment is simply too close to that intermediate state of indifference that lies between pleasure and pain.[16] Just as an unexercised body becomes slack and lethargic, desiring the exertion of its muscles, so the mind can become too relaxed. Encounters with pain, danger, and other fear-provoking situations shake up the mental works in a healthy and enlivening way, even as they cause us to dwell on forces that threaten our safety and raise our mortality to the forefront of awareness. Ironically, the ultimate object of contemplation that is so enlivening is death, and Burke calls the most profound pain an "emissary to that king of terrors."[17]

Burke's own catalog of sublime objects includes a large and disorderly collection of examples from natural events to passages from the Bible. He lists various qualities an object might have that inspire terror, awe, reverence, respect, astonishment—all emotions that can be components of the feeling of the sublime. Vastness, danger, desolation, infinity, great size, difficulty, and magnificence all have their sublime exemplars, and what they share is a degree of power that puts their might above that of a human being. "I know of nothing sublime which is not some modification of power," Burke remarks.[18] Things over which we exercise control may be physically stronger than we are, but they

---

15. Edmund Burke, *A Philosophical Enquiry into the Origin of Our Ideas of the Sublime and Beautiful* (1757), ed. James T. Boulton (Notre Dame, IN: University of Notre Dame Press, 1958), 39. "Delight" is the term Burke uses to convey the positive magnetism of the sublime despite its pain; Kant calls this phenomenon "negative pleasure," and the oxymoron he chooses sums up the paradox of aversion. I return to theories of the sublime in chapter 5.

16. Burke, *Philosophical Enquiry*, 134–45. See also Paul Crowther, *Critical Aesthetics and Postmodernism* (New York: Oxford University Press, 1993), chap. 6.

17. Burke, *Philosophical Enquiry*, 40.

18. Burke, *Philosophical Enquiry*, 64.

are not sublime. A beast of burden may be immense, but it does our bidding and inspires neither fear nor awe. "We have continually about us animals of a strength that is considerable, but not pernicious. Amongst these we never look for the sublime: it comes upon us in the gloomy forest, and in the howling wilderness, in the form of the lion, the tiger, the panther, or rhinoceros."[19]

Burke himself draws the line at disgust, claiming that animals that are aversive but not fearsome are merely odious and more likely to arouse disgust than sublimity.[20] Although I aim to make a case for certain parallels between sublimity and terrible eating, there are obvious factors that initially seem to separate eating from anything akin to sublime status. In some way or other, the perceiver must achieve some distance from the object of the aversive emotion in order to experience delight. Vision and hearing permit the apprehension of terrifying objects from a distance, affording a physical margin of safety from which dread and terror can be converted into delight. By contrast, distance seems to be what taste will not permit because objects of taste are always literally close to one. Touch and taste are contact senses and require reduction of physical distance; even smell quickly disappears as one begins to move away from an object.

Moreover, the reversed power relations that obtain between the objects one eats and the objects that inspire awe and terror would seem to preclude eating experiences from comparability with the sublime. By the time something has landed on our plate, it is thoroughly subdued; we the eater are in control. Therefore, it would seem that there is no possibility that we might encounter qualities that exhibit analogous aesthetic import. But this conclusion relies overmuch on the fact that our dinner poses no immediate danger. Its presence may nonetheless remind us of that king of terrors, as well as other intimations of mortality and loss, evidence that the fourth conversion harbors disturbing and potentially profound aesthetic experience.

This point is bolstered by the role of food and drink in art. Still life painting, including the genre known as the gamepiece, has often been used to fore-ground rot and decay, transience, loss, and ultimate mortality—ideas manifest in forms where difficult emotions such as fear and disgust are harmonized with artful composition and iconographic tradition. These themes appear at their most extreme in the grisly *vanitas* picture, with its grimacing skulls loll-ing amid the detritus of human endeavor (figure 3.2). Decay and transience are more decoratively present in pretty flower and fruit paintings when they include spotted and browning peaches, spilled drink, or scavenging vermin (figure 3.3). The gamepiece with its depiction of bloodstained, disemboweled deer and hare virtually celebrates slaughter, a harvesting of the bounties of

19. Burke, *Philosophical Enquiry*, 66.
20. Burke, *Philosophical Enquiry*, 86.

FIGURE 3.2. Pieter Claesz, *Vanitas—Still Life*. 1656. Kunsthistorisches Museum, Vienna. Erich Lessing/Art Resource, NY.

FIGURE 3.3. James Peale, *Still Life: Apples, Grapes, Pear*. Ca. 1822–25. Oil on wood, 18 3/16 × 26 3/8 in. Museum purchase in memory of William C. Murray, who served the Munson-Williams-Proctor Institute from 1955 to 1977. Munson-Williams-Proctor Arts Institute, Utica, New York. Munson-Williams-Proctor Institute/Art Resource, NY.

FIGURE 3.4. Jan Fyt, *Still Life with Fruit, Dead Game, and a Parrot.* Late 1640s. Oil on canvas. © National Gallery, London/Art Resource, NY.

nature commemorated in paintings that might hang on the walls of tastefully decorated dining rooms (figure 3.4)[21]

Any worry over undue inference from art to practice is assuaged by similar illustrations of dead game and cuts of meat often found in cookbooks, which, because themselves informed by the genres of still life, provide a segue from paint to plate. A notable example of this is provided by the *Four Seasons Cookbook* (1971), whose photographic illustrations include a gamepiece composition bearing the caption "Superb Richebourg celebrates autumn game birds and 20-gauge over/under that downed them" (figure 3.5). Another—in explicit homage to William Michael Harnett's *After the Hunt* (figure 3.6)—is captioned "Hare (in composition after Harnett) provides saddle in specialty by Chef Chantreau" (figure 3.7)[22]

Leon Kass refers to the "great paradox of eating, namely that to preserve their life and form living forms necessarily destroy life and form."[23] As

21. Kenneth Ames, *Death in the Dining Room* (Philadelphia: Temple University Press, 1982).

22. Charlotte Adams, *The Four Seasons Cookbook* (New York: Ridge Press/Holt, Rinehart and Winston, 1971), 48–58 and 116–17. The photographs are by Arie deZanger. A reciprocal transition from art to kitchen is provided in the double publication of an exhibit catalog and a cookbook: Donna R. Barnes and Peter G. Rose, *Matters of Taste: Food and Drink in Seventeenth-Century Dutch Art and Life,* packaged with Peter G. Rose, *Matters of Taste: Dutch Recipes with an American Connection* (Albany/Syracuse, NY: Albany Institute of History and Art/Syracuse University Press, 2002).

23. Leon Kass, *The Hungry Soul: Eating and the Perfecting of Our Nature* (New York: Free Press, 1994), 13.

FIGURE 3.5. "Superb Richebourg celebrates autumn game birds and 20-gauge over/under that downed them." *Four Seasons Cookbook*, 1971. Photograph by Arie deZanger.

Margaret Visser observes, "Animals are murdered to produce meat; vegetables are torn up, peeled, and chopped; most of what we eat is treated with fire; and chewing is designed remorselessly to finish what killing and cooking

FIGURE 3.6. William Michael Harnett, *After the Hunt*. 1884. Oil on
canvas. Collection of the Butler Institute of American Art, Youngstown,
Ohio.

began."[24] The addition of chewing to this catalog implicates us all in the
process of destruction. Not all this violence is apt to disturb, and indeed for
some people none of it does. But certain meals seem deliberately to harbor an
awareness of the fact that to sustain one's own life one takes another. This
intuition looms especially close to consciousness when the object of one's
dinner fits into the third category introduced earlier: another animal whose
form is still recognizable as its living body. Indeed, this kind of eating can
appear brutish, and one might surmise—prematurely—that it disgusts
because of the absence of the kind of distance that separates civilized human
from brute.

One means to quell this discomfort is to remove the object one is eating
from noticeable signs of its origin. Consider the following passage from the
novel *Cold Mountain*, by Charles Frazier. This narrative is set in the waning

24. Margaret Visser, *The Rituals of Dinner: The Origins, Evolution, Eccentricities, and Meaning of Table Manners* (New York: Penguin, 1991), 3–4.

FIGURE 3.7. "Hare (in composition after Harnett) provides saddle in specialty by Chef Chantreau." *Four Seasons Cookbook,* 1971. Photograph by Arie deZanger.

years of the American Civil War at a time when scarcity and winter take vast tolls on the resources of the defeated. At a point toward the end of the story, four characters find themselves stranded snowbound in the mountains, where they have trapped some squirrels and roasted them for dinner.

All they had left was a little bit of grits and five squirrels that Ruby had shot and gutted and skinned. She had skewered them on sticks and roasted them with the heads on over chestnut coals, and that evening Ruby and Stobrod and Inman ate theirs like you would an ear of corn. Ada sat a minute and examined her portion. The front teeth were yellow and long. She was not accustomed to eating things with the teeth still in them. Stobrod watched her and said, That head'll twist right off, if it's bothering you.[25]

25. Charles Frazier, *Cold Mountain* (New York: Atlantic Monthly Press, 1997), 347.

This passage does not detail an object of haute cuisine but a piece of meat desperately needed to avert starvation, and in context it may seem as if the presence of body parts such as teeth is what renders this meal particularly brutal. Twisting off the head removes some of the uglier evidence of the killing required to sustain human life. And in fact, some instances of developed cuisines do go to extraordinary lengths to remove not only meat but other foods from their original condition, such as by chopping and stewing, or molding or hiding in dough casings such as ravioli or wontons. It would be premature, however, to conclude that *fine dining* is distinguished from *brute eating* by the degree of unrecognizability of its objects or their remove from the apparent natural state in which they lived. Indeed, the dramatic opposite is the case. Consider the elaborate dressings of suckling pigs and boar heads, or the displays of meats stuffed back into skins that graced the medieval dining table.[26] Indeed, one can discover within those same categories of foods that initially disgust and repel, both the distancing of the disgusting and repellent qualities to make the food palatable, and the cultivating of the disgust and repulsion into a form of deliberate and purposeful dining. Items that disgust at first may be transformed into foods that we savor—for the very qualities that initially repel. Uniting the several categories of the disgusting, this phenomenon is manifest both in the sensory realm and in the meanings that foods possess.

Consider objects with tastes that offend the senses at first: very hot spices and peppers, which burn; alcohol, which sickens. All these substances one can learn to like through practice and maturity (for the tongue and its receptors develop into adulthood), and once these tastes are cultivated, substances without them appear bland. Certain vegetable foods are difficult to eat because of their sensory properties, and for that reason they have become the focus of contests that challenge contenders to eat them in formidable quantities (incidentally confounding the role of surfeit in eating and disgust).[27] Ramps, the strong wild leeks of the eastern mountains of the United States, are but one example of foods celebrated in reeking festivals of superconsumption. The durian fruit of Indonesia presents a particularly puzzling case of a taste that both disgusts and delights. It has such a repellent odor—reportedly like vomit and rotten onions—that it is banned in public places, but it has a delectable taste. An English traveler to Indonesia in the mid-nineteenth century was an enthusiastic convert to durian:

---

26. Revel observes that these decorative aspects of meals bordered on the inedible because the original skins of animals that housed the cooked meat were often beginning to rot and to emit foul odors, which required heavy perfumes to accompany the meal. This adds an additional element of disgust to the scene, though evidently one that was neither welcome nor cultivated. *Culture and Cuisine*, 134.

27. Items in the second category, tastes that disgust because of surfeit, seem different from the others, all of which permit scope for the fourth conversion. Surfeit indicates an abuse of taste that requires scaling back rather than exploitation.

The pulp is the eatable part, and its consistency and flavour are inde-
scribable. A rich butter-like custard highly flavoured with almonds
gives the best general idea of it, but intermingled with it come wafts of
flavour that call to mind cream-cheese, onion-sauce, brown sherry, and
other incongruities. . . . In fact to eat Durians is a new sensation, worth
a voyage to the East to experience.[28]

The unusual combination of flavors plus the divergent valences provided by
taste and smell supply their own paradox: because taste and smell are close
companions, such that a large percentage of taste is supplied by the olfactory
sense, this aesthetic division in the case of durian is curious. It appears to be a
food with approach and avoidance built into its very sensory qualities.

These examples represent foods the very sensuous properties of which
must be overcome and then cultivated; but those tastes represent only themselves, as it were. They do not have any additional meaning that may be repugnant. But certain foods both vegetable and animal come packaged with toxins
or repellent substances that need to be washed away to make the food edible,
and the tastes of these substances *mean* danger or foulness. At the same time,
sophisticated preparation often deliberately retains some of the noxious substances. In his *Grand Dictionnaire de Cuisine*, Alexandre Dumas asserts that
kidneys are at their best when they are prepared so that a whiff of urine flavor
remains in them.[29] In this case, something one would gag to drink is retained
as flavoring—but only for the kidney, not for any other meat. It is a reminder of
the origin of the food that stays within its very taste. Similarly, gamy meat harbors a flavor of decay that renders it stronger and more pungent. In both these
cases, it is not only that the taste initially disgusts, but that it signals the presence of something that has a repugnant meaning: waste, death. Yet, the most
sophisticated mode of preparation is one that retains rather than expunges the
sense qualities that remind the diner of the borderline state of the food.

Perhaps the most famous example in this category is fugu, the puffer fish,
so poisonous that in Japan, where it is commonly eaten, only a licensed chef
who knows what organs to remove and how to get rid of the toxins is permitted
to prepare it. Yet reportedly, the most sophisticated diner is also the one prepared to risk the most to savor the taste of fugu, for by request enough of the
neurotoxin can be left in the fish that the diners' lips and tongue are slightly
numbed, reminding them of the presence of danger and death. (And sometimes overwhelming them, for this is a dangerous meal, and every year people
die from eating fugu.)

Some foods are substances that are so alien that they seem to represent a
category that simply should not be consumed. Insects, which in swarms are

28. Alfred Russel Wallace, *Borneo, Celebes, Aru*, (from *The Malay Archipelago*) (London: Penguin, 2007), 56.
29. Alexandre Dumas, *Dumas on Food: Selections from Le Grand Dictionnaire de Cuisine*, trans. Alan Davidson and Jane Davidson (London: Folio Society, 1978), 152.

commonly featured on lists of disgusting items, are quite nourishing and are eaten in many parts of the world. To others, it is nearly impossible to imagine putting them into one's mouth. These differences in eating habits are usually just noted as varieties of cultural practice, but this overlooks something very interesting: disgusting foods do not appear only in the diet of the Other. We all have categories such as these that we do eat, foods that we recoil from or treat very cautiously in nature that we learn to consume quite readily. That which is disgusting is not just that which other people eat; it appears on our own tables, transformed into the delicious. Of course, once this transformation occurs it is hard to recall the initial disgust, which is why we ordinarily consider only unfamiliar foods disgusting.[30]

Perhaps the most interesting conversion of the repellent or disgusting to the delectable occurs when the presentation of foods mimics them in life, for it is then that the attentive eater can hardly fail to notice his participation in a death-dealing activity. This is particularly vivid when the death of the animal occurs in the presence of the diner: raw shellfish just dredged from a seabed; live oysters opened at the table and served with their flesh still pulsing. Or the cup of warm cobra blood and the still-beating heart of the snake that globe-trotting chef Keith Floyd reports he was offered in a Vietnamese kitchen.[31]

In times past, the heads of animals have been considered delicacies and have been brought to the table prepared for eating but still in their original containers, perhaps decorated or even bejeweled. This taste has passed in North America, though we still carve whole fowl at the table, which are quite recognizable even without their wattles and claws. Though we now often remove the heads and tails of fish, we can buy fish platters that thoughtfully trace heads and tail fins in their design so that the succulent middle can be placed between. All these devices remind us of the original state of what we eat. Although this reminder often goes unnoticed, at times our realization is enhanced to a point that achieves a parallel with sublime experience, and sometimes it lapses into horror. Here are two examples.

Richard Gordon Smith was an Englishman who lived in Japan in the early years of the twentieth century. He recounts a meal he requested in a remote part of that country, where he asked the cook at an inn to prepare a carp in the traditional way that was reserved for the nobility. Delighted at the request, the cook prepared a live fish, still gasping on the plate, surrounded with tasteful symbolic decorations that mimicked the look of the bottom of a sandy ocean. At first it did not occur to Gordon Smith that the fish had already been readied

---

30. Just as the food of others can be disgusting, the disgust of others can be perplexing. I once repelled a German visitor with a pumpkin pie. Cynthia Freeland told me of an Icelandic acquaintance to whom honey—"bee-spit"—was disgusting.

31. Keith Floyd, *Far Flung Floyd* (New York: Citadel Press, 1994), 59–60.

for eating; he writes: "The dish was really pretty in spite of the gasping fish which, however, showed no pain, and there was not a sign of blood or a cut." But the artistry of the chef was only revealed when he dribbled a little soy sauce into the fish's eye:

> The effect was not instantaneous: it took a full two minutes as the cook sat over him, chopsticks in hand. All of a sudden and to my unutterable astonishment, the fish gave a convulsive gasp, flicked its tail and flung the whole of its skin on one side of its body over, exposing the underneath of the stomach parts, skinned; the back was cut into pieces about an inch square and a quarter of an inch thick, ready for pulling out and eating. Never in my life have I seen a more barbarous or cruel thing—not even the scenes at Spanish bull fights. Egawa [Smith's Japanese companion] is a delicate-stomached person and as he could eat none, neither could I. It would be simply like taking bites out of a large live fish. I took the knife from my belt and immediately separated the fish's neck vertebrae, much to the cook's astonishment and perhaps disgust.[32]

I wonder if this meal is markedly more cruel than any other. The startling revelation of the flayed body aside, Gordon Smith's revulsion seems to be chiefly a matter of timing. He was invited to eat a being whose life had not yet expired, but had the fish been killed just minutes earlier, the collision of life and death would not have occurred to him. And yet it would have lingered there in the very fresh taste of the recently killed fish. The freshness of fish, the agedness of gamy meat: both announce themselves *in their very tastes* to the reflective diner. (Roland Barthes suggests that such meals are memorials of sorts: "If Japanese cooking is always performed in front of the eventual diner (a fundamental feature of this cuisine), this is probably because it is important to consecrate by spectacle the death of what is being honored.")[33]

My final example also represents the re-creation of a meal that is now uncommon and that formerly was prepared only for the elite of a culture. When President François Mitterand of France knew that he was dying, he resolved to finish his mortal days by eating one final meal that summed up the best that can be presented to the senses. The centerpiece of that meal was ortolan, a small warbler, a migratory wild bird, which is now prohibited by French law from the table. It is said to represent the soul of France, and consuming it is a sin. But Mitterand prevailed in his last wish and served a remarkable meal to more than thirty guests.

32. Richard Gordon Smith, *Travels in the Land of the Gods: The Japan Diaries of Richard Gordon Smith*, ed. Victoria Manthorpe (New York: Prentice Hall, 1986), 205. This part of the diary is from 1906–1907. Mark Meli drew this account to my attention.
33. Roland Barthes, *The Empire of Signs*, trans. Richard Howard (New York: Hill and Wang, 1982), 20.

The tiny birds are caught in the wild and kept in the dark to fatten. When ready, they are drowned in Armagnac brandy and plucked. They are roasted and served whole, wings and legs tucked in, eyes open. They are brought to the table straight from the fire, and one must consume the entire bird. The diner traditionally eats them with a large linen napkin draped over his head. The napkin traps the aroma of the dish, even as it hides the shame of the feast from the eyes of God.

Mitterand's last meal was re-created and consumed by a curious American writer, Michael Paterniti, who offers this description of eating ortolan:

> Here's what I taste: Yes, quidbits of meat and organs; the succulent, tiny strands of flesh between the ribs and tail. I put inside myself the last flowered bit of air and Armagnac in its lungs, the body of rainwater and berries. In there, too, is the ocean and Africa and the dip and plunge in a high wind. And the heart that bursts between my teeth.
>
> It takes time. I'm forced to chew and chew again and again, for what seems like three days. And what happens after chewing for this long—as the mouth full of taste buds and glands does its work—is that I fall into a trance. I don't taste anything anymore, cease to exist as anything but taste itself.
>
> And that's where I want to stay—but then can't because the sweetness of the bird is turning slightly bitter and the bones have announced themselves. When I think about forcing them down my throat, a wave of nausea passes through me. And that's when, with great difficulty, I swallow everything.[34]

Both these examples involve meals that virtually force the diner to contemplate the sacrifice of his or her dinner. (Or even, perhaps, to entertain the possibility that this kind of eating approaches decadence, so far has it come from mere necessity.) This suggests that part of the experience of this kind of a meal involves awareness, however submerged, of the presence of death amid the continuance of one's own life. And it seems to me most improbable to account for the development of such cuisine simply in terms of the search for a really good taste pleasure. It is better understood as an aesthetic transformation of an aversion into a pleasure—the disgusting into the delicious. Just how this transformation occurs is complex, involving educated tolerance for ingesting unusual things and receptivity to their tastes. Even more, it requires reflective eating regarding the relationship between the eater and the eaten. Admittedly, such insights are not always very ready to consciousness. Other habits of mind, including the purely practical demands of eating, form

34. Michael Paterniti, "The Last Meal," *Esquire* 129, no. 5 (May 1998): 117.

insulating layers over these matters, a factor that reminds us of the intensely functional circumstances that remain to distinguish even the most recherché foods from artworks.

Animals that qualify as sublime, such as the tiger, the panther, and the rhinoceros, are fearsome precisely because they might attack, kill, or eat *us*. The power relation is reversed when we are the eaters, and one of the privileges of being at the top of the food chain is that we rarely must defend ourselves against becoming another creature's meal. Yet we are certainly edible, and we are as mortal as any other living being. Preparation that foregrounds an awareness of the life and death of our meal does not arouse fear for our own safety, but it prompts meditation on the cycles of life and death that we all undergo by forcing reflection on the very moment where we participate in that cycle. The gasping carp puts us in the presence of death. The fragrances that summon up the life of the ortolan are compressed into its taste, a taste that is both nauseously difficult and ecstatically delectable. It would reach neither extreme were it not for one's intense, bodily awareness of this moment when a life and a death are commemorated in a taste.

With the sense of taste the shift from disgust to savor transforms the aversion to an enjoyable affective state. Ironically, it would appear that the primary role for disgust—to monitor ingestion of noxious substances—also represents the very situation where disgust can convert to an actual pleasure. The roles for disgust in art are considerably more variable, for there the disgusting may become aesthetically valuable and even savorable, while yet sustaining its ability to arouse genuine aversion. I now turn to the presentation, expression, and evocation of disgust in art.

4

Varieties of Aesthetic Disgust

The previous chapter has confirmed one dimension of the complicated commerce between disgust and attraction, for sometimes substances that possess a disgust quotient can be transformed into foods that are highly savored. When it comes to eating, however, the manipulation of the disgusting into the delicious brings about a marked change in the affect under study. Disgust loses its aversive features and is transformed into pleasure, though there may be a residue of what once was disgusting that lingers both in taste sensation and in meaning. Because this residue deepens flavor and the experience of eating, by the time that sort of food is prepared for the hungry diner, it no longer functions as a proper object of disgust. On the basis of food examples alone, therefore, it might appear that when the disgusting exerts an appeal, it is an invitation to discover that something is really not an object of disgust at all. In other words, perhaps the appeal of disgust is always—or at least typically—toward an object that fails to prompt that emotion by the time that it comes to be savored. If this were indeed the case, an aspect of the Enlightenment analysis of the artistic use of disgust would be vindicated.

This judgment would be hasty, however, as we can readily see when attention turns to works of art, for when disgust is aroused by art it often stays disgusting. Though usually mixed with—or even masked by—other emotions, the characteristic revolt remains in place, becoming itself an element of aesthetic recognition. In such cases, whatever conversion of affect occurs, it does not transform the disgusting into another category altogether. In maintaining the contrary, Enlightenment philosophers were certainly wrong. As I have already noted, the exploitation of a disgust response in art is possible to a large degree because as a rule the primary bodily senses of smell and taste are engaged only in imagination, and visual or imaginative evocations of disgust do not enjoin the same need to convert into sensory pleasure in order to be physically tolerable.[1] These widened parameters of aesthetic disgust invite an enormously increased range for artistic employment of this response.

This chapter has three main objectives. The first is simply to intensify recognition that disgust in art manifests a prodigious diversity, a point to be made with the aid of numerous examples. It is worth reviewing this diversity in some detail because it will be important to bear in mind for the next chapter when theories of the "enjoyment" of disgust are considered. Second, a close look at particular cases confirms that disgust can come in small doses; that the recoil of disgust is not an all-or-nothing affair; and that this basic emotion has varieties sufficiently subtle that their kinship with strong core disgust can go unnoticed. I shall be arguing on behalf of maximum variety of all elements of aesthetic disgust: of the qualia of the affect, of the significance disgust achieves in art, of the degrees of affect aroused, and of the plausible accounts for the satisfactions it can deliver.

The variations of disgust evident even in rather similar artistic contexts lead to the third point to be advanced, namely, that emotions, and in particular aesthetic emotions, are partially constituted by their specific intentional objects. This will complicate the general picture of emotions outlined in the first chapter, but it is necessary to account for the aesthetic plasticity of disgust (and, for that matter, other emotions as well). Along the way, this argument will provide a perspective on the famous and contentious singularity of aesthetic judgments—the idea that aesthetic responses are virtually unique to their particular objects.

I begin with a reminder that when I refer to aesthetic disgust I mean the arousal of disgust in an audience, a spectator, or a reader, under circumstances where that emotion both apprehends artistic properties and constitutes a component of appreciation. Obviously, art can also arouse nonappreciative disgust. If one walks out of a movie because one is too revolted to sit there any longer— perhaps because of its seamy subject matter or mean-spirited humor—this counts as an arousal of disgust but not an appreciation. It constitutes a judgment about the quality of art, but it is not a species of the difficult apprehension marked by aesthetic disgust. Therefore, it will not occupy me here. Rather, I am interested in affective responses that are virtually required by artworks in order that they be fully apprehended and valued.

---

1. This generalization obtains even though there are a number of contemporary artists who produce work that more directly engages the bodily senses, exploiting touch, smell, and even taste.

To illustrate with a familiar example, the creature in the *Alien* movies, with its huge, slobbering maw, arouses disgust that both correctly grasps its axiological (value-laden) properties and appreciates such a horror spectacle. One who watches *Alien* without feeling disgust (and fear and a host of other emotions) could hardly be said to appreciate the movie. Insofar as an artwork prompts disgust as part of its appropriate effect, then aesthetic disgust is a significant feature of aesthetic judgment. If the overall judgment is positive—that the work is valuable, successful, worthy—then the disgust is a component of recognition of that value. Understanding does not necessarily eventuate in positive assessment, but it is a prerequisite for sound verdictive judgment.

Disgust can be aroused by most art forms, though the majority of cases probably occur with visual and narrative arts. With the latter, as with many aesthetic emotions, disgust on the part of an observer or reader may mirror an affect that a fictional character undergoes. Because so much disgust is deployed in horror, stories in which characters are caught in terrifying and revolting situations, some of the most familiar instances of aesthetic disgust do match the emotions of a character. For example, the victims of Dracula experience fear and disgust when the vampire nears them, and so do the readers of the stories or viewers of the movies. As Noël Carroll describes horror fiction:

> The emotions of the audience are supposed to mirror those of the positive human characters in certain, but not all, respects . . . the characters' responses counsel us that the appropriate reactions to the monsters in question comprise shuddering, nausea, shrinking, paralysis, screaming, and revulsion. Our responses are meant, ideally, to parallel those of characters.[2]

This structure of response is not restricted to horror, for many fictions in which characters are disgusted (frightened or otherwise disturbed) arouse a version of the same emotion in audiences.

This does not adequately describe all disgust responses, however. Just as often the audience is disgusted but a character is not—as, for example, when a gruesome autopsy is being conducted by a doctor inured to the scene, presently a popular device of television forensic dramas. One of the conceits of such scenes is precisely to disgust the audience, even prompting one to turn away while the team of forensic scientists carries on undisturbed. The device can be amusing, heartless, and clever. It can also keep a reminder of the fragility of life at the forefront of attention without articulating an explicit declaration.

Scenes like these can feed the skepticism about the reliability of disgust that I have been arguing against throughout this study. A disgust skeptic might contend that the doctors present at an autopsy no longer are disgusted

---

2. Noël Carroll, from *The Philosophy of Horror, or Paradoxes of the Heart*, excerpted in *Aesthetics: The Big Questions*, ed. Carolyn Korsmeyer (Malden, MA: Blackwell, 1998), 276.

by dismembered bodies and the stench of decaying flesh. Therefore disgust does not locate objects in the world that are really foul, it is just we oversensitive viewers who find them so. Again, I maintain that such resistance slights the very purpose of the artistic use of this strong emotion. Obviously, forensic pathologists do become inured to the difficult circumstances of their work. One can learn to quell disgust partly because sensory shock diminishes with exposure. (It helps that smell has a low overload threshold.) But we are examining the scene in a drama, and equally obviously the very point of such staging is to disturb viewers, dramatizing the contrast between the audience response and that of the oblivious scientists.

Not only can audiences react with disgust when characters display an absence of affect, but also aesthetic disgust can be a response to something terrible to which a character responds with entirely different emotions, perhaps anger or grief. Examples of these differences will be introduced shortly. In all cases, the transparency of disgust makes the aesthetic response especially vivid, often to the point even of sickening the audience.

The very purpose of some art is to upset. Arthur Danto refers to the phenomenon of what he calls "disturbatory" art: "This is art that does not just have disturbing contents. . . . Disturbatory art is intended, rather, to modify, through experiencing it, the mentality of those who do experience it."[3] He has especially in mind politically motivated art that seeks to change social norms, and he notes that performance art, with its radical decrease of aesthetic distance between artist and audience, is particularly adept at disturbance. Perhaps all serious artists strive to alter our mentality to some degree, at least for the short time in which we remember their works. Aesthetic disgust is a vivid way to do just that.

Disgust: A Sampler

How to determine which artworks disgust? To avoid assembling a merely idiosyncratic list, I refer here to art that makes use of what are identified as the typical elicitors of core disgust reviewed in chapter 1. These include eating things that are taboo: inappropriate substances such as worms and spiders and—most vilely—another human being; foul intrusions into the mouth or other bodily orifice; extrusions from the body such as excrement, pus, blood, or vomit; violations of the bodily envelope that occur with mutilating injuries or infected wounds; swarms of vermin, especially those that invade the body; putrefying organic materials; and other dissolutions of bodily integrity. These themes can be deployed to present both the alien and the familiar. They contribute to the

3. Arthur C. Danto, "Bad Aesthetic Times," in *Encounters and Reflections: Art in the Historical Present* (Berkeley and Los Angeles: University of California Press, 1990), 299. For discussion of performance and shock art, see Robert Rawdon Wilson, *The Hydra's Tale: Imagining Disgust* (Edmunton: University of Alberta Press, 2002), chap. 1.

imaginative formation of monsters and their foul deeds. They confront us with the indignities of the end of life in its inescapable disintegration. And if they are presented as the outcome of violent or purposive action, they evoke questions of responsibility and motivation. When the disturbing situation is the result of human agency, we move into territory where core disgust mingles with moral disgust.

What follows is a set of lists of works that potently, importantly, and deliberately arouse disgust. Some set out to shock and revolt, and there is an enormous catalog of gross-out works that do little else. These are interesting to consider insofar as they exert an attraction, but they are so unsubtle that I shall ignore them for the moment, taking up the question of whatever allure they possess again in the next chapter. More important here are works that disgust because of the treatment their difficult subjects demand. With some, the arousal is so slight and subtle that it may seem only weird, though I maintain that whenever a particular visceral queasiness ensues disgust is present, exerting its own brand of aesthetic power. The extent and variety of this assembly indicate the range of ways that disgust can be aroused, from revulsion to subtle discomfort, sorrowful pathos, eroticism, satire, horror, and humor. The lists are organized by art form. They are of necessity partial, and they will hopefully prompt numerous additions.

> *Movies*: Horror movies featuring monsters or alien species. Movies that feature human monsters who mutilate and kill, such as the infamous Hannibal Lecter in *Silence of the Lambs*. Adventure sagas such as *Conan the Destroyer* or *Starship Troopers* with its hideous brain bug (figure 4.1).

FIGURE 4.1. Film still, *Starship Troopers*. Dir. Paul Verhoeven. TriStar Pictures, 1987.

David Lynch's *Eraserhead* with its monstrous baby. Holocaust depictions such as portions of *Schindler's List.*

Television: Science fiction tales such as *The X-Files* that introduce monsters and dwell upon their unfamiliar and threatening forms. Forensic and medical dramas that graphically depict mutilations such as *NCIS* or *House*. Crime dramas that foreground sadistic murders and rapes such as *CSI* and *Law and Order: SVU*.

Prose literature: Horror narratives such as Bram Stoker's *Dracula* or Mary Shelley's *Frankenstein*, Bataille's *Story of the Eye* with its voyeuristic and excretory eroticism. Works by Stephen King and Clive Barker. Portions of J. K. Rowling's *Harry Potter* series. War narratives such as Sebastian Faulks's *Birdsong* (discussed later). J. G. Ballard's *Crash*, in which mutilations of bodies multiply the orifices for sexual penetration. Rabelais's scatological stories of Gargantua and Pantagruel. Jean-Paul Sartre's *Nausea* and Albert Camus's *The Plague*, in both of which disgust evinces existential horror at being itself.[4]

Poetry: War poetry such as that of Wilfred Owen, which describes the effects of mustard gas on soldiers ("the blood/Come gargling from the froth-corrupted lungs".)[5] The ancient Scottish poem "Twa Corbies," also a song, in which two ravens find the body of a fallen knight and discuss how they will pluck out his pretty blue eyes.

Theatrical arts: Sophocles' *Philoctetes* ("His foot was festering, oozing pus/ From a foul wound./Even at festivals/We hardly dared touch the wine or meat.")[6] *Antigone*, in which a brother's corpse is picked apart by carrion birds. The gruesome background and murderous plotlines of Aeschylus's *Oresteia*. Aristophanes's *Peace*, with its giant dung beetle and proportionate stinking comestibles. Shakespeare's *King Lear*, whose character Gloucester suffers his eyes gouged out ("Out, vile jelly!"), and *Titus Andronicus*, whose character Queen Tamora is made to eat of the bodies of her two sons.[7]

Sculpture and installation: Cellini's bronze statue of Perseus, in which the hero stands over the decapitated Medusa, the blood still spurting from her neck (figure 4.2). Kiki Smith's *Tale*, which features a crawling woman trailing a rope of excrement. Marc Quinn's portrait bust, *Self* (discussed later). Giacometti's *Disagreeable Object*. Works variously utilizing dead and dying animals by Hermann Nitsch, Damien Hirst, and

---

4. Robert C. Solomon, "Facing Death Together: Camus's The Plague," in *Art and Ethical Criticism*, ed. Garry L. Hagberg (Malden, MA: Blackwell, 2008), 163–83.

5. Wilfred Owen, "Dolce et Decorum Est," in *The Oxford Book of War Poetry*, ed. Jon Stallworthy (Oxford: Oxford University Press, 1984), 189.

6. Sophocles, *Electra, Antigone, Philoctetes*, trans. Kenneth McLeish (Cambridge: Cambridge University Press, 1979), 109.

7. Wilson provides numerous examples of disgust elicitors in Shakespeare in *The Hydra's Tale*.

FIGURE 4.2. Benvenuto Cellini, *Perseus*. 1545–54. Bronze. Loggia dei Lanzi, Florence. Alinari/Art Resource, NY.

Sun Yuan and Peng Yu. Wim Delvoye's *Cloaca*, a large installation that mimicks digestion and displays the conversion of gourmet meals into shit.

Paintings: Titian's *Flaying of Marsyas*, in which the satyr's skin is being removed from his body, his blood collected in a bucket. Artemisia Gentileschi's *Judith and Holofernes* with its sawn neck and blood-soaked mattress (figure 4.3). Caravaggio's *Doubting Thomas*, in which the apostle Thomas inserts his grimy fingers into the wound on Christ's side (discussed in chapter 7). Gèricault's painting of severed limbs, a study for *The Raft of the Medusa* (figure 4.4). Odd Nordrum's finely finished depictions of amputations and excrement. Many of the works of Francis Bacon. Jenny Saville's paintings of distorted and bloated female flesh. The paintings of Saturn devouring his children by Rubens and by Goya (discussed later). Rubens's giant painting, *The Feast of Herod*, in which Salome displays the severed head of John the Baptist on a serving dish while her mother, Herodias, sticks a fork in his protruding tongue.

FIGURE 4.3. Artemisia Gentileschi, *Judith and Holofernes*. Ca. 1620. Oil on canvas. Uffizi, Florence. Scala/Art Resource, NY.

Photography: Joel Peter Witkin's still life arrangements that include body parts as disturbingly literal memento mori pieces. Cindy Sherman's photographic compositions of vomit, decay, and monstrosity. Judy Chicago's *Red Flag* and Chen Lingyang's *Twelve Flower Months*, both of which foreground menstrual blood.

Music: Richard Strauss's *Salome*, when Salome triumphantly kisses the mouth of the decapitated head of John the Baptist. The third movement of Mahler's Second Symphony, in which a passage he labeled a "Cry of Disgust" is intended to express loathing of the pointlessness of social existence.[8]

Several points emerge from this list. First, it could be much longer. I offer it only as a starting point, for it could extend indefinitely. Second, the examples

8. See chapter 2, note 31.

FIGURE 4.4. Thèodore Gèricault. Body Parts. Study of arms and legs for *Raft of the Medusa*. 1818 or 1819. Oil on canvas. Musée des Beaux Arts, Rouen. Bridgeman-Giraudon/Art Resource, NY.

span history from antiquity to the present. Despite its prevalence in current television and movies, aesthetic disgust is neither a contemporary stunt nor an emotion exploited to pander to the lowest common denominator in popular art forms. The employment of disgust extends from high-culture fine art to mass-market entertainment. Moreover, examples of disgusting art can be found in virtually all genres, although they are scarcer in music than in other art forms because of the relatively weak role of hearing as a sensory mode of disgust. Indeed, lyrics and performance styles (e.g., punk rock) probably provide most of the disgust in music.

These examples could equally well be organized according to the kinds of collateral emotions with which aesthetic disgust mingles. Some of them are comic, linking Rabelais's stories and Aristophanes' play with campy horror movies. Giacometti's *Disagreeable Object*, which severally resembles larva, penis, and turd, has lately taken on kinship with Mr. Hankey of *South Park*. Some combine disgust with pity and sympathy, such as portions of *Schindler's List* and *Birdsong*. Some are erotic, joining the shockingly odd sexuality of *Crash* and *The Story of the Eye* with Perseus's triumph over the Gorgon, a conquest depicted as both sexual and heroic.[9] The sexual, the monstrous, and the comic

9. For an analysis of the political meaning and eroticism of this sculpture, see Yael Even, "The Loggia dei Lanzi: A Showcase of Female Subjugation," in *The Expanding Discourse: Feminism and Art History*, ed. Norma Broude and Mary Garrard (New York: HarperCollins, 1992), 126–37.

are combined in the movies *Conan the Barbarian* and *Starship Troopers*, both of which blatantly enlarge male and female genitalia in the creation of monsters. Some works evoke disgust to intensify the violence or wickedness of characters and situations, such as ancient tragedies and contemporary crime television shows. Some works enlist disgust in expressions of social or existential angst, such as Mahler's symphonic passage and the novels of Sartre and Camus. And many cases do not fit clearly into any standard descriptive category and bear only glancing similarities with other examples.

Perhaps most important, the ways that disgust is aroused and the function it serves in any specific work give each instance of the emotion a distinctive feeling quality and meaning. Disgust is aroused for vastly different artistic purposes. It functions one way in comedy, another in satire or politically provocative art, another in tragedy, and each instance differs from the others. Aesthetic disgust establishes different and sometimes unpredictable attitudes of the audience toward the subject matter of art. Comedy, for instance, often prompts emotional distance and an absence of sympathy, especially for a character who is depicted as disgusting. As many have noted, one standard way for people in outsider groups to be marginalized is to portray them as disgusting, a ploy that effectively maintains a category of social otherness.[10] The same kind of claim has been made for laughter, the typical response to comedy. Henri Bergson called laughter a killer of emotions, by which he meant the emotions that bind people together in sympathy.[11] If both disgust and laughter can blunt sympathy, the wide use of disgust in comedy may be a contributor to the idea that it is an untrustworthy emotion when it is deployed to sustain social norms.

Tragedy, on the other hand, arouses sympathy and sorrow for the characters. Aristotle identified the tragic emotions as terror and pity, though the examples here indicate the presence of aesthetic disgust in tragedies as well. Although disgust repels, when a character is made so because of brutal and deplorable circumstances, this need not bring about distance between character and audience at all. In Spielberg's movie *Schindler's List*, for example, there is a scene where a little boy flees from the Gestapo and plunges into a camp latrine. We see him neck deep in excrement, his face and lips splashed with the diarrhea of sickened and terrified inmates; and while the horrid stench of the scene emanates from the screen, sympathy is at its height.

Disgust can have a moral and a political use, and in fact is a frequent component of the apprehension of feminist art and of the "disturbatory" art that Danto writes about. It is an upsetting emotion that is deployed by artists just for

10. This is a reason that Martha Nussbaum asserts that disgust is never a reliable foundation for a moral judgment. See Nussbaum, *Hiding from Humanity: Disgust, Shame, and the Law* (Princeton, NJ: Princeton University Press, 2004). Also Sara Ahmed, *The Cultural Politics of Emotion* (New York: Routledge, 2004), chap. 4.

11. Henri Bergson, *Laughter: An Essay on the Meaning of the Comic*, trans. Cloudesley Brereton and Fred Rothwell (Copenhagen and Los Angeles: Green Integer Books, 1999), 10. Also John Morreall, "Amusement and Other Mental States," in *Philosophy of Laughter and Humor*, ed. John Morreall (Albany: State University of New York Press, 1987), 221–22.

that reason—to upset and unsettle comfortable attitudes and conceptual frameworks.

For all these reasons, depending on the artistic context, disgust may mingle
with diametrically opposed emotions: with pity and sorrow, with amusement
and contempt, with sexual arousal or repulsion, with wonder and curiosity.

The consequence of the multifarious occasions of aesthetic disgust is that
one and the same emotion—the one labeled "disgust"—feels markedly different when aroused in different contexts. And the differences can be profound:
instances of aesthetic disgust differ in valence (i.e., in whether they are felt as
pleasure or pain, as negative or positive), in the degree and tenor of somatic
arousal, in the emotions that accompany them, in their meanings, in the attitudes they ground, and in their roles in genres and works of art. Even the more
specific term of use, "aesthetic disgust," is misleading, for it may imply that
there is a single type of affect that is evoked by multitudinous works of art, as
though similar qualia are occasioned by variant works. On the contrary, each
aesthetic affect is different; each registers a distinct meaning and element of
art. The rest of this chapter is devoted to fragmenting aesthetic disgust into as
many pieces as there are works that arouse it.

Singularity and Aesthetic Disgust

As a preface to this section, I again address the question of the predictability of
disgust responses. Here is a tempting counterclaim regarding the list I have
offered: not everyone is going to be disgusted by these works of art. And even
those who are might just walk away. The arousal of disgust is so culture-bound
and so geared to individual reactions that any such list will be perennially de-
batable. What is so disgusting about some of those examples, anyhow, such as
Owen's poem or Quinn's portrait bust?

I suspect that some of the source for this objection has to do with the fact
that many of the works on my list of disgusting art are also gripping, powerful,
or sad. They do not repel; they invite attention. Their emotional affect is subtle
and reflective. How can they be disgusting as well? Isn't the invitation to ponder, wonder, and admire evidence that disgust has receded? At least some of the
impulse to remove works from the disgusting category can be palliated by
pointing out that disgust has many degrees, gradations, and subtleties, even
though our vocabularies usually do not label them as such.

Is the notion of subtle disgust oxymoronic? Some would say yes, for scientific, philosophical, and critical theories of disgust tend to treat the emotion as
a radical aversion, as the review of theorists in chapters 1 and 2 indicates. It is
also likely that among the items on the lists here there are some borderline
entries. Is the affect aroused by Owen's poem or Shakespeare's plays really a
species of disgust? The inclination to answer in the negative, I surmise, is

prompted by the expectation that disgust comes in only one dosage. If we insist on this strong reading of the emotion, then there will be few cases of aesthetic disgust beyond horror, stories of war and terrible crime, and confrontational performance. But this conclusion would set disgust oddly apart from other emotions.

Unlike other difficult emotions such as fear and anger, varieties and degrees of disgust are not readily identified in our linguistic practice. Think of the multiple variants on fear that are recognized in the long list of types of fears familiar to all: panic, terror, fright, alarm, dread, apprehension, worry, phobia, anxiety, concern, trepidation, foreboding, timidity, misgiving, nervousness, uneasiness. Or of anger: rage, fury, wrath, outrage, indignation, irritation, umbrage, vexation, acrimony, exasperation, annoyance, resentment, miff. The lists for both emotions include both extremely strong versions and milder variants. There are comparatively few synonyms for disgust—revulsion, loathing, execration, abomination—and they all connote strong responses; it is hard to think of terms that indicate milder varieties. Queasy, perhaps. But the paucity of terms (at least in English) referring to degrees of this emotion is notable. Both emotion theorists and our linguistic practice usually treat disgust as an all-or-nothing recoil. Similarly, psychological studies tend to class disgust as one of the more primitive affects that is always aversive.

Is it the case, however, that disgust comes in only one powerfully nasty form? If this were indeed so, then it would make sense that its only aesthetic role would be in powerfully nasty art such as horror. But the catalog of artworks in this chapter demonstrates that disgust has many degrees and varieties; it can be funny, pathetic, contemptible, sympathetic, and uneasy. It can be delivered in shocking doses that leave one sick or in fleeting qualms that intensify other impressions. And whether in extreme or subtle modes, disgust can be evoked to register not only foul objects—from which we rightly recoil—but also the very fragility of existence, which inspires recoil at the same time that it compels acknowledgment.

Closer consideration of one of the preceding examples will supply us with an amplified vocabulary. Marc Quinn's portrait bust *Self* (1991) (figure 4.5) is a life-sized head molded from a cast of the artist's own features. It sits in a transparent cube equipped with a refrigeration unit because of the unusual medium: nine pints of the artist's own blood, collected over a period of weeks, poured into the mold, and frozen. As it sits on display, its surface slowly becomes crazed with ice crystals that adumbrate its eventual disintegration. Here is how Peter de Bolla describes encounters with *Self*:

> I have come across viewers who, on seeing *Self* for the first time, describe a sensation akin to tingling, a kind of spinal over-excitation, or a curious shudder—that involuntary somatic spasm referred to in common speech by the phrase "someone walking on one's grave." And for some these immediate somatic responses may quickly give

FIGURE 4.5. Marc Quinn, *Self*, 1991. Blood (artist's), stainless steel, perspex, and refrigeration equipment. 81 7/8 × 24 13/16 × 24 13/16 in. (208 × 63 × 63 cm.). © The artist. Photo Stephen White. Courtesy White Cube.

way to a variety of thoughts associated with formally similar presentations of the human head or face: the death mask, waxwork, funerary sculpture, embalmed body, or anatomical model. When this happens, the frisson of the physical encounter rapidly mutates into a jumble of thoughts, as if an impulse—call it a spark of affect—sets in motion a series of reactions that leave their trace in whatever permeable surface they encounter.[12]

12. Peter de Bolla, *Art Matters* (Cambridge, MA: Harvard University Press, 2001), 2.

This reaction is prompted by shock at the unusual medium. More important, it recognizes the horrid tenuousness of individual life, the fragility of mortal being. De Bolla's term "somatic spasm" neatly supplements the clumsy and now inadequate "disgust" as a descriptor of the visceral reaction to such a work. But we still have here, I maintain, a particular instance of the generic emotion we call disgust. The elicitors of disgust need not be *merely* lowly and foul. All organisms are subject to decay and putrefaction, ourselves included. Insofar as disgust plays a role in such insights, it places us in intimate contact with mortality—for we do not simply think about the transience of existence, we register its inevitability in our very viscera. The art that conveys such meanings may be horrible, but it need not be only that. Indeed, disgust can be even beautiful in its own disturbing way. Here is where the foul meets the fair. I shall appropriate the term "somatic spasm" to describe other works, for it aptly captures visceral responses to art, including those that are extremely subtle and require attention to detect and identify the source of their disturbance.

The works examined in the final two chapters will foreground subtle examples of artistic deployments of disgust. Now I turn to the third of this chapter's goals: to establish the necessity of including specific intentional objects in describing the arousal of aesthetic disgust.

The Qualia of Disgust: Six Examples

Chapter 1 reviewed different approaches to understanding emotions, all of which commonly acknowledge that emotions are characterized by the salient traits of their intentional objects. For example, the property that occasions fear is danger, the property that triggers disgust is foulness. These characterizations illuminate the complex event that is an emotion. But they are general accounts of emotion types, and in experience emotion occurs in very particular circumstances. When those circumstances are supplied by works of art with all their stylistic and substantive individualities, the affective triggers become so diverse that any general account falters. Aesthetic disgust comes in too many forms to be exhausted by the idea that its objects are simply foul, contaminating, or rotten. Disgust deployed by art can be confrontational, disturbatory, pathetic, funny, gross, erotic, curious, and all manner of additional qualifiers.

One might point out that the same kind of specification by circumstances occurs in practical experience, and that therefore all emotions achieve aspects of their felt qualia with reference to their intentional objects.[13] I think a case

---

13. Spinoza says little about disgust, but he does note that disgust is aroused with very specific thoughts of its object. Of the affinity of sexual jealousy and disgust he says: "He who thinks of a woman whom he loves as giving herself to another will not only feel pain by reason of his own appetite being checked but also, being compelled to associate the image of the object of his love with the sexual parts of his rival, he feels disgust for her." *Ethics*, trans. Samuel Shirley (Indianapolis, IN: Hackett, 1982), Scholium, Proposition 35, p. 125. See also the role of the target object in Ronald de Sousa's *Rationality of Emotions* (Cambridge, MA: MIT Press, 1987).

can be made for this view, but it is particularly pertinent to emotions in their aesthetic forms for two reasons, or more exactly for one reason with two aspects. Works of art fix the targets of emotions and their contexts in ways that remain there to be reflected on and pondered. While many art productions are formulaic, very skillful works are unique. The affects they inspire are a way to register this individuality. Moreover, the emotive qualities of works of art are also aesthetic properties that characterize a particular work and contribute to (or detract from) its success and impact. The ability of Owen's poem to evince a kind of biting regret, for example, describes a property of the poem that only that poem with its particular arrangement of words achieves. (Regret aroused by another poem might be maudlin or chauvinistic.) Insofar as emotive properties are aesthetic properties, and insofar as those emotive properties are registered by the arousal of affect, aesthetic emotions are individuated not just by characteristic traits of a type of object but also by specific artworks. Supporting argument for this point will again proceed with examples.

Several of the disgust researchers reviewed in the first chapter note that the mouth is a particularly sensitive zone of disgust. Tasting and drinking are potentially risky activities, and one basic function of disgust is to patrol safety for what enters the body. When that safety net fails, it is the mouth that pours forth vomit, registering disgust, producing disgust, cleansing the interior, and reversing the course of food through the body. The mouth and its activities are also near-universally twinned with sex, an association that links eating and its risks with eroticism and its vulnerabilities. There are too many examples of art that exploit the union of eating and sexuality to enumerate, but I am interested here in pointing out the differences in what general terminology would label aesthetic disgust. Here are two utterly different instances where eroticism and disgust combine with peculiar voluptuousness.

Peter Greenaway's movie *The Cook, the Thief, His Wife, and Her Lover* (1989) features encounters between the wife of the thief and her lover, abetted by the sympathetic cook at an elaborate artifice of a restaurant. The thief (played by Michael Gambon) is personally disgusting from his gross table manners to the spew of verbal abuse that marks his conversational style. Amid and between the courses of sumptuous dinners, his wife, Georgina (played by Helen Mirren), sneaks out for trysts with her lover. Just about all of the disgust elicitors are employed: the envelope violation of an excruciatingly excised navel, vomiting at the dinner table, sex in a toilet stall, and a truckload of rotting meat into which the lovers flee naked—oddly reminiscent of Cranach's Adam and Eve and the expulsion from the Garden. The movie unfolds at Greenaway's trademark glacial pace, so one is induced to dwell intensely on what is happening. The capstone of plot, artifice, and disgust comes at the very end. The lovers are discovered, and the man is slowly murdered, choked with the pages of a book from his library. In revenge the grief-maddened Georgina persuades the cook to prepare a macabre feast. She invites her husband to dinner in the opulent setting of the restaurant and presents him with her roasted lover. This is a twist on an old theme: the classic revenge plot where a betrayed husband tricks his wife into eating a dish prepared from her lover's heart (a theme to be explored in chapter 6). The final scene triggers a virtual spectrum of disgust responses.

We recoil from the image of the roasted man, but our eyes stray back, prompted by the camera that pans up and down the length of his crisp flesh (figure 4.6) The sight is given a measure of aesthetic distance by the formality of the scene, for the man is laid out like a figure on a sarcophagus. We are fascinated at the fact that not only has he been cooked but also apparently glazed. What is more, because we are looking at meat that has been elaborately prepared for the table, there may be a terrible synaesthetic tremor on the tongue: *What would he taste like?* This is hardly delectation, but it is a somatic apprehension of the horror laid upon the table.

Just when we are getting used to looking at the screen, the Thief is handed a knife and fork and compelled at gunpoint to take a slice from just under the ribs. One feels the fork in one's own side. It is a relief when Georgina shoots her choking husband. "*Cannibal*," she whispers.

This movie manages to engage the audience in particularly intimate ways, largely because of the somatic responses elicited. The synaesthetic evocations of taste are but one example of how the film penetrates the imagination, making us both participate in the horrid feast before us and recoil from it in utter revulsion. There is a teasing quality to the combination of gourmet preparation and disgust, and this itself is an aspect of the movie that one can appreciate, perhaps alongside doses of notable nastiness. I think that few audience members would challenge the description of the final scene as disgusting, but

FIGURE 4.6. Film still, *The Cook, the Thief, His Wife, and Her Lover*. Dir. Peter Greenaway. Miramax, 1989.

if one has suffered through the movie that long, it is also a scene to be admired. Without the arousal of disgust, a portion of what is to be admired is absent, for this is a superbly manipulative scene. We are more than disgusted, and not only because there are many other affects competing for attention. Here it is as though disgust has become its own subject. Calling the emotion a brand of aesthetic disgust is merely a way to understand the general forces at work over our sensibilities.

My next example may not at first seem to disgust at all. I believe, however, that it is a telling example of how disgust can operate with great subtlety. The painter Jenny Saville is well known for her works featuring her own large body and those of friends and family. Often classed as a feminist or postfeminist artist, she is frequently interpreted as both challenging and changing contemporary norms of feminine beauty. Certainly the atmosphere of feminist theory surrounds Saville's work, for the depiction of the nude female body is such a staple of painting that some art historians have claimed that it virtually defines Western art since the Renaissance.[14] Saville's work, like that of so many contemporary painters, defies the standard norms of the nude with her portrayal of bodies overflowing their garments with bulbous extrusions of fat. Because an opposite of beauty and its attraction is disgust and its revulsion, the female body is a primary site for interrogation of beauty.[15] Whether Saville's work seeks to alter the concept of beauty or defy it; to insert a variant body type into contemporary norms, or accept exclusion and challenge viewers for their complicity in that exclusion, is not completely clear from regarding her works, though that they raise these issues is pretty evident.[16] Some commentators stress the extended range of beauty; others note the power that disgust holds with her work.[17]

The painting that I choose for my example of the subtle arousal of disgust is far from a standard nude: *Host* (figure 4.7). This horizontal figure is presented in close-up, the head off-canvas, the torso displayed in the time-honored position of a reclining Venus. But the breasts are replaced with a set of teats, the waist is swollen, and it is not immediately clear to what species this torso

14. Lynda Nead, *The Female Nude* (London: Routledge, 1992).

15. Menninghaus incorporates this point into his analysis of disgust in *Disgust: Theory and History of a Strong Sensation*, trans. Howard Eiland and Joel Golb (Albany: State University of New York Press, 2003), chap. 2.

16. The artist herself says: "Beauty is always associated with the male fantasy of what the female body is. I don't think there is anything wrong with beauty. It's just that what women think is beautiful can be different. And there can be a beauty in individualism. If there is a wart or a scar, this can be beautiful, in a sense, when you paint it. It's part of your identity. Individual things are seeping out, leaking out." Quoted in David Sylvester, "Areas of Flesh," in *Jenny Saville* (New York: Rizzoli, 2005), 15.

17. Diana Tietjens Meyers singles out beauty in "Jenny Saville Remakes the Female Nude," in *Beauty Revisited*, ed. Peg Brand (Bloomington: Indiana University Press, 2011). Michelle Meagher explores the role of disgust in "Jenny Saville and a Feminist Aesthetics of Disgust," in "Women, Art, and Aesthetics," ed. Peg Brand and Mary Devereaux, special issue, *Hypatia* 18, no. 4 (2003): 23–41. For a more critical feminist approach to work such as Saville's, see Cynthia Freeland, "Against Raunchy Women's Art," in *Art and Social Change*, ed. Curtis L. Carter, International Yearbook of Aesthetics 13 (Milwaukee, WI: Marquette University Special Editions, 2009), 56–72.

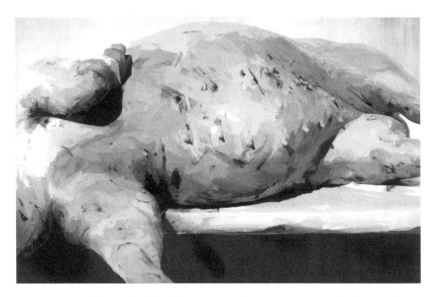

FIGURE 4.7. © Jenny Saville, *Host*. 2000. Oil on canvas. 120 × 180 in. (304.8 × 457.2 cm.). Courtesy Gagosian Gallery. Photo by Robert McKeever.

belongs. The Saatchi Gallery provides this explanatory note to the painting, supplying narrative illustration: "*Host* is based on the novel *Pig Tales* by Marie Darrieussecq, a story of a woman who finds herself slowly turning into a pig as her libido grows more liberated and gratifying. Jenny Saville paints the sensuous belly of a lady-swine, ripe and swollen for suckling."[18] Not only the painting but also the title and the accompanying note contribute to the somatic spasm that I think apprehension of this painting warrants. It is not that it is gross or revolting. But it does grab at the gut, and it does so because of the particular way in which disgust elicitors are deployed. First, there is the title, *Host*, which already suggests something feeding off something else in the way that a stomach is host to a tapeworm. But there is also ambiguity in the tenor of the title, for the lady-swine (a choice of words itself to be pondered) willingly makes herself available for suckle, playing the hostess, as it were.

Second, the identity of the body is in transition. It is neither human nor pig but something of both—as such qualifying as a classic monster. The border of human and animal is challenged, a border that, as we have seen, is patrolled by disgust.[19]

18. www.saatchi-gallery.co.uk/imgs/artists/saville (accessed September 17, 2009).

19. Matthew Kieran has this comment about another of Saville's paintings: "The queasy sense of disgust and repulsion arises from the sense, intrinsic to the visual experience, of confronting something which is essentially human and yet which threatens our categorical assumptions about how the living human face and its features should look." Kieran, *Revealing Art* (London: Routledge, 2005), 81.

Third, there is voluptuousness and eroticism in this painting, although it is hard to call it alluring. Unlike the traditional nude, the flesh here is not smooth and supple. There are too many protrusions, too many nipples, perhaps in fact they are growths. The body has lost its feminine shape, and yet it is not definitively a pig either. In this case, the complex employment of disgust also prompts thoughts about the animal nature of human being, the elasticity of desire and pleasure, and perhaps even the temptation to relinquish human rationality for the rhythms of nature and sense. One can put this point in existentialist terms, interpreting the painting to present an invitation to abandon transcendence with its relentless demand for freedom and to give in to the stupefied calm of immanence. This is not an utterly fanciful stretch, remembering the affinity of Saville with feminist theory.[20] Simone de Beauvoir makes similar observations, albeit much more critically, in *The Second Sex*. Her diagnosis of woman's "situation" targets the fact that for most of history women have been harnessed to their bodies because of their role in reproduction, rendering them slaves to the species. But only human striving toward projects that transcend natural animal functions can create value in the world. In Beauvoir's words,

> Giving birth and suckling are not *activities*, they are natural functions; no project is involved; and that is why woman found in them no reason for a lofty affirmation of her existence—she submitted passively to her biologic fate. The domestic labors that fell to her lot because they were reconcilable with the cares of maternity imprisoned her in repetition and immanence.[21]

Saville's painting registers but seductively defies this sentiment, with the sow-woman voluptuously acquiescing to her animal maternity, perhaps questioning the ultimate value of transcendent effort. Aesthetic disgust, in this case, plays a Janus role, revolting and enticing, both pointing to the compromised border between human and pig and teasing our curiosity about what lies on the other side. Or such, I contend, is a possible response to this painting. As de Bolla notes, the somatic spasm prompted by art gives way to a variety of thoughts.

The Singularity of Aesthetic Disgust

Examples such as these support the claim that an aesthetic affect must include its intentional object as a constituent of the emotion in order to be recognized accurately. The general accounts of emotion reviewed in chapter 1 serve to

20. The website of the Saatchi Gallery says this about Saville: "These works direct the traditional objectification of the female nude by suffusing painterly skill with feminist theory." www.eyestorm.com/saatchi/saville. asp (accessed October 3, 2001).

21. Simone de Beauvoir, *The Second Sex* (1949), trans. H. M. Parshley (New York: Random House, 1989), 63.

outline the parameters of different emotions, and it is understood that context of arousal influences the degree and even quality of the affect. Emotions as appreciative aesthetic responses require acknowledgment of yet more specific identifiers. As I assert earlier, in the case of aesthetic emotions, that object is specifically the particular work of art, not just an object with the general axiological quality characteristic of disgust—foulness. Here are two more comparisons, each of two works of art, that further demonstrate the singularity of aesthetic disgust. They are selected because the works are in many respects quite similar, yet disgust—the tenor of the visceral apprehension—is palpably different in each.

The first comparison is of two visual works: the famous paintings on the subject of Saturn devouring his children depicted by Peter Paul Rubens and Francisco Goya (figures 4.8 and 4.9). The themes are identical: the classical legend of the god who, fearing one of his children would displace him from power, devoured them at birth. Both pictures feature a large male figure and

FIGURE 4.8. Peter Paul Rubens, *Saturn Devouring His Son.* 1636. Museo del Prado, Madrid. Scala/Art Resource, NY.

FIGURE 4.9. Francisco de Goya y Lucientes, *Saturn Devouring One of His Sons*. 1821–23. Oil on canvas. Museo del Prado, Madrid. Scala/Art Resource, NY.

one child in the act of being bitten; both are horrific, difficult to contemplate, and geared to arouse the signature visceral response of disgust. And yet they are also very different, and that difference is registered in the qualia of the appreciative affect.

Goya's *Saturn* is an exaggerated picture of the god, whose figure exhibits some of the standard traits of horror. His huge body is elongated and gaunt, his hair disheveled and overgrown, his eyes staring and insane. He holds in his bony hands his child, whose body has adult form and looks rather like a toy. The head is already consumed, and only a bloody stump of neck remains. With the gaping mouth about to consume the rest of the child, the painting directs the somatic spasm of the viewer to the throat, prompting a kind of appreciative gag.

Rubens's version of the legend pictures Saturn in a more standard form for a Greek god. He is a well-muscled, aging adult male, large and strong, though his bulging eyes are unsettling. He cradles in his left arm one of his infant children, whose body is plump and smooth. This child has not been decapitated, and his head is flung back in agony, his mouth distorted in a scream. His father's teeth have just begun their work, and a pulled piece of skin on the chest indicates the first bite. One almost feels that sharp tug on one's own side as the skin begins to rip away from the baby's ribs. Viewers' responses will differ, though Rubens's picture has my own vote for the more effective because of that focus on the first bite, the first split of the skin, the first realization that the child is doomed, and the specificity of the somatic response of the viewer who can virtually feel the baby's skin tear.

Both paintings are horrifying, and registering their horror enlists a gut twinge. But the pictures are markedly different in style and rendition of the story, and that difference is also noted in the different affects aroused. We can call both responses instances of aesthetic disgust; we can call both somatic spasms. But such terms remain general. The exact emotion aroused cannot be pinpointed without reference to the paintings themselves in all their particularity.

With these two paintings, disgust is aroused in viewers without a mimetic correlate. That is, the gods are not disgusted. They are occupied with their grisly fare, and the children are either dead or terrified and in pain. It is the viewers who respond with a visceral spasm at the paintings. The next comparison is of two passages of narrative art where aesthetic disgust on the part of readers mirrors the emotions that the fictional characters are depicted as also experiencing. The mirror is a distorting one, for a reader is not in exactly the same position, even imaginatively, as a character. Nonetheless, the appreciative affect is a sort of empathy, echo, or simulation of the emotions experienced by the characters.[22]

Both quotes are from long novels. One section is from a narrative of war, Sebastian Faulks's *Birdsong*. The other is from the opening pages of Martin Cruz Smith's detective thriller *Havana Bay*. I choose these two passages because of the marked similarity of their subject matter, including details of emphasis, yet they produce palpably different tenors of affective responses. In both, we find extended, graphic descriptions of human bodies falling apart from putrefaction. The evocation of smell and touch is vivid in each, and also in each a character responds by vomiting. These passages detail indisputable disgust elicitors and typically extreme disgust reactions. Nonetheless, the aesthetic disgust aroused is noticeably different; the affect aroused—the somatic spasm—*feels* different.

22. A number of philosophers employ simulation theory to account for the arousal of emotions by fictions. See, for instance, Gregory Currie, "Imagination and Simulation: Aesthetics Meets Cognitive Science," in *Mental Simulations*, ed. Martin Davies and Tony Stone (Oxford: Blackwell, 1995), 151–69; Susan L. Feagin, *Reading with Feeling: The Aesthetics of Appreciation* (Ithaca, NY: Cornell University Press, 1996), esp. chap. 4.

Birdsong, set during World War I, contains a moving, extended, and graphic description of the infamous trench warfare of that conflict. It is vividly evocative of some extremely uncomfortable feeling states, including claustrophobia, for one of the specialized tasks of the main characters is to tunnel deep into the earth and lay explosives under enemy lines. Faulks is especially sensitive in his descriptions of damages inflicted on the human body. Here is a passage from a section that takes place above ground and that describes soldiers returning to a battlefield to collect the corpses of dead comrades:

> They tracked out toward a shellhole, the sun bright, a lark above them. Blue sky, unseen by eyes trained on turned mud. They moved low toward a mine crater where bodies had lain for weeks uncollected. "Try to lift him." No sound of machine guns or snipers, though their ears were braced for noise. "Take his arms." The incomprehensible order through gas mouthpiece. The arms came away softly. "Not like that, not take his arms *away*." On Weir's collar a large rat, trailing something red down his back. A crow disturbed, lifting its black body up suddenly, battering the air with its big wings. Coker, Barlow shaking their heads under the assault of risen flies coming up, transforming black skin of corpses into green by their absence. The roaring of Goddard's vomit made them laugh, snorting private mirth inside their masks. Goddard, releasing his mask, breathed in worse than he had expelled. Weir's hands in double sandbags stretched out tentatively to a sapper's uniform, undressing the chest in search of a disk which he removed, bringing skin with it into his tunic pocket. Jack's recoil, even through coarse material, to the sponge of flesh. Bright and sleek on liver, a rat emerged from the abdomen; it levered and flopped flatly over the ribs, glutted with pleasure. Bit by bit on to stretchers, what flesh fell left in mud. Not men, but flies and flesh, thought Stephen. Brennan anxiously stripping a torso with no head. He clasped it with both hands, dragged legless up from the crater, his fingers vanishing into buttered green flesh. It was his brother.[23]

This description is compact with emotional charge: anguish, pity, grief, horror, bewilderment, disgust. Not all the emotions of the characters depicted in this passage are the same as the emotions aroused in the reader. The soldiers are anguished and bewildered, grief-stricken and horrified. The reader is pitying, horrified, perhaps fascinated, but not bewildered or grief-stricken. Disgust is an emotion shared by both.

This does not mean that the feel of aesthetic disgust matches the affect aroused on that battlefield. Despite the vivacity and the synaesthetic arousal of horrid sensations, we the readers are still shielded from the actual smell of

---

23. Sebastian Faulks, *Birdsong: A Novel of Love and War* (New York: Vintage, 1997), 336–37.

rotting flesh; we imagine smell but do not smell. The images conjured up by the description act as the sensory elicitor, and they are sufficient. The notion of a mental image suggests that when we imagine what is visible, we also see with the mind's eye. The imaginative sensations from the other senses are not absent, but they tend to be less vivid. We imagine our fingers sinking into the "buttered flesh" of Brennan's brother. We are truly disgusted, but our disgust is more tolerable than that of the soldiers because the immediate, primary sensations that trigger disgust are absent.[24] Moreover, while no one would willingly return to that battleground horror, one might read the passage over and over, perhaps even to admire and wonder at the disgust so poignantly aroused. The fact that one would reread the book to reexperience the painful affect indicates that there is something uniquely insightful about that aesthetic emotion not supplied by any other object.

I do not expect that everyone will agree with my description of this passage, which in any event is too brief to measure up to a careful critical reading. My point is not to suggest a particular interpretation but to call attention to the fact that despite notable similarities of description, two passages in two different novels are equally disgusting but strikingly different in affective tone. Some of the difference is owing to the fact that a war narrative is a different genre from detective fiction, and the reader anticipates a different purpose. Nonetheless, the particular passages exploit their disgust-elicitor themes in manners that are quite parallel, and yet with affective outcomes that are importantly different.

Compare the war narrative to this passage from *Havana Bay*. At the opening of the story the Russian detective Arkady Renko has arrived in Havana after news of the disappearance of a former colleague who has been tentatively declared dead, a victim of accidental drowning. A body is found floating in an inner tube in the bay and hauled out. A short time later it is opened for autopsy. Thus the start of the book doses the reader with horrific scenes.

> A diver in a wet suit slid off the police boat while an officer in waders dropped over the sea wall. They clambered as much as waded across crab pots and mattress springs, mindful of hidden nails and septic water, and cornered the inner tube so that it wouldn't float away. A net was thrown down from the seawall to stretch under the inner tube and lift it and the body up together. . . .
> The diver stepped into a hole and went under. Gasping, he came up out of the water, grabbed onto first the inner tube and then a foot hanging from it. The foot came off. The inner tube pressed against the

24. The fact that aesthetic emotions are often muted has led many to conclude that in a way they are not "real" or "genuine" emotions. This is not a necessary conclusion, although emotions aroused by fictions lack some of the dimensions of emotions aroused in practical situations, such as an absence of the kind of behavior prompted by emotions in real life. However, aesthetic emotions are partially constituted by their intentional objects, and their intentional objects are fictional, so no behavior is appropriate.

spear of a mattress spring, popped and started to deflate. As the foot turned to jelly, Detective Osorio shouted for the officer to toss it to shore: a classic confrontation between authority and vulgar death, Arkady thought. All along the tape, onlookers clapped and laughed. . . .

The inner tube was sinking. An arm disengaged. Shouts flew back and forth between Osorio and the police boat. The more desperately the men in the water tried to save the situation, the worse it became. . . . As the diver steadied the head, the pressure of his hands liquefied its face and made it slide like a grape skin off the skull, which separated clearly from the neck; it was like trying to lift a man who was perversely disrobing part by part, unembarrassed by the stench of advanced decomposition. A pelican sailed overhead, red as a flamingo.

"I think identification is going to be a little more complicated than the captain imagined," Arkady said.[25]

So far this macabre scene has maintained a shockingly comic tone. It is abetted by the fact that both the readers and the main character are able to maintain a bit of distance from the person who was this unfortunate body, for at this point it is not identified, and there is little sympathy generated for the individual it once was. The Russian detective along with the police divers are chiefly concerned with retrieval. They do not express disgust in this scene. Mainly, they are trying without much success to keep the evidence intact. At the same time, the horrid comedy is striking, and the reader is likely squirming with delighted nausea.

Later at the autopsy even Renko succumbs:

Usually, an examiner cut at the hairline and peeled the forehead over the face to reach the skull. Since in this case both the forehead and the face had already slipped off and bade adieu in the bay, Blas proceeded directly with a rotary saw to uncover the brain, which proved rotten with worms that reminded Arkady of the macaroni served by Aeroflot. As the nausea rose he had Rufo lead him to a tiny, chain-flush lavatory, where he threw up, so perhaps he wasn't so inured after all, he thought. Maybe he had just reached his limit.[26]

Both these passages detail the disintegration of a body undergoing similar stages of decay. Hands sink into flesh, limbs fall away, characters vomit helplessly. Yet how different are the tenors of aesthetic disgust aroused in the reader. The first is appalled, sorrowful, pitying. The second is horridly comic. There is far more to be said of each, and again I am not offering a thorough reading of the novels or even of these specific passages. Nonetheless, I hope that these two examples

25. Martin Cruz Smith, *Havana Bay* (New York: Random House, 2008), 4–5.
26. Cruz-Smith, *Havana Bay*, 7–8.

provide a kind of demonstrative proof of the nuance, variety, and singularity of aesthetic disgust even with objects that are in certain ways quite alike. Despite their thematic and descriptive similarity, the somatic responses prompted by these passages could never be mistaken for each other.

This diversity has critical implications for emotion theory because it enjoins caution when generalizing about emotions extracted from the contexts in which they are aroused. And it has equally important implications for the solution to the paradox of aversion in the case of disgust and the theoretical accounts of the satisfactions that disgust affords in art. This diversity indicates that any solutions formulated for the paradox of aversion ought to accommodate the vastly different instances of aesthetic disgust. No single answer to Mendelssohn's question, "Whence this peculiar satisfaction?" will be adequate. Oddly enough, there do seem to be cases where there is a relish in dwelling in disgust, one that perhaps ought to count as a pleasure akin to the *haut goût* of cuisine. In other cases disgust is better accounted for in terms of its role as a means to further another aesthetic emotion and to increase understanding. It can be a feeling the acceptance of which is morally dubious, and also a feeling to embrace and relish.[27] All these possibilities need to be examined before we decide if there are common grounds that obtain in all examples of aesthetic disgust that would serve to account for its insight, appreciative sensibility, and even its savorability. These points will be pursued in the next chapter.

---

27. The sheer amount of contemporary art that seeks to disgust is worth pondering. For two critical philosophical perspectives, see Kieran, *Revealing Art*, 83–86; and Carole Talon-Hugon, *Goût et dégoût: L'art peut-il tout montrer?* (Nîmes: Éditions Jacqueline Chambon, 2003), introduction and passim.

5

The Magnetism of Disgust

Having reviewed numerous examples of aesthetic disgust and taken note of their heterogeneity, we are now in a position to consider why one might return again and again to such experiences. How is it that disgust, a paradigmatic aversion, can sometimes also attract? Is there pleasure to be found from encounters with disgusting art? If so, exactly what is the nature and object of that pleasure? If not, then how to account for the allure of this sort of difficult art and the value it possesses?

Such questions cluster around what I have been calling the "paradox of aversion," the mystery of why seemingly normal human beings willingly seek out experiences that deliver unpleasantness, even pain. It is an old question, and it is often called the "paradox of tragedy" because in the *Poetics* Aristotle first posed it of that art form and the arousal of the painful emotions of pity and terror that he considered the hallmarks of tragedy. Both tragedy and sublimity have been the standard targets for examining the paradox, and Mendelssohn's question, "Whence this peculiar satisfaction?" was posed in the course of wondering about the sublime and its emergence from terror. The outlines of this problem have already been presented in chapter 2, along with modern philosophy's singular exclusion of disgust from the emotions to be rendered in beautiful art. Now I return to the topic and consider the array of possible solutions that have been proposed when the paradox of aversion focuses on its putatively most difficult entrant.

A number of related questions can be unpacked from the paradox, which most generally queries how an affect that seems by its very nature to be an *aversion* manages to exert an *attraction* in aesthetic encounters.[1] This question presumes that aversion and attraction are not only opposites but also contraries: if one occurs, the other cannot (or ought not). Sometimes aversions and attractions are put in terms of pains and pleasures: How does a pain become a pleasure? Indeed, the language of pleasure has dominated discussion, and I shall sort through the complications of this concept shortly.

While we need to inquire about the pleasure that disgust can deliver, there is another set of more exact—and to my mind more important—questions to pose: What does disgust, as an aesthetic emotion, provide that other affects do not? What values does this emotion register when it is deployed in art? How does the meaning of this emotion—or, better, how do the meanings of the multitudinous instances of aesthetic disgust—manifest in art? How does its signature physical response become a mode of aesthetic apprehension? While there is considerable agreement about the general meanings attributed to disgust, there is also substantial disagreement about how and why disgust operates aesthetically.

I begin by considering the concept of pleasure and how it should be understood in order to illuminate the appreciation of art that arouses difficult emotions. This treatment will permit departure from purely hedonic approaches to the paradox of aversion and emphasize a more cognitivist perspective that stresses the insights afforded by aesthetic emotions, insights that gratify but perhaps do not actually please in the familiar sense of the word. It is this latter perspective that affords the richest account of aesthetic disgust. Moreover, I believe this approach is sufficiently flexible to accommodate insights developed out of other theoretical points of view. This chapter does not posit a single explanation for aesthetic disgust but rather endorses insights from a number of perspectives, an eclecticism in keeping with the myriad manifestations of disgust in art.

Pleasure

In order to defend this eclecticism, I need first to make a case for the multivalence of pleasure.[2] The previous chapters have indicated the line of argument I intend to pursue. Encounters with aesthetic disgust are extremely variant and do not all possess the same affective tenor. Even when they evince hedonic elements, they

1. Aaron Smuts sorts through different formulations of the paradox in "Art and Negative Affect," *Philosophy Compass* 4, no. 1 (2009): 39–55.

2. On desiderata for an account of aesthetic pleasure, see Jerrold Levinson, "What Is Aesthetic Pleasure?" in *The Pleasures of Aesthetics* (Ithaca, NY: Cornell University Press, 1996), chap. 1.

may not please for the same reasons. Therefore, it would be an error to try to locate the same foundation for the pleasures they occasion. The particularism of aesthetic disgust argued for in the last chapter needs to be matched by a particularist account of enjoyment. Or—since "enjoyment" does not always describe taxing aesthetic encounters—a particularist account of appreciative aesthetic absorption.

Aristotle's discussion of the paradox of tragedy has been enormously influential for subsequent generations of theory, and his solution provides a model useful for considering disgust as well, as we shall see later. Although most of his analysis of pleasure was formulated independently of aesthetic considerations, his treatment of that subject also provides an excellent guide for understanding the different ways that an object or an activity can please.[3] His examination supports the conclusion that pleasure is not a unitary phenomenon in any substantial respect. Different instances of pleasure do not have similar causal conditions; pleasure does not designate an identifiable sensation or feeling state; and it is not directed to objects that share particular pertinent features. This is true of pleasures in general, he claims, and by extension it is true of the pleasures that art affords.

Clearly pleasure is not always experientially the same in the way that the acute burning sensation is the same each time one is stung by a bee. Enjoying poetry and enjoying a chamber music concert *feel* different, and neither feels like enjoying a suspenseful movie. Accordingly, as Aristotle notes, pleasures differ with their objects. We take pleasure in nature, in works of art, in activities, in experiences of our senses. Some activities are undertaken for pleasure, such as sitting down to a fine meal; others are enhanced by the pleasure they bring, such as the absorption of a mathematician in her work. Consequently we can see that "as pleasant things differ, so do the pleasures arising from them" (1153a6–7).[4] "Each of the pleasures is bound up with the activity it completes" (1175a29–30; X: 5). Thus Aristotle's analysis of pleasure runs parallel to the case I made in the previous chapter that aesthetic emotions take their tenor from their particular objects.

What is more, pleasures differ because we ourselves change. "There is no one thing that is always pleasant, because our nature is not simple but . . . we are perishable creatures" (1154b21–22). The unstable nature of the human constitution means that some pleasures come about because of antecedent discomforts that are alleviated.[5] When we are very hungry, for example, we take

3. There are two chief sites for the treatment of pleasure in the *Nicomachean Ethics*, and while those at the beginning of Book X are generally considered more mature and final than those that appear at the end of Book VII, both provide insights that are usefully extended to an understanding of aesthetic pleasure.

4. Quotations from Aristotle's *Nicomachean Ethics* are taken from the translation of W. D. Ross revised by J. O. Urmson, *The Complete Works of Aristotle: The Revised Oxford Translations*, vol. 2, ed. Jonathan Barnes (Princeton, NJ: Princeton University Press, 1984).

5. Aristotle calls pleasures that arise from the alleviation of prior discomforts qualified pleasures; pleasures that arise independently are unqualified or pleasurable in themselves.

pleasure in eating. If we are full, eating is no longer pleasant. Rest is pleasant after fatigue but boring after the body regains energy. Other things give plea-sure independently of any prior discomfort, such as the scent of flowers or a glowing dawn. Pleasures become more difficult when they mix responses, such as a deep massage that may make one gasp but still qualifies as a pleasure when it releases tension. A simple melody may be pleasant, but so are dishar-mony and complexity in some music. Plays that make one laugh, that make one cry, that terrify or disturb, all these can be the occasions for experiences that can qualify as pleasures. (Of course, this is the very fact that generates the paradox.)

Whether pleasure arises from the alleviation of antecedent conditions such as pain or desire, or whether it is an independent phenomenon has remained a point of perennial contention.[6] Enlightenment theories of the aesthetic wrested pleasure free from antecedent states of self-interest and advocated a notion of disinterested pleasure. Only this kind of feeling, they maintained, could separate beauty from the satisfaction of desire. Other theorists, including those who favor psychoanalytic perspectives, keep pleasure firmly welded to prior conditions.[7] Aristotle sensibly maintains that it depends. Some pleasures operate one way, some the other.

Pleasure enhances activity, he observes. Thus a person who enjoys math-ematics will concentrate more fully and to better effect than a person who considers it drudgery. Because pleasures absorb the character of their objects, they cannot be characterized *tout court*, a point demonstrated by the fact that pleasures can conflict with each other. A mathematician who also loves flute music may discover that she is so distracted by music that she cannot attend to her calculation. If pleasure were always the same thing, then just any plea-sure would enhance activity. The flute in the background would not distract the mathematician but deepen her concentration. However, the pleasure of music shoulders aside the pleasure in mathematics, indicating that the two phenomena, while both labeled pleasure, must be different. In short, pleasure is not a unitary psychological event, and we do not speak univocally when we report enjoying, liking, appreciating, and taking pleasure in different things. Pleasure takes enough of its quality from its objects that it is more accurate to say that it differs from case to case than that there is a common subjective phenomenon called pleasure that attaches itself to all instances of being pleased.

6. The history of theories of pleasure is usefully reviewed in H. M. Gardiner, Ruth Clark Metcalf, and John G. Beebe-Center, eds., *Feeling and Emotion: A History of Theories* (New York: American Book Company, 1937).

7. Because Freud treats pleasure as always consequent upon antecedent desire, his account would seem automatically to discount the possibility of aesthetic pleasure of the disinterested sort. Terry Eagleton declares that for "conventional aesthetic theory, Freud is exceedingly bad news," insisting that even formal beauty is rooted in libidinal impulses (Eagleton, *The Ideology of the Aesthetic* [Oxford: Blackwell, 1990], 265). This assertion, however, begs the question about the nature of aesthetic pleasure.

In his essay "Pleasure" (1954), Gilbert Ryle pursued these points, concluding that pleasure is nothing above and beyond the activity that we enjoy. In addition, he pressed the asymmetry between pleasure and pain still further. While he does not have aesthetic pleasures solely in mind, Ryle's argument addresses the phenomenon of enjoyment of difficult art forms, a situation that, he observes, generates puzzles only when one starts to generalize:

> There are many overlapping fields of discourse in which, long before philosophizing begins, generalities about pleasure are bound to be mooted and debated. The moral educator in inculcating standards of conduct, the psychologist in trying to classify the springs of human action . . . and the art-critic in comparing the appeals of different works of art, all must talk in general terms about, among many other things, the pleasure that human beings do or should take in different things. It is in the interplay of these and kindred generalities, of whose truth, when considered separately, we have no general doubts, that our characteristic problems arise.[8]

In trying to construct general principles for human behaviors, Ryle maintains, theorists often make the fundamental mistake of trying to analyze reciprocal pushes and pulls on actions in terms of pleasures and pains. This not only incorrectly separates pleasures from their objects and activities but also leads to the misleading thesis that pleasures and pains are opposites—one impelling action, the other impeding it.

Compounding this false opposition is the temptation to try to understand pleasure in the same terms that it is natural to understand pain—namely, as a sensation. Not only is pleasure a poor candidate for a sensation (as Aristotle too points out), but trying to conceive of it as such intensifies the misleading opposition between pain and pleasure. Pain, which in its foundational sense is a sensation with specific bodily location, is not really an opposite of pleasure at all. Ryle concludes with the observation that "the concepts of enjoying and disliking have been wrongly alleged to be of the same category with having a pain."[9] Effectively, this dissolves the paradox of aversion, for we encounter a real paradox only if the "painful" content of art is in principle incompatible with the aesthetic "pleasure" it occasions. But pleasure and pain are neither opposites nor contraries, and the concepts of aesthetic satisfaction or dissatisfaction fit poorly with the language of sensation implied by a pleasure-pain dichotomy.[10]

8. Gilbert Ryle, "Pleasure," chap. 4 of *Dilemmas* (Cambridge: Cambridge University Press, 1954), 56.

9. Ryle, "Pleasure," 66–67. For a critique of Ryle and further discussion of the problem of considering pleasure a sensation, see Murat Aydede, "An Analysis of Pleasure vis-à-vis Pain," *Philosophy and Phenomenological Research* 61, no. 3 (2000): 537–70.

10. See also Smuts "Art and Negative Affect," 43; Alex Neill, "On a Paradox of the Heart," *Philosophical Studies* 65 (1992): 53–65. Many have observed that pleasures in general are not well understood as sensations, though as the argument has been made repeatedly, it seems difficult to jettison this assumption once and for all.

Commenting on Ryle's observations, Anthony Kenny advances even more emphatic reasons why it is incorrect to define pleasure in general as a sensation, although he correctly observes that some sensations arouse pleasure. He returns to Aristotle's arguments by noting that while some theorists treat pleasure as distinct from the action it accompanies, others (including Ryle) claim it is identical with the act with which it is associated. Kenny agrees that pleasure is not "some extra activity over and above the activity in which it is a pleasure," but it does not follow that the pleasure and the action are simply identical. Aristotle surmised that pleasure might be understood as "unimpeded activity" (*Nicomachean Ethics* VII: 1153a15), and Kenny takes up this point, observing that what we label pleasure can equally well be called *absorption* in an activity.[11] It is this idea of absorption—fascination, concentration, rapt attention—that I shall adapt in my own treatment of pleasure. Whether we speak of fascination and curiosity, emotional engagement, rapture, or just plain old enjoyment, to say that one takes pleasure means that one is occupied with a singular keenness and ardor. Rather than rendered as a noun, "pleasure" seems to behave more like a *modifier of attention*, intensifying for a host of reasons some experience that the participant would rather have continue than not.

From these three philosophers we have several useful conclusions regarding the concept of pleasure that can be applied to consideration of aesthetic disgust. The venerable paradox of aversion can be set aside as not a true paradox at all, even though the psychological puzzles it raises are not so easily put to rest (and will be pursued further later). Although it would be awkward to dispense altogether with the language of pleasure, we do not need to think of pleasure as anything like a sensation or as a kind of additional event that arises with encounters with art, nor need we think of aesthetic satisfactions as phenomena that require parallel explanations in all cases.[12] We can cease worrying about a common causal source of pleasure and redirect attention to the idea that what satisfies is also what absorbs attention in artworks. What is it about the object of attention that so absorbs us that we stick with it rather than turning away when it becomes difficult? This takes us directly to the question posed earlier: What does aesthetic disgust deliver that other emotions do not? Because there is no single answer to that question, it will take a bit of time to sort through the possibilities.

---

11. Anthony Kenny, "Pleasure," in his *Action, Emotion, and Will* (London: Routledge and Kegan Paul, 1963), 137. Kenny goes on to consider problems with this as a definition of pleasure and to discuss standards for being pleasurable, but I develop the point in a different direction.

12. "The pleasure of experiencing an artwork is just that: it is typically a pleasure in *doing* something—listening, viewing, attending, organizing, projecting, conjecturing, imagining, speculating, hypothesizing, and so on—rather than just allowing things to happen to one on a sensory plane." Levinson, "Pleasure and the Value of Works of Art," *Pleasures of Aesthetics*, 13. For two other approaches to the problem of aesthetic pleasure and multiple objects, see Eva Schaper, "The Pleasures of Taste," and R. A. Sharpe, "Solid Joys or Fading Pleasures," both in *Pleasure, Preference and Value*, ed. Eva Schaper (Cambridge: Cambridge University Press, 1983), 39–56 and 86–98.

Even if we do not have an actual paradox to resolve, we are still left with the perplexing question of why many people are attracted to painful works of art, especially to works that arouse disgust. Understanding pleasure in terms of absorption in activity does not remove this question. Why would one be absorbed in something revolting? As William Alston notes, "Enjoyment or satisfaction seems to take whatever felt quality it has from what one is enjoying or getting satisfaction from."[13] But why would not the felt quality of satisfaction in disgust be itself merely disgusting? I begin considering this problem with the most difficult and least elevating examples of art—those that simply set out to revolt.

Yuck and Eew

> I recognize terror as the finest emotion and so I will try to terrorize the reader. But if I find that I cannot terrify, I will try to horrify, and if I find that I cannot horrify, I'll go for the gross-out.[14]

So says novelist Stephen King, master of the literary gross-out. The gross-out is the deliberate arousal of disgust for its own sake by means of images, description, special effects, or confrontational performance. As the invitation to wallow in the loathsome with no promise of compensatory enlightenment, it is the hardest variety of aesthetic disgust to account for. There are numerous horror movies and videos that employ the gross-out, and now there are entire websites devoted to it. It is often dismissed as the preoccupation of low or juvenile sensibilities, but in fact the gross-out also appears in gallery exhibits and installations, as with some of Cindy Sherman's work. It is the hallmark of performance artist Paul McCarthy. And even if it were a symptom of immaturity, it would still demand explanation. Some artists who specialize in the gross-out may have a higher theoretical purpose—perhaps to confront us with the unimaginable Real that defies all rational order, or to test absolute limits of tolerance. But for the moment let us just diagnose what might appeal in the sheer arousal of disgust for its own sake.

To many the answer to this query will be simple: Absolutely Nothing. A taste for the gross-out is far from universal, and in fact most of the impetus behind the paradox of aversion presumes that there is no enjoyment that a sane person would take in the irredeemably disgusting. To add to this puzzle, from an evolutionary perspective such a propensity seems bafflingly counteradaptive. If disgust responses evolved to protect us by inducing recoil, there ought to be no appeal at all.

13. William Alston, "Pleasure," in *Encyclopedia of Philosophy*, vol. 6, ed. Paul Edwards (New York: Macmillan, 1967), 344.

14. Stephen King, *Danse Macabre*, 22–23, quoted in *Arguing about Art: Contemporary Philosophical Debates*, ed. Alex Neill and Aaron Ridley, 3rd ed. (Oxford and New York: Routledge, 2008), 293.

Nonetheless, willful encounters with all kinds of aversion have their defenders. Many people admit to a liking for the thrill of fear or the pathos of sorrow, and there are also some who acknowledge the allure of the disgusting. One who has pondered this psychological oddity thoroughly is Aurel Kolnai, who, as I have already noted, locates in the structure of the emotion an aesthetic dimension. "There is without doubt a certain invitation hidden in disgust as a partial element," Kolnai remarks, "I might say, a certain macabre allure."[15]

It is the attention to sensuous qualities that leads Kolnai to call disgust "aesthetic," not its deployment in art. But his disclosure of the pause between reactive recoil and that second curious look is an expedient foundation for understanding how this particular aversion can invite reflection. Emotions often just happen to us; they come upon us unbidden, prompting responses that we are helpless to control. It is this dimension that courts the synonym "passions" —that which makes us passive—and it is a description that is especially apt for those reactive modular emotions that include disgust. But even the most reactive emotions are occasions for reflection on the fact that they have occurred at all. Both the pause built into disgust and the reflective aftermath of emotions afford scope for what some have identified as a second-order pleasure in aversion.

Susan Feagin looks to reflection on emotional responses for an explanation of the paradoxical enjoyment of disgust when it is aroused by art forms such as horror. We do not necessarily experience disgust as a pleasure, she surmises. Rather, the fact that we are the kind of person capable of undergoing a difficult experience and of expanding our own emotional repertoire may be the object of gratification when the emotion itself is aversive: "Suppose that it is appropriate . . . to take pleasure in having the feeling components of fear and disgust. If such pleasures are appropriate, if it is part of appreciating horror fiction for what it is that one have such pleasures, one may take pleasure in the fact that *one takes pleasure in* these feelings."[16] So understood the appreciation—or at least its pleasurable part—is a metaresponse directed to our own emotional capacities.

The metaresponse answer to the paradox of aversion has been criticized for redirecting attention unduly away from the artwork itself.[17] But it has the advantage of acknowledging the uncomfortable features of the experience without trying to mute them. Even more, it puts the reflective element of the apprehension of art squarely in the center of analysis. The fact alone that one can endure disgust is not a sufficient account of the value of that reflective

15. Aurel Kolnai, "Disgust" (1929), in *On Disgust*, ed. Barry Smith and Carolyn Korsmeyer (Chicago: Open Court, 2004), 42.
16. Susan Feagin, "Monsters, Disgust, and Fascination," *Philosophical Studies* 65 (1992): 83. This article and Alex Neill's "On a Paradox of the Heart" in the same issue comment on Noël Carroll's theory of horror. Feagin first developed the metaresponse theory to address tragedy in "The Pleasures of Tragedy," *American Philosophical Quarterly* 20, no. 1 (1983): 75–84.
17. Smuts, "Art and Negative Affect," 49. Smuts also believes such metaresponses are rare.

pause, however, which affords the leisure to indulge a terrible curiosity. I venture that the gross-out can be a kind of self-exploration that teases the edges of our tolerance, bringing us to the brink not only of our individual psyches but also of what creatures such as ourselves can countenance.[18] In its palpable visceral force disgust declares itself a fundamental aversion, a reaction designed to keep the species alive. It commands me to leave. And I won't. I have caught disgust in the act and won't let it go. The childish "Eeew" indulges in just that—holding on for a moment to that which should be shunned. One wallows in what nature commands that one reject.

The degree to which this account accommodates aesthetic disgust is important but limited. It also raises questions about the value of artworks that exploit the sheer arousal of this emotion for its own sake alone. Although we can discover an important role for the apprehension afforded by disgust throughout the history of art, in most instances the emotion has a larger role to play than its mere arousal. However, a good deal of contemporary art in both gallery and popular venue appears to have as a main purpose the stimulation of disgust. Indeed, Carole Talon-Hugon identifies the sheer arousal of disgust stripped of larger narrative contexts as an artistic phenomenon beginning in the twentieth century.[19] While such works demand individual evaluation, it is worth noting that one of Lessing's objections to disgust comes into play in considering the aesthetic effects of the arousal of strong emotions. If a difficult artwork arouses a distressing emotion at its height, then the imagination has nowhere further to go.[20] Imagination can extend the portrayal of anguish far more effectively if the moment of distress is depicted at its beginning rather than its culmination. If (*if*) an art work has as its purpose the mere arousal of disgust, it will probably fall prey to this observation, and something similar obtains with other emotions such as fear, anger, or sorrow as well. A merely terrifying narrative is little more than a house of horrors; a story that only manipulatively tugs at the heart is soppily sentimental.

Nonetheless, although one should not make too much of the gross-out, which is a pretty crude experience, speculation about its aesthetic power leads to deeper and more important territory: the realization that there is something made available by means of disgust that lies beneath the surface of both the recoil of revolt and the loathsome presentational qualities of objects. Something that exerts what Kolnai describes as a "macabre allure," a "superimposed attractedness of the subject towards that object."[21] At least part of the enticing nature of disgust is the impression that it possesses an elusive significance:

18. Cf. Ralph Rawdon Wilson on Bataille, *The Hydra's Tale: Imagining Disgust* (Edmonton: University of Alberta Press, 2002), 76. Bataille himself was interested in Kolnai's philosophy. See Georges Bataille, *Oeuvres Complètes* Vol. II (1922–40) (Paris: Gallimard, 1970), 438–39.

19. Carole Talon-Hugon, *Goût et dégoût: L'art peut-il tout montrer?* (Nimes: Édition Jacqueline Chambon, 2003), 13–14.

20. Gotthold Ephraim Lessing, *Laocoön* (1766), trans. Edward Allen McCormick (Indianapolis, IN, Bobbs-Merrill, 1962), chap. 3.

21. Kolnai, *On Disgust*, 42.

The object of disgust is prone to be connected with something which is concealed, secretive, multilayered, uncanny, sinister, as well as with something which is shameless, obtrusive, and alluring; that is, in sum, to be something which is taunting. Everything that is disgusting has in it something which is at one and the same time both striking and veiled, as is, say, a poisonous red berry or a garishly made-up face.[22]

To investigate what lies behind that veil we need to consider what disgust means, and the insights that it alone affords when it is deftly evoked in art. Pursuing this direction, we can discover additional explanations for aesthetic disgust, including how on occasion aversion can convert to attraction.

What Disgust Signifies

That the fundamental disgust elicitors offend the senses in a particularly nau-seating way is by now more than familiar. Philosophers and psychologists alike agree on the basic things that trigger this aversion—the filthy and foul, the insides of the body that have burst free from their containment, the loss of bodily integrity and the means by which it came about, objects that infect and contaminate. So far, however, we have explored the meanings of this emotion only in general and, as it were, from a distance.

The stench of a rotting carcass is powerfully awful, and the reaction to the smell is automatic and virtually uncontrollable. Even in the grip of recoil, however, it means more than an offense to the nose. It means decay, putrefaction, disintegration: death. Disgust is a constant signifier of death. More must be said, however, for fear can mean the same thing, yet disgust and fear are not the same emotion, nor do they signify in the same way.

Kolnai vividly states that disgust is "pregnant with death," but in his comparison of fear and disgust he got it wrong. He states that the objects of disgust, being inferior to us in power and stature, revolt but do not threaten our being; fear, in contrast, registers a direct threat to our individual existence. Maggots disgust; a tiger terrifies. However, insofar as this obtains, it does so only in the short run, for objects that disgust pose long-term threats that are all the worse for being absolutely inexorable. Disgust is more of a response to the transition between life and death—to that which has recently died and is falling apart, to waste that was food and is now used up, to the mindless life-forms that invade and complete the process of disintegration.

22. Kolnai, *On Disgust*, 47.

The fact that disgust registers the process that death initiates rather than the state of being dead marks another difference between disgust and the other affects that take note of mortality. Bones are relatively clean and permanent; flesh is not. Thus installations such as Gunther von Hagens's Body Worlds, which features human bodies stripped of skin and preserved in plastic, neither emit nor evoke the soft, oozy stench of decay. While decidedly uncanny, even creepy, these exhibits are rarely found to be disgusting. Similarly, ossuaries are full of the presence of death, but it is death long past, the piles of bones mutely testifying to the huge numbers of dead, their individual identities long lost.[23]

It is common to refer to the objects that disgust as low, base, and inferior to us. Excrement is food that is used up and discarded, carrying with it an infusion of bacteria that makes it more than waste—it is filth. Once expelled it is no longer part of us. We bury it or flush it away. The same with pus from wounds, mucus from noses, discharged menstrual blood. As soon as possible these objects are discarded. Coprophages, those creatures whose diet is dung, help with the cleanup and are themselves unclean. Thus maggots, worms, roaches, flies in the swarms and masses needed to cleanse the amount of filth expelled by us and our fellow animals—they too are disgusting. It is an aid to health that disgust rejects such objects, but perhaps the violence of that rejection masks our intimate connection with that which is cast away. William Ian Miller posits such an idea when he asserts:

> We hold no animal feces as disgusting as human feces. . . . Our bodies and our souls are the prime generators of the disgusting. What the animals remind us of, the ones that disgust us—insects, slugs, worms, rats, bats, newts, centipedes—is life, oozy, slimy, viscous, teeming, messy, uncanny life. We needn't have recourse to the animals for that reminder; all we need is a mirror.[24]

Disgust recognizes the communion of death with the process of disintegration, along with the subsequent devolution to life-forms where discrete individual identity is insignificant, giving way to swarms, nests, hives, infestations. In this respect disgust signals a less dynamic—and certainly less exciting—variety of Nietzsche's Dionysian impulse, which similarly violates the principle of individuality and surrenders to orgiastic flux. Reflection on the emotion leads to the nasty realization that the time will come when our own integrity will suffer the same indignities, that the exalted human will become one with the worm. This is not an

23. There is a borderline here that is hard to fix. On the threshold of a chapel near Prague constructed from thousands of bones of victims of the Black Plague, I had to pause to let a wave of dizzying nausea wash through me before entering. Once this was accomplished, it did not return.

24. William Ian Miller, *The Anatomy of Disgust* (Cambridge, MA: Harvard University Press, 1997), 49–50. Colin McGinn emphasizes the significance of death as an object of disgust in his *The Meaning of Disgust: Life, Death, and Revulsion.*

idea that uplifts, nor does it cause joy or happy anticipation. It is, however, an idea that inspires curiosity, fascination, and the absorption that provides a good way to understand the grip of attention that misleadingly is called "pleasure."

Aesthetic Cognition

Recasting pleasure as an intense absorption in an object that induces us to continue rather than halt an experience supports a cognitivist account of aesthetic apprehension, yet without abandoning the notion of pleasure altogether. (That is, pleasure is redescribed rather than discarded.) The term "cognitivist" is used in several ways philosophically, so I need to be clear what I mean when I describe my views in this way. In aesthetics the term can be used as it commonly is in ethics, to refer to theories that hold that critical judgments can be true or false (as opposed to merely expressions of subjective response).[25] Also, as we saw in chapter 1, "cognitivist" is used in emotion theory to refer to the view that emotions are partly constituted by beliefs or propositional attitudes that can be assessed for truth and falsity. Neither of these meanings is in play now. But there are two additional senses of "cognitivist" that are closely related, both of which are accounts of aesthetic satisfaction.

One version of cognitivism maintains that it is the knowledge gained by means of the arousal of difficult emotions that imparts pleasure to aesthetic encounters. Once again, it is Aristotle who provides us with this model. In the famous opening lines of the *Metaphysics* he asserts that everyone has a desire to learn and takes pleasure in information from the senses, and he begins the *Poetics* by observing that humans are naturally imitative and gain great pleasure from learning by means of representation. This approach is designed to permit us to retain talk about pleasure while keeping the disgusting object thoroughly aversive. Philosophers such as Noël Carroll have followed this route and argued that disgust and pleasure occur in sequence as curiosity about a gruesome plot is piqued and its mysteries resolved. Horror stories and movies rely on the arousal of disgust and fear triggered by the monsters that populate the fictions that Carroll dubs "art horror." It is counterintuitive to try to locate pleasure in aversion. Therefore, the pleasure we take in horror is best understood as a cognitive delight taken in discovering the nature of the monstrous entity that propels a plot. So understood, the disgust aroused in the audience "might be seen as part of the price to be paid for the pleasure of their disclosure. . . . Disgust, so to say, is itself more or less mandated by the kind of curiosity that the horror narrative puts in place."[26]

25. Elisabeth Schellekens, "Towards a Reasonable Objectivism for Aesthetic Judgments," *British Journal of Aesthetics* 46, no. 2 (2006): 163–77. Also Nick Zangwill, *The Metaphysics of Beauty* (Ithaca, NY: Cornell University Press, 2001), 26.

26. Noël Carroll, *The Philosophy of Horror, or Paradoxes of the Heart* (New York: Routledge: 1990), 184. One goal of cognitivism, especially in film studies, where theories of the unconscious have dominated critical interpretation, is to square interpretive theory with current neuroscience. See the introduction to Noël Carroll and David Bordwell, *Post-Theory: Reconstructing Film Studies* (Madison: University of Wisconsin Press, 1997). Cynthia Freeland discusses the cognitivist option for understanding pleasure in horror movies in *The Naked and the Undead: Evil and the Appeal of Horror* (Boulder, CO: Westview Press, 2000).

This approach stresses the fact that the engagement of audiences is complex and requires exercise of different mental facilities both emotive and intellectual. Carroll does not need to explain how painful affects convert to aesthetic pleasure because by his lights they do not. Thus he endorses an account in which disgust, fear, and pleasure coexist but retain their distinct valences.[27] For those who shut their eyes at gore but enjoy the plots of horror, it is a persuasive account. And I think it is wise to grant that there are many works that sustain this kind of diagnosis of their enjoyment.

On the other hand, this variety of cognitivism can backfire, for it is also the case that discovering too much about an object of horror can be deflationary. A degree of the thrill of horror is supplied by the imagination roaming into regions that are not made explicit. Slavoj Žižek, adding a Lacanian twist, remarks that monsters (he has the shark in *Jaws* in mind) remain outside the "formal symbolic moment": "What resists absorption into meaning, is the horrifying power of fascination that pertains to the presence of the shark itself. . . before signifying something, before serving as a vessel of meaning, monsters embody enjoyment qua the limit of interpretation, that is to say, *nonmeaning as such*."[28] And as Burke remarked, "Aclear idea is another name for a little idea."[29] I shall come back to the implications of this sentiment in a moment.

If we understand pleasure in the particularist way suggested earlier, the rivalry between pleasure in learning and pain in disgust does not arise, and we need not locate enjoyment only in the learning component of the experience. Instead, we have a situation of concentrated absorption in works that arouse difficult thoughts and feelings that at the same time supply a kind of insight and experience that would be absent without them. The emotions aroused by art provide aesthetic apprehension, some of which is horrible to contemplate, yet they deliver intense satisfaction—inseparable from the difficult emotions aroused.[30]

In embracing this variant of cognitivism, one must also acknowledge that it is not easy to describe just what is "cognized" by aesthetic means because it is difficult to parse what is "known" by means of art. Nor is it entirely clear who the "knower" is. (Peter de Bolla remarks that sometimes it seems oddly as though the artwork itself knows something.)[31] There are a number of reasons for this, including the fact that art is simply not the obvious place to go for

27. This "coexistentialist" account retains the separation of pain and pleasure. Critics of Carroll tend to favor "integrationist" accounts. See Gary Iseminger's comments about sequence versus blending in "How Strange a Sadness," *Journal of Aesthetics and Art Criticism* 42, no. 1 (1983): 81–82.

28. Slavoj Žižek, "Grimaces of the Real, or When the Phallus Appears," *October* 58 (1991): 64.

29. Edmund Burke, *A Philosophical Enquiry into the Origin of Our Ideas of the Sublime and Beautiful* (1757), ed. James T. Boulton (Notre Dame, IN: University of Notre Dame Press, 1968), 63.

30. There are a number of ways to formulate cognitivist aesthetic values. For an insightful analysis of "Aristotelian" and "pragmatist" grounds for this approach, see Cynthia A. Freeland, "Art and Moral Knowledge," *Philosophical Topics* 25, no. 1 (1997): 11–36.

31. Peter de Bolla, "Toward the Materiality of Aesthetic Experience," *Diacritics* 32, no. 1 (2002): 25.

learning.[32] Second, often what one grasps from an aesthetic encounter is a truism that one already knows, for art's insights are not particularly revelatory when stated in general terms. Wise observations such as "We are all mortal" are flat and robbed of the punch that they have when delivered in a vivid and distinctive manner, for it is the acute impression of a particularly skillful or eloquent artistic rendering of a truth that brings it home.[33] I shall take up this point again in the next chapter, providing some examples that I believe demonstrate why it can take a difficult emotion such as disgust to deliver forceful recognition of what is a banal truism when uttered in a simple proposition. Third, and perhaps most important, an aesthetic apprehension imparts the impression that one is on the brink of an intuition that eludes articulation in plain language and can only be approached by means of the artwork that induces it. This is something like what Kant refers to as an "aesthetic idea," by which he means "a presentation of the imagination which prompts much thought, but to which no determinate thought whatsoever, i.e. no [determinate] *concept*, can be adequate, so that no language can express it completely and allow us to grasp it."[34] An aesthetic idea leads the mind toward the ineffable. Or, in more postmodern terms, it evokes what Lyotard refers to as the "unpresentable."[35]

The idea that aesthetic value includes a brand of insight, understanding, or knowledge is thus not new. It lies at the heart of the modern coinage of the very term "aesthetic," as I noted in the introduction. And although this understanding is sometimes sidelined by an emphasis on pleasure (i.e., on accounts of pleasure wrong-footed by a sensation paradigm), it appears widely in the literature in aesthetics. It is not that aesthetic insight substitutes for pleasure; rather, pleasure modifies the compressed insight that is the mark of the aesthetic. Nelson Goodman makes this point in terms that are especially apt for considering disgust when he notes that aesthetic emotions function cognitively:

> In contending that aesthetic experience is cognitive, I am emphatically not identifying it with the conceptual, the discursive, the linguistic. Under "cognitive" I include all aspects of knowing and understanding, from perceptual discrimination through pattern recognition and emotive insight to logical inference.[36]

32. This is one reason that Peter Lamarque rejects a cognitive account of aesthetic value in "Cognitive Values in the Arts: Marking the Boundaries." A pendant essay arguing the contrary is Berys Gaut, "Art and Cognition," both in *Contemporary Debates in Aesthetics and Philosophy of Art*, ed. Matthew Kieran (Malden, MA: Blackwell, 2006), 127–39 and 115–26. See also Stephen Davies, ed., *Art and Its Messages: Meaning, Morality, and Society* (University Park: Pennsylvania State University Press, 1997).

33. As Matthew Kieran puts it, "Works can get us to grasp certain truths, insights or possibilities, and make us realise their import in psychologically immediate ways, in ways pure reason rarely does." *Revealing Art* (London: Routledge, 2005), 120.

34. Immanuel Kant, *Critique of Judgment* (1790), trans. Werner S. Pluhar (Indianapolis, IN: Hackett, 1987), 182. The aesthetic idea is the counterpart to a "rational idea," a generally expressed idea for which no particular imaginative intuition is adequate.

35. Jean-François Lyotard, "Presenting the Unpresentable," *Artforum*, April 1982, 64–69.

36. Nelson Goodman, "Reply to Beardsley," *Erkenntnis* 12, no. 1 (1978): 173. See also Goodman, *Languages of Art: An Approach to a Theory of Symbols* (Indianapolis, IN: Bobbs-Merrill, 1968) esp. sec. 6.

Disgust can signify many things, and the collateral affects that often accompany it—such as amusement or erotic arousal—often overtake in immediate awareness its more difficult meanings. Therefore, I do not offer a picture of all instances of aesthetic disgust with a single description. However, I think we shall find that in its more profound uses, at the root of the apprehension afforded by the arousal of disgust is recognition of the aspects of death that are the least heroic: stench and bodily disintegration presented with particular intimacy and nearness. The emotion is unlikely to occur by itself, but it has many potential companions: bemusement, sorrow, dread, terror, and even acquiescence.

Psychoanalysis, Disgust, and Desire

While general solutions to the paradox of aversion are aimed at a set of uncomfortable emotions, psychoanalysis actually targets disgust.[37] Although this approach has not had many advocates among analytic philosophers, psychoanalytic perspectives dominate the critical disciplines of literature and film studies. I have noted from time to time the tendency among emotion theorists to treat disgust in ways that are not commensurate with other emotions, assigning to it only extreme degrees of intensity, for example, or placing it as an unyielding antithesis to beauty. Freud also distinguishes it from other emotions when he singles out disgust (and shame) along with morality as reaction formations obscuring infantile sexual desire that must be sublimated for a mature self to develop. He traces the allure of disgust to its genesis from repressed desire, the emotion retaining the residue of that original primal impulse.

For Freud, pleasure and pain (or unpleasure: *Unlust*) are conceptually inseparable, for pleasure occurs with the release of tension or discomfort. The central case is tension built up from an unsatisfied sexual impulse. Because infantile sexual instincts, such as the desire on the part of boys for union with the mother, must be repressed and sublimated in order for the organism to mature, there is a block to the immediate satisfaction of pleasures implicit in the very development of the individual. When the tension built up is released by indirect means (fantasy, jokes, dreams, works of art), the result is registered as pleasure. One is not able to access the nature or source of that pleasure directly because it is buried in the unconscious, for according to Freud's tantalizing observation, the feelings of pleasure and unpleasure, which "act so imperatively upon us," issue from "the most obscure and inaccessible region of the mind."[38]

37. Freud wrote a brief comment on the paradox of tragedy, noting that sometimes the enjoyment of difficult dramatic emotions is aimed simply at blowing off steam; Freud, "Psychopathic Characters on the Stage," in *The Complete Psychological Works of Sigmund Freud*, Vol. VII (1901–5), ed. James Strachey (London: Hogarth Press and the Institute of Psycho-analysis, 1953), 305–10.

38. Sigmund Freud, *Beyond the Pleasure Principle* (1920), trans. James Strachey (New York: Norton, 1961), y. For an appreciative critique of Freud, see Karmen MacKendrick, *Counterpleasures* (Albany: State University of New York Press, 1999).

There is an array of such theories in use, which despite differences are united in certain basic assumptions. All conceive of pleasure as the relief of some antecedent condition, often identified with the blanket term "Desire." As I have argued earlier, this approach erroneously assumes that pleasure must indicate the removal (whether actual or imagined) or some discomfort, and because Desire is erotically charged, the notion of pleasure is further flawed by being modeled on sensation.[39] These general missteps about what pleasure must entail limit the applicability of psychoanalytic diagnoses. Nonetheless, these approaches have some acute things to say about the attraction of disgust that are worth pondering even if one does not accept their overall theory of mentality.

One of the most influential texts for the interpretation of aesthetic disgust is Julia Kristeva's *Powers of Horror: An Essay on Abjection*. Kristeva develops her theory of abjection from Freud, Lacan, and the structuralist anthropologist Mary Douglas.[40] While abjection is not identical with disgust, her treatment deepens both the psychological and the existential signification of that emotion. Kristeva agrees with the common analysis of disgust as an emotion that recognizes the threat of slimy, oozy, life-generating and death-dealing decay, which is not only an offense to the senses but also a threat to identity. She pursues the nature of the threat by analyzing just how disgusting objects represent the overtaking of form by formlessness, of distinction by undifferentiation. They call to mind the tenuousness of our own identity, under siege from the first moments of its formation.

Kristeva's approach is distinctive in that she directs her analysis to the maternal role in the development of a conscious self. Each developing consciousness forms its own identity through distinguishing itself from other things. The unconscious comes into being in the process of repression and sublimation, whereby the initial sense of oneness and lack of differentiation from the world—figured as the maternal body—is ruptured as the infant begins to develop a sense of separate identity. With recognition of this separation—the abjection of the mother—comes an awareness of loss, lack, the desire to return to the plentitude of prenatal union. But this return is not only impossible but also in opposition to the need to separate and become independent. The desire to regain the union with maternal oneness is sublimated as the child enters the symbolic order and develops a mature self. But a profound and transgressive magnetism lingers in desire that is tantalized though never satisfied in images that return the self to its undifferentiated state. The maternal body lurks beneath consciousness as invitation to regain this state of oneness,

---

39. Ermanno Bencivenga seeks to recast and restore some of the insights of Freud regarding pleasure in "Economy of Expression and Aesthetic Pleasure," *Philosophy and Phenomenological Research* 47, no. 4 (1987): 615–30.

40. Mary Douglas's *Purity and Danger: An Analysis of the Concepts of Pollution and Taboo* (London: Routledge and Kegan Paul, 1966). Both Kristeva and Carroll invoke Douglas's work to support their theories.

but at the same time this invitation is a horrific threat to the formed self that would lose identity were it to succumb to its lure. The abject is thus at once disgusting and alluring—a "vortex of summons and repulsion."[41]

Kristeva's perspective vividly amplifies the signification of disgust by foregrounding the counterpart of death: birth. There is no more intimate relation than that between mother and unborn child, and at birth we come into the world trailing not clouds of glory but blood and viscous tissues. Birth is messy and sticky. What was perfect union has fallen apart and cannot be reunited. The substances surrounding birth may arouse disgust after they are extruded and become waste, but they also signify what once was absolute proximity—union with a sustaining presence now lost to possibility. Although I have argued against the general theory of pleasure Kristeva assumes, her theory offers a separable picture of disgust that is compelling in its description of how one universal event can be surrounded by both disgust and longing. The abject body repels because of its threat to identity; it lures as relief from the burden of individual selfhood.[42] Kristeva presents a provocative aspect of the terrible intimacy that disgust can signify.

What is more, the theory of abjection is widely employed in both criticism and art. It is invoked to understand the power of horror movies, especially those in which the image of the devouring mother appears.[43] The linkage of disgust with the maternal and with femaleness itself has been employed by feminist and other contemporary artists who explore the meanings of the body and its material vulnerabilities.[44] These uses of disgust are consequential with or without agreement with their background theoretical premises, and they form an important part of the cultural jigsaw that includes aesthetic disgust. The centrality of the maternal in Kristeva's theory provides an additional way to understand the attention to sexuality and the body that is a prominent feature of many current works of gallery and theater. Indeed, the appropriateness of abjection for a good deal of contemporary art reminds us that aesthetic satisfactions have cultural form and moment.[45] At present, this particular species of

41. Julia Kristeva, *The Powers of Horror: An Essay on Abjection*, trans. Leon S. Roudiez (New York: Columbia University Press, 1982), 1.

42. Late in his writings Freud introduced the death drive at the heart of the unconscious. Death—the return to a state without individuation—is the ultimate release of tension. See Ellie Ragland, *Essays on the Pleasures of Death: From Freud to Lacan* (New York: Routledge, 1995).

43. For instance, Barbara Creed, *The Monstrous Feminine: Film, Feminism, Psychoanalysis* (London: Routledge, 1993); Laura Mulvey, *Fetishism and Curiosity* (Bloomington: Indiana University Press, 1996). See also Claire Kahane, "Freud's Sublimation: Disgust, Desire, and the Female Body," *American Imago* 49, no. 4 (1992): 411–25. For a critique of the use of abjection in film interpretation, see Freeland, *The Naked and the Undead*, 17–21 and passim.

44. Craig Houser, Leslie C. Jones, Simon Taylor, and Jack Ben-Levi, *Abject Art: Repulsion and Desire in American Art* (New York: Whitney Museum, 1993); Carolyn Korsmeyer, *Gender and Aesthetics: An Introduction* (New York: Routledge, 2004), chap. 6.

45. See suggestions of Daniel Hurwitz, "Pleasure," in *Encyclopedia of Aesthetics*, vol. 4, ed. Michael Kelly (New York: Oxford University Press, 1998), 1–6. See also essays in the volume *Formations of Pleasure* (London: Routledge and Kegan Paul, 1983).

disgust is playing out in the worlds of art and entertainment more or less glob-
ally. The confluence of preoccupations with femaleness and the grotesque body
affords another way to discern disgust as a culture-creating passion, to use
Miller's apt phrase.

Disgust and the Sublate

Thus far we have a picture of disgust that beguiles in several ways. It teases
consciousness and the limits of tolerance, and it acquaints us with the common
denominator of organic life and eventual loss of identity. Such apprehensions
can occur with the valences available from different art forms and narrative
contexts—whether comic, tragic, horrid, or just fascinating. Both cognitivism
and the idea that disgust can be accounted for in terms of a metaresponse
countenance the idea that what might be termed pleasure in aesthetic disgust
is displaced from the immediate arousal of the emotion. That is, disgust
remains aversive and as such an emotional "pain," but the knowledge gained
by means of it affords enjoyment, as does the second-order reflection on one's
toleration of the disgusting. Such accounts explain a range of examples of aesthetic disgust. But the picture is not complete. Probing more deeply, we may
discover how what is ordinarily an aversion sometimes may *convert* in affective
tenor to an aesthetic attraction.

Classic conversion accounts come in two forms. As responses to the paradox of tragedy, they focus on how an unpleasant subject that provokes painful
emotions can become beautiful in the hands of a skilled artist. Hume offers a
famous conversion account in his short essay on tragedy, though it is widely
criticized for not being clear about just how the eloquence of expression converts a pain to a pleasure. Although it is difficult to provide—and unreasonable
to expect—a formula for such conversion, Hume is surely right to observe that
the "uneasy passion" of difficult art, "unaccompanied with any spirit, genius, or
eloquence, conveys a pure uneasiness and is attended with nothing that can
soften it into pleasure or satisfaction."[46] That is to say, we would ignore the
artwork unduly if we did not acknowledge that the mode by which difficult
passions are aroused is crucial to understanding their aesthetic value and
import. So far I have said little about beauty, and since this is the subject of the
last chapter I shall save consideration of that value until then. In any event, the
more relevant point of comparison for disgust is the one already introduced:
fear and the conversion of that emotion to the rival pinnacle of aesthetic value,
the sublime.

---

46. David Hume, "Of Tragedy," in *Essays Moral, Political, and Literary*, vol. 1 (1882), ed. T. H. Green and T.
H. Grose (Darmstadt: Scientia Verlag Aalen, 1964), 265.

As a rule, aesthetic emotions (i.e., those that constitute appreciative arousal) are varieties of everyday emotions: anxiety, sorrow, dread, anticipation, happiness, and so forth, although they may alter in their aesthetic form from the ordinary variety. Grief is muted by cognizance of the fictionality of its objects, for instance. With certain emotions, however, aesthetic transformation is so profound that an entirely new affective experience is brought into being. The most famous example of this is the emotion identified as the sublime, widely theorized as founded upon terror, though transmogrified into thrill and awe. In chapter 3 I teased out a parallel with the sublime to make a case for a conversion of the disgusting into the delicious. Now I shall try to nudge disgust in another direction, for just as fear can be the foundation for encounters with the sublime, so disgust can achieve its own aesthetic counterpart. It does not have a name, but if a label is needed I recommend we call it the "sublate."

This term plays upon the senses of "sublime" in both philosophy and chemistry. In the latter discourse, "sublime" refers to a substance when it passes directly from solid to gaseous state with no interval of liquid. The term originates in the language of alchemy.[47] The metaphor of heavy turned to light, and of solid and confined turned to vaporous and expansive, suits well both the rhetorical sense of "sublime" meaning lofty and great that originates with Longinus, and the modern philosophical use of the term to signify an experience of boundlessness, might, and mystery. The term "sublate," which is seldom used any more in chemistry, is the opposite of "sublime," indicating something turning directly from gas to solid. It has a remote etymological connection with words meaning "burden," a weight to be removed.[48] Philosophy houses the term too, for Hegel's *Aufhebung*—the negation of a concept that transforms it into a component of a higher-order relation—is often translated "sublation." This meaning is not entirely at odds with my use of "sublate," though I have in mind a far more specific phenomenon. Just as the experience of sublimity is likened to an elevation and expansion of spirit—free from earthly weight—so the sublate signals aesthetic insight in a bodily, visceral response.

Although disgust did not figure in the formulation of those Enlightenment theories that transmute terror into the sublime, a parallel case can be made for metamorphosis of affect for that aversion too. I have already argued for a conversion of disgusting into delicious. With eating, however, the successful transformation of a dubious substance into gourmet delight or recondite cuisine also converts a difficult response into a positive pleasure, such that while a trace of the disgusting may linger, the substance no longer provokes the emotion itself. This is a conversion of sorts, but it has limited extension into the

47. Edmund Andrews, *The History of Scientific English* (New York: Richard R. Smith, 1947), 247.

48. Eric Partridge, *Origins: A Short Etymological Dictionary of Modern English* (New York: Macmillan, 1958), 724–25.

worlds of art because the close ties to sensory experience place physical limits on how far dubious substances can be exploited. (Some of the pleasures of eating are obviously directed at sensations, but we do not want the presence of sensory considerations to divert us back to a mistaken general model of pleasure as sensation.) With the sublate a conversion occurs that bears closer parallel with sublimity.

Again, the theorist of the sublime whom I shall most use to make this case is Burke, for his work converges insightfully with that of Kolnai, whose observations about disgust are now familiar. Although Kant's sublime has had greater influence, it is Burke who takes serious account of the bodily sensations that accompany fear.[49] And as Kolnai notes, "Both fear and disgust manifest a close linkage with the body and—not independently of this—a psychic 'depth,' a power which, at least temporarily, fills out the personality."[50] Both Burke and Kolnai also acknowledge a certain allure in the emotions they examine. Kant, in contrast, argued that by the time we experience the emotion of the sublime we are no longer scared. Since I intend to keep the somatic spasm of disgust intact, this observation is out of tune with the aesthetic uses that I think disgust provides.

That the difficult emotion lingers in the positive apprehension indicates just what is being "converted." It is not that disgust and fear lose their nature altogether in the process of aesthetic conversion, such that in their aesthetic form they are no longer members of those classes of emotion. Rather, it is that what was an aversion is put to use in the kind of attentive absorption that seems to be the best way to understand aesthetic apprehension and its pleasures.

To review the case for fear as the emotional foundation for the sublime: Burke presumes that there are three basic feeling states that always accompany experience—pleasure, pain, and indifference. Pleasure is the zone where beauty operates, and beautiful objects typically possess untaxing qualities such as daintiness, delicacy, curviness, and relatively small size. Beautiful things are bounded and limited, and they can be grasped in their entirety by both perception and imagination. But the aesthetic scene also includes experiences grounded in "pains" —which Burke surmises are more powerful than pleasures. He identifies acute fear or terror as the deepest emotional pain. Terror recognizes power, and proximate power threatens to engulf or annihilate the perceiving subject. But because it also inspires awe, that which arouses terror is also capable of becoming the object of the sublime, the "strongest emotion which the mind is capable of feeling."[51]

49. See also Richard Shusterman, "Somaesthetics and Burke's Sublime," *British Journal of Aesthetics* 45, no. 4 (2005): 323–41.
50. Kolnai, *On Disgust*, 33.
51. Burke, *Philosophical Enquiry*, 39.

but should I this book
tell us how it happens ?

A person in the grip of actual terror enjoys nothing; the emotion overwhelms and produces intolerable distress. However, if it is possible to regard a mighty and fearsome object from a position of relative safety, or to achieve psychological distance that lessens the grip of fear, then one may observe terrifying things and be stirred with the thrill of the sublime, recognizing might, magnificence, and the ineffable endlessness of the cosmos. In fact, anything of great size, including the concept of infinity, fills the mind with what Burke calls "delightful horror."[52] The sublime is not itself an experience of terror—at least not only terror. But without the underlying terror that its objects inspire, there would be no experience of the sublime. Here a supremely uncomfortable and aversive emotion is transmogrified into powerful and transportive aesthetic insight. Just how this occurs is hard to fathom, but that it occurs is indisputable. Burke speculates that the human constitution has a limited tolerance for the neutral state of indifference and simply demands to be stirred and stretched. Mere pleasures induce languidness and content, requiring the energizing discomfort of fears and pains to reignite dynamic engagement with life.[53]

What can disgust provide that stands in counterpoint to the sublime? At first glance, not much. Burke refers to objects such as toads and spiders—his only mention of things often considered disgusting—as "merely odious," and he clearly does not think that they are philosophically very interesting (although he allows that poetic descriptions of intolerable stenches can contribute to sublime literary effects). However, as we saw in chapter 2, aesthetics at that point in history had an agenda that overdetermined the exclusion of disgust from artistic consideration, and there is no reason to accept Burke's peremptory judgment. In contemporary theory the stricter parameters of earlier aesthetics are no longer endorsed, which also means that the bodily responses occasioned by art are more frequently acknowledged as aesthetically legitimate. Now, therefore, it may be easier to discern the roles that disgust has always played in art, including its subtle presence in the sublate.

Although strong emotions occasion physical turmoil, they are not just sensations or internal commotions but also means of insight. Terror is the ground for the sublime because it registers the overwhelming character of its objects. The presence of a specific emotion at the foundation of the sublime contributes an important asymmetry to the beautiful and the sublime—so often considered balanced opposites. Because beauty is identified as a pleasure with no particular emotional content, the sublime is not merely the more difficult counterpart experience. It is cognitively more significant because it has built into it a particular range of meaning supplied by the foundation of terror. Cynthia Freeland describes it this way: "We might say that the sublime object presents us with a sensory and emotional experience of some sort that is so

52. Burke, *Philosophical Enquiry*, 73.
53. Burke, *Philosophical Enquiry*, 135.

extreme, unsettling, or intense that it would be disturbing on its own. But in its context it forces us to shift into another mental mode, cognition, or thought."[54] I prefer to call the mental mode another type of aesthetic emotion, but whether we label it sublime or sublate, or eschew new labels, the important thing to stress is that the experience gives rise to an *apprehension*, a grasp of an idea that is so imbedded in affective response to the work that provokes it as to be virtually inseparable.

The objects of both fear and disgust pose threats to the perceiving subject, though threats of a different order and immediacy. Fear indicates imminent danger; disgust registers a threat of contamination that is likely only in the longer term. Not all instances of fear give rise to the sublime, of course; and certainly not all instances of disgust yield the sublate. The sublime and the sublate operate differently from other aesthetic emotions, for the aversions at the basis of those aesthetic modes are not experienced as such. The fear underlying the sublime is transmuted into awe and exaltation. I now need to make a case for a counterpart transformation of disgust into the sublate.

Terror is aroused by the natural upheavals, cosmic vastness, infinity itself—anything that signifies human powerlessness and possible annihilation. If that realization goes no further, we are only scared. If our attention manages to leave our own peril and become directed to the powerful forces at hand, we may be rewarded with the thrill and awe of the sublime. Death is realized differently in the experience of disgust. Here we have not the destructive sweep of mighty forces but the dismemberment, putrefaction, or the slow and demeaning disintegration of individual bodies, even the most complex forms of which are eventually overtaken by hordes of proliferating microbes and vermin. Disgust apprehends not just destruction but reduction—of the noblest life to decaying organic matter in which all traces of individuality are obliterated.

Fear and disgust thus can yield kindred, complementary insights. Their general import, however, is rarely revelatory. We already know that we are mortal, that generations pass, that civilizations are finite. But as a rule we know these things only in the abstract, and when stated in bald paraphrase, such insights usually flatten into truisms. However, it is the nature of aesthetic encounters to be singular; they bring home general truths in a particularly vivid manner, deepening their apprehension more profoundly than straightforward statement can accomplish. When strong emotions come into play, these insights are grasped not only with the mind but also with palpable somatic resonance.

This conversion is by no means the only aesthetic role that disgust can play. More than one account of this emotion is required to accommodate its immense variety. What I label the sublate is among the ways that disgust performs in art, and it is the principal one that permits this emotion to join the

54. Cynthia Freeland, "The Sublime in Cinema," in *Passionate Views: Film, Cognition, and Emotion*, ed. Carl Plantinga and Greg M. Smith (Baltimore: Johns Hopkins University Press, 1999), 68.

as a key underlying term
but can 'appreciation' be measured

roster of affective attributes that achieve particularly high artistic value. It puts the finish on the argument against the traditional exclusion of disgust from aesthetic importance. The emotion's distinctive power is recognized as capable of attaining a unique transformation.

With this latter point in mind, I conclude with a corrective observation. In articulating a counterpart of the sublime, I find that I have been tempted in a direction that I have resisted throughout this study, and that is to focus on the type of disgust that is an extreme emotion that discloses extreme insights. Sometimes indeed this is the case. The Dionysian creative impulse so vividly described by Nietzsche, which in its pure form overpowers not only rational order but the principle of individuation itself, is as close kin to the sublate as to the sublime. But Kristeva's opening example of the abject is a humble object: the skin on a glass of milk. Unlike the sublime, the sublate can come in small and subtle doses—little indignities, wry insights, furtive curiosities, comic interruptions. We need not always yank at the veil of Isis, descend into *jouissance*, or contemplate nonmeaning as such in order to register the somatic spasm of aesthetic disgust. The worm in the rose can appear in modest guise, prompting only a slight intake of breath, a squirm, a hesitation, a queasy little—oh.

6

Hearts

The overall approach to understanding aesthetic disgust has been presented in the previous chapters. I hope to have established that this emotion, so often regarded as assuming only extreme forms, manifests degrees and shades, blending with, deepening, and complicating other affects experienced in art. Emotions in general take much of their phenomenal flavor from their particular objects, and with the artistic uses of disgust this contribution is especially notable. Aesthetic disgust not only possesses a subjective quality that is part of "appreciation" but also is the prime mode by which a range of meaning is apprehended. In the last chapter I argued that the bedrock of that meaning is death and its aftermath, but that by no means reduces all meanings to one, for it leaves open very different attitudes and emphases that mark the subject. Aesthetic disgust holds open-ended possibilities of tenor and valence from dismal to hilarious, melancholy to erotic. The visceral response is crucial, but it too varies from slight twinge to horrified nausea. Whatever form it takes, aesthetic disgust lends intimacy and immediacy to its encounters.

We have before us a sense of the values and significance that disgust registers, and we also have a list of the standard objects that provoke its occurrence. However, despite certain demonstrable constants in the qualities of disgusting objects and in physiological responses to them, it is clear that the arousal of this emotion is far from a matter of simple cause and effect. These affective encounters are highly variant, as we have seen from the heterogeneous array of art that manifests or provokes disgust. Notwithstanding a common general emotive character, aesthetic qualities differ markedly depending on the genre, the style, the context, the purpose, and the import of the individual works. (It also needs to be remembered that appreciation is always influenced by audience familiarity with genres, tastes for different kinds of art, and tolerance for psychological extremes.)

In previous chapters I assembled examples to demonstrate how disgust takes many forms. I now adopt a reciprocal tactic and consider just one motif that has been employed with stunningly different meanings and valences. This strategy will deepen our grasp of the elasticity of responses even to objects that qualify among the central disgust elicitors, and it will provide further examples to confirm the various accounts of the satisfactions that this somatic aversion can uniquely provide.

I select as the focus for this discussion the human heart, an organ with intense symbolic power and a long cultural history. Because the heart is an organ of the body, it is an automatic candidate for disgust elicitor when it is removed from its proper place in the chest. Violation of the bodily envelope and evisceration are among the primary triggers of disgust identified by psychologists and philosophers, as we saw in chapter 1. The newly removed, still-beating heart is often exploited in images of sheer horror, such as in graphic scenes in the macabre and gruesome film *Angel Heart* (figure 6.1). One might suppose that an image such as this one is bound without exception to revolt. But even a heart ripped from a living body is capable of prompting a fair variety of aesthetic reactions, depending on the preparation of

FIGURE 6.1. Film still, *Angel Heart*. Dir. Alan Parker. TriStar Pictures, 1987.

SVBLATIZ higher tone?

audiences for its display, its role in narrative, and—most important—the significance it possesses within the artwork in question. Sometimes, as I argued
in the last chapter, disgust operates quite like the terror that lies beneath the
sublime. When this occurs, we have an instance of the conversion of disgust
into an aesthetically significant quality that has an emotive tone all its own,
for which I offered the name sublate. Shortly I shall present some examples
that I believe illustrate the subtle power of the sublate in narrative. By no
means does this transformation leave the emotion itself behind. On the contrary, any account that would convert disgust into another affect altogether
loses reference to the potency of that somatic spasm. What is converted is
not the emotion itself but its valence; the insight it affords by means of the
particular artistry with which it is delivered is central to its aesthetic import
and value.

To initiate consideration of the artistic uses of the heart, we need first to consider the extent of its cultural applications in image, metaphor, and practical usage.
Of all the viscera, the heart has probably been assigned the most persistent and
deepest symbolic value. It is an immediate and easily discernible signal of life. A
mere touch at the pulse points of the body can detect the beating of the heart, reas-
suring one that life persists. The fact that the heart both represents and literally is
an immediate sustainer of life disposes it to be used in a kind of natural symbolism: when the heart beats, there is life; when it ceases, there is death. Obviously,
it is not the only internal organ that ceases activity with death, but most of the
others cannot be detected without the aid of technology. The flat-lining electroen-
cephalograph indicating the cessation of brain activity, for example, is a relatively
recent entry into the symbol systems that attest to the persistence or the end of a
life. But although I have asserted a disposition to natural symbolism, it is the ac-
crual of practices and meanings around the heart that establish that symbolic
usage. We can see this by comparison with the peristaltic action of the stomach,
which can also be easily detected from the outside simply by putting one's ear to
another person's midsection. But the squish and gurgle of digestion has not
entered our symbolic vocabulary as a signal of life or death. Even natural symbols
require a cultural boost.

Just how pancultural or local this symbolic usage may be is a question for
anthropologists and historians. Certainly it appears in the artistic motifs of very
diverse cultures: European, Persian,[1] West African, native North American, to
mention just a few. Aztec statuary depicts the goddess Coatlicue wearing a
necklace of human hearts, hands, and a skull (figure 6.2). And the meanings
ascribed to the heart are often consonant across history and culture. In ancient
Egypt—as today—the heart was regarded as the seat of morality. The Egyptian
Book of the Dead pictures the god Anubis weighing the heart of the deceased

1. Annemarie Schimmel, *The Triumphal Sun: A Study of the Works of Jalaloddin Rumi* (Albany: State University
of New York Press, 1978), 138–39.

FIGURE 6.2. Coatlicue, the Earth Mother. Aztec, late fifteenth century.
Museo Nacional de Antropologia e Historia, Mexico City. Werner Forman/Art
Resource, NY.

against the feather of truth (figure 6.3). In the broad-based "Western" cultural
tradition within which these words are written the appropriation of the heart to
carry meaning far beyond its duties as a bodily organ is indelible and pandemic.

In English, the very term "heart" metaphorically signals the core, the essence of
something ("the heart of the matter"). Reference to the heart declares authenticity and
sincerity ("heartfelt"). It stands for a deeply held kind of knowledge ("I know in my
heart") that is sometimes private and guarded ("Mary pondered them in her heart").
Memory permits one to "learn by heart."[2] The pulse, that soft drumbeat emanating
from the heart's pumping rhythm, is one of the body's internal agitations that is most
evident to the subject, and therefore the heart is often invoked in declarations of passionate response, whether elation ("My heart leaps up when I behold . . .": Word-
sworth) or terror ("Her heart was in her mouth"). Perhaps most commonly, it stands
for love ("dear heart") and for longing ("heart's desire"). The heart breaks under the
weight of great loss. The heart may stand for life, love, honesty, self, essence.[3]

2. This locution is "a relic of the medieval link between heart and memory," embedded also in the word "record"
(from Latin, where *cor* = heart). Eric Jager, *The Book of the Heart* (Chicago: University of Chicago Press, 2000), xv–xvi.

3. These meanings are embedded in wide linguistic practice. Paul Stoller observes that among the Songhay
of Niger, to say that someone feels with two hearts is to accuse him of duplicity or hypocrisy; Stoller, *Fusion of the
Worlds: An Ethnography of Possession among the Songhay of Niger* (Chicago: University of Chicago Press, 1989), 161.

FIGURE 6.3. Psychostasis (Weighing of the Souls). The Book of the Dead of the Priest Aaner. Papyrus. New Kingdom. Museo Egizio, Turin. Alinari/Art Resource, NY.

The heart is unique among the viscera in having a well-established schematic symbol: ♥, a figure that was in wide use by the European Middle Ages.[4] This design abstracts and makes symmetrical the two chambers of the heart and omits many of its functional components such as valves and arterial connections. Now a motif for decoration and for the bland holiday of Valentine's Day, this pretty design is about as far from disgusting as one can imagine. And it can be funny. In cartoons the beating heart of an infatuated character leaps from his chest in comical exuberance. In more sentimental treatments, the expression "hearts and flowers" invokes only sweetness, the flower valence taking over the deeper, tougher meanings of the heart. (An actual flower with a heart-shaped blossom, *Dicentra spectabilis*, has the folk name "bleeding heart.") Even so, the schematic heart may also be displayed with equally schematic tear-shaped drops of blood, indicating that the design retains reference to the literal organ. (The flower also has pendant "drops" on the bloom.)

Few of the metaphorical invocations of hearts listed here are even on the horizon of disgust, even though—taken literally—they would be. Think of the expression "Eat your heart out." The cultural symbol is so well entrenched that the oddity of the expression is barely noticed. Calling attention to it has its own artistic uses, for changing from metaphorical to literal heart imagery produces an interplay of affects that can switch abruptly from tenderness to horror to humor. For example, an episode of the television series *Buffy the Vampire Slayer* includes this exchange between Buffy and her vampire lover Angel:

4. Jager, *Book of the Heart*, 82.

ANGEL   I saw you before you became a slayer. You walked down the steps and I loved you.

BUFFY   Why?

ANGEL   Because I could see your heart. You held it before you for everyone to see, and I worried that it would be bruised or torn, and more than anything in my life I wanted to keep it safe. To warm it with my own.

BUFFY   That's beautiful. [Pause] Or taken literally, incredibly gross.[5]

In short, we have with the human heart an object that can be simultaneously, sequentially, or selectively an organ, an icon, a metaphor, a decorative design, a symbol.

It is also a dish.

Love in Disguise

Once again a culinary context provides the entry point for considering an artistic motif. Like brains, kidneys, livers, and other organs, hearts are cooked and eaten. In English they are usually classed in the old-fashioned category of "offal," a term that literally means "off-fall" and refers to the parts of a carcass that fall away when the choicer flesh is selected.[6] Therefore heart—of pig or calf or chicken—is rarely considered the best type of meat, but that by no means makes it inedible. Today in North America it is rarely consumed, and although the very idea of eating heart is disgusting to many, this revulsion is more a signal of its current unfamiliarity than its taste.

A dish made from an organ is often prepared in such a way that the organ retains its original shape, and its distinctive flavor bears evidence of its identity even after it has been cooked and served. This promotes its latent representational function, for it readily calls attention to its original purpose. As noted earlier, there is a way to prepare kidneys that retains the merest hint of urine in the taste, a mode of cooking approved by many gourmet eaters. The heart, with its rich symbolic history, is literally the engine of life of an animal and metaphorically the core of that life. Hence even dressed and served on a plate, a heart issues a standing invitation for the diner to ponder his or her dinner, its origin in a living creature, and its meaning. As we saw in chapter 3, that pondering can range from the whimsical to the terrible. Consider this description of an old recipe for hearts. Significantly, it has a title:

5. *Buffy the Vampire Slayer*, season 3, episode 12, "Helpless."
6. John Ayto, *The Diner's Dictionary: Food and Drink from A to Z* (Oxford: Oxford University Press, 1993), 236. The term "offal" is derived from the Dutch *afval*. See also Jeremy MacClancy, *Consuming Culture: Why You Eat What You Eat* (New York: Henry Holt, 1992), chap. 19.

Love in Disguise

A disgusting Victorian euphemism for what seems to modern sensibilities a fairly disgusting Victorian dish: a calf's heart wrapped up in minced veal, coated in a layer of crushed vermicelli, and then baked. The outlandish name is based on the symbolism of the heart for "love."[7]

More detailed recipes for this dish permit pigs' hearts rather than calf. Several also recommend the use of a tomato sauce. Both the coating of vermicelli and the red sauce amplify the macabre wit provided by the title of the dish, for the former hints of worms and the latter a dribble of blood.

The interpretation of the title as a euphemism that cloaks the disgusting quality of the dish is baseless, however, as is another surmise that the name "masks the origins" of the heart dish and permits the diner to eat without thinking of the organ being chewed.[8] Indeed, the exact reverse is the case, for rather than mask, the title actually calls attention to the fact that one is eating a heart. It does so with the same kind of wicked humor that goes into the names for other dishes that—far from averting disgust—seek to create it. This is, after all, the cuisine that produced "toad in the hole," a dish of sausages baked in Yorkshire pudding. The more American "pigs in a blanket" to describe hotdogs wrapped in bread has much the same function. The title is not needed as a disguise to tempt the squeamish to eat something vile. To those initiated into the culinary tradition it is either droll or barely noticed, as is the repellent "boiled baby" to refer to suet pudding.[9] To the less familiar, the title dangles disgust—the culinary gross-out—before one as a kind of dare in a teasing, amusing, and faintly nasty manner. Perhaps such titles operate as conceptual spice, lending a frisson of risk to an otherwise commonplace dish.

Calves' and pigs' hearts were commonly eaten when Love in Disguise was named. Indeed, if one surveys cookbooks in English from the late nineteenth century to the present, one finds three or four heart recipes in the older ones, perhaps one in the mid-twentieth century, and none today. A dish needs no euphemism if it is so familiar that disgust is unlikely to arise. On the contrary, the title is a witty direction to the diner to think of the meal in stronger terms than simply "stuffed heart" invites. Moreover, a host of allusions come to mind from ancient myth and fairy tale. As bygone diners sliced into the baked heart, they might have thought of the many tales of revenge in which an unfaithful wife is fed the heart of her lover. If so, perhaps they stopped eating. Or maybe they ate with greater relish spurred by romantic imagination. The dish called

7. Ayto, *Diner's Dictionary*, 198.

8. "Fancy names were traditionally given to offal dishes like this one in order to mask their origins." Website for PBS documentary on the "demon barber" Sweeney Todd: http://www.pbs.org/kqed/demonbarber/recipes/loveindisguise.html (accessed November 4, 2003).

9. See Barbara Pym, *No Fond Return of Love* (New York: Harper and Row, 1984), 95.

"Love in Disguise" is wit with a bite and with a long and macabre history lying behind its name, as we shall see in due course.

Relic Hearts

The heart has a history in philosophy and medicine that contributes to the way it is used to signify various aspects of self and character. According to Robert Erickson:

> By the early modern period, the word "heart" had come to mean a variety of things: the center of all vital functions, the source of one's inmost thoughts and secret feelings or one's inmost being, the seat of courage and the emotions generally, the essential, innermost, or central part of anything, the source of desire, volition, truth, understanding, intellect, ethics, spirit. It was the single most important word referring both to the body and the mind.[10]

Christian iconography underwrites much of the meaning that the heart has accrued in Western culture. Multiple passages in both the Old Testament and the New Testament prepare the way to view the heart in terms of the relationship between God and humankind. Over time, understanding scripture became figured as knowledge inscribed on the book of the heart. The heart was the seat of learning, recollection, and understanding God's word. Saint Augustine described his *Confessions* as writing on the heart, and medieval artists depicted the two folding parts of a codex as the twin lobes of the heart.[11]

These symbolic uses can carry an erotic charge, for the devout heart was described as having been penetrated by the finger of God. Within medieval Catholicism there developed the legend of the sacred heart of Jesus, sometimes depicted in paintings as a literal heart in his open chest, sometimes surrounded by a crown of thorns and dripping blood, sometimes schematically rendered and held before his chest (figure 6.4). These motifs, combined with the clustering of emotions and the identification of the self around this organ, intensify the association of the heart with love both romantic and divine.

The symbolic uses of the human heart are by no means restricted to representations. The actual heart, bearing all the meanings mentioned earlier, has often been removed after death and given special burial. It is a way to extract the essence of the person, preserve it as a memento of a loved one, or carry it to a special place for final interment. The practice of heart burial is no longer common, but it was for centuries. Sometimes the heart was kept in a reliquary and not buried, or kept for so long before it reached its grave that only a desiccated fragment was finally laid to rest.

10. Robert A. Erickson, *The Language of the Heart, 1600–1750* (Philadelphia: University of Pennsylvania Press, 1997), 11.

11. Jager, *Book of the Heart,* 36–43.

FIGURE 6.4. Pompeo Batoni, *Sacred Heart*, 1757. Il Gesu. Rome. Scala/Art Resource, NY.

Among the many famous figures whose hearts were buried separately from their bodies are numerous kings, including Richard I and Edward I of England, and Louis IX, XIII, and XIV of France. The hearts of many Hapsburgs rest separately in a chapel in Vienna. The heart of Queen Marie of Romania, a daughter of Queen Victoria, is carved into a mountainside in Transylvania. Chopin's heart is entombed in a pillar in a church in Warsaw, and Shelley's was snatched from his pyre and given to his widow, buried only much later.[12] Rumor has it that the novelist Thomas Hardy's heart suffered a less dignified fate. His body was buried at Westminster Abbey, but his heart was removed for burial next to his wife. While awaiting interment the heart, temporarily stored in a biscuit tin, was discovered by a rummaging cat, which made a grisly feast. If this story is true, and if the cat finished its morsel, then it may be a pig's heart resting by Hardy's beloved wife.[13]

12. Sir Walter Raleigh's widow kept her husband's embalmed head after his execution. Keeping a body part as a memento of a loved one has a long and sometimes bizarre history. Russell Shorto, *Descartes' Bones* (New York: Doubleday, 2008), presents the strange sequence of proprietary disputes over Descartes' skeleton, especially the skull that housed the *cogito*. For anecdotes of preserved or buried hearts and heads, see "Bits and Pieces," http://www.historic_uk.com/HistoryUK/England_History/BitsandPieces.htm (accessed July 14, 2009).

13. http://www.britainexpress.com/History/bio/hardy.htm (accessed July 14, 2009).

One of the most enduring stories of heart burial concerns the Scottish king Robert the Bruce (1274–1329). Robert had always wished to take part in a crusade, but battles at home kept him too occupied. On his deathbed he requested of his loyal knight, Sir James Douglas (the "Black Douglas"), that his heart be taken from his chest and embalmed, then carried to the Church of the Holy Sepulcher in Jerusalem for burial. The words recorded by the medieval chronicler Froissart reflect several meanings of the heart expressed in Robert's last wishes: "And sith it is so that my body cannot go or achieve that my heart desireth, I will send the heart instead of the body to accomplish mine avow instead of myself."[14] Douglas had a casket made of silver in which he placed the embalmed heart, ever thereafter carrying it on a chain around his neck. (It must have made a substantial necklace.) Unfortunately, on his way to the Holy Land to fulfill his mission, Douglas was killed in battle against the Moors in Spain. The heart was recovered and returned to Scotland, where it was buried at Melrose Abbey.

The story of the heart of Robert the Bruce was retold in Johne Barbour's long narrative poem, *The Brus* (1375). Thus the literary heart perpetuates the meaning already bestowed on the literal heart. Today the traditions of both are carried on by means of yet another cultural object, for the story is repeated on bottles of Scottish ale:

> Black Douglas™, a dark ruby traditional ale with a soft full crystal malt flavour, is named after Sir James Douglas, trusted friend of Robert the Bruce.

> Black Douglas, a powerful knight and one of Scotland's heroes whose daring exploits often brought him to the Border country of Scotland, home of Broughton Ales, is famous for carrying the Bruce's heart into battle on the Crusades.[15]

A heart removed from the body of a king, an embalmed organ enshrined in precious metal, history related in epic narrative, a bottle label. The transition from literal viscera to poetic reference is nearly seamless.

Hearts in Art and Literature

With a sense of the enormous depth of context imparting meanings to the human heart, let us now turn to a few examples in art.

Outside the gallery, there are greeting cards produced for Valentine's Day (figure 6.5). These supply the largest quantity of heart images, from

---

14. Quoted in James A. Mackay, *Robert Bruce King of Scots* (London: Robert Hale, 1974), 179.
15. Bottle label, Black Douglas Ale, Broughton Ales Limited, Scotland.

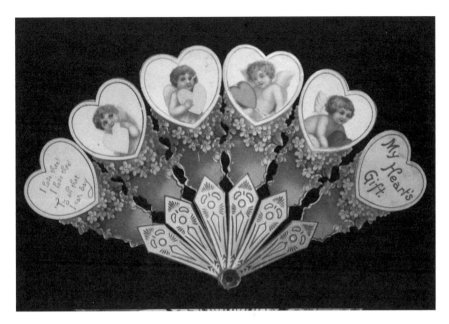

FIGURE 6.5. Victorian valentine, ca. 1880. Courtesy of Ann Colley and Irving Massey.

simple schemata to elaborate lace confections with accompanying sentimental verse.

Pop artist Jim Dine has a series of paintings that utilize the heart motif.

In 2007 Jeff Koons's steel and enamel sculpture *Hanging Heart* (1994–2006) sold at auction for $23.5 million. For a time this colossal, valentinish heart was also the most expensive contemporary artwork ever sold.

Carlos Estevez's *Homo absconditus* (Hidden Man) (1994) is a large wall sculpture in the openwork shape of a heart, behind which stands the smaller figure of a man (figure 6.6). Forty-four glass holders attached on the front contain candles.

In the multipart exhibit entitled Golem: Objects as Sensations (1979–82), Jana Sterbak included a work called *Heart Series* (1979), which consists of seven molded hearts (figure 6.7). As they are arranged right to left, one can see that the hearts are increasingly constricted as by the pressure of a hand.

The valentine design is abstract and decorative, sentimental to the point of kitsch. This kind of image is so prettified and familiar that linking it to anything even remotely disgusting seems preposterous. Koons's sculpture is deliberate kitsch, a postmodern comment on that very phenomenon. Its outlandish size and polished finish make it look like a giant decoration for a Christmas tree. Both of these pieces make use of the symmetrical, iconic heart shape. Estevez's and Sterbak's hearts are closer to anatomical shape. Estevez's

FIGURE 6.6. Carlos Estevez, *Homo absconditus* (Hidden Man). 1994. 79 × 79 × 12 in. Mixed-media wall sculpture. Collection of the artist.

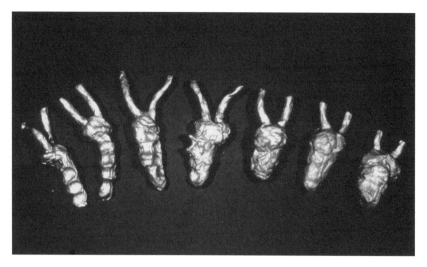

FIGURE 6.7. Jana Sterbak, *Heart Series*, from Golem: Objects as Sensations (1979–82). Collection Musée des Beaux Arts de Nantes, France.

These are almost life-size "hearts"

piece is huge, the heart dwarfing the man. The kinship of the glass candle-holders with votives lends a religious, specifically a Roman Catholic, overtone to the piece. Perhaps it suggests that human essence is hidden in the heart of a person—the spiritual core. Sterbak's molded hearts are close to life-sized. Their shapes are not abstract and in photographs may be taken to be real desiccated viscera.

All these works invoke the heart as a symbol of love, though to quite different aesthetic effect. The idea of love surrounding Estevez's piece is perhaps remote, but it suggests divine love protecting the person. The valentine is sweet and rather pedestrian. Koons's work is exaggerated and invites the suspicion that there is irony lurking about somewhere, if only in the act of appreciation. Sterbak's hearts invite reflection on the perils of love and failed romance. With her work the relative verisimilitude of the shapes and their gradual distortion reach into more disturbing territory, and the appreciative viewer might well experience a slight constriction in the chest. This is the faint disturbance of a somatic spasm, the merest hint of the sublate. While this work appears utterly different in design, execution, and purpose compared with the valentine-style hearts, its depth of meaning is only enhanced by the prevalence of easier hearts in our cultural repertoire.

These works make use of the visual image of the heart, but part of its disposition as a natural symbol stems from the fact that it is also audible. The sound of the beating heart may be incorporated into music, and pulselike drumbeats in the soundtracks of movies are employed to arouse audiences, an effective device even if they are only dimly aware of the sound.[16] The imagined beating heart of his victim so plagues the guilty narrator of Poe's story "The Tell-Tale Heart" that, tormented by its increasing volume, he blurts out his crime to his surprised visitors. I suspect that part of the power of hearing heart rhythms is personal memory, for doubtless everyone has experienced fear or anxiety so acute that it seems one's own heartbeats thud loudly enough for all to hear.

Three of the preceding examples do not occasion disgust at all, and the others arouse it with different, sometimes relatively subtle, tenors. Poe's story is close to horror, and the imagined beat of the heart is used effectively to build tension—a tension in the narrator that is echoed in the appreciative reader. Only with the movie *Angel Heart* do we have an indisputable arousal of standard disgust. When confronted with the first, unexpected image of a heart resting on a doily-draped side table, the most likely appreciation lies with how the appalling scene propels the plot. For a select few, there may also be an indulgence in the gross-out. I surmise that for most, there is a sequence of revulsion followed by curiosity and, eventually, satisfaction, for as the story unfolds there are mounting hints of a diabolical metaphysics in play.

---

16. Jean Harrell speculates about music and memory of prenatal experience of maternal heartbeats in *Soundtracks: A Study of Auditory Perception, Memory, and Music* (Buffalo, NY: Prometheus Books, 1986) chap. 1.

Conversions

Between kitsch and horror, is there a register that qualifies for conversion into an aesthetic quality such as beautiful, sublime, or sublate? We can find affirmative examples not only by examining the middle ground between images that are sweet and those that are revolting, but even in the extreme ranges of the horrid. Here are some examples from narratives in which the heart is both disgusting and . . . something else entirely.

The popular television series *The X-Files* (1993–2002) blended horror, adventure, and science fiction. An episode from season 6, "Milagro" (first aired April 18, 1999), supplies us with an illustration of the direction that aesthetic conversion travels, for it contains two scenes that are visually nearly identical but aesthetically markedly different.[17] The episode opens with a slow shot of a rather ordinary-looking young man wearing an expression of intense concentration. Slowly, he reaches inside his shirt. Blood begins to leak through the fabric. With a slight grimace, he pulls out a gelatinous, dark mass (figure 6.8). It is his own heart, bloody and palpitating in his hand. The audience has no preparation for this event. We do not know why he performs this macabre act, nor how he does so. The initial audience response is likely to be disgust of the most recognizable, reactive kind. It is accompanied by startle and intense curiosity.

The young man is Phillip Padget, a writer whose literary imagination is so powerful that he conjures into existence whatever he writes, including a psychic surgeon whose fingers can penetrate the human chest and remove the hearts of his victims. Padget is writing a love story, and the surgeon removes the hearts of those suffering unrequited love. Because what Padget imagines actually comes to be, he is suspected of several murders that match the plots of his manuscript. Padget has developed a passion for Agent Scully and has written her into the novel as the main character. One day he follows her to a church, and before a painting of the sacred heart of Jesus he relates the tale of Saint Mary Margaret, who loaned her own heart to Christ that it might burn with divine love. This exchange hints at part of Padget's own design: to love with similar intensity.

The two FBI agents Mulder and Scully set up a surveillance operation in hopes they will see Padget and the man they surmise must be his accomplice in the murders. All they see throughout the night is Padget sitting still before his typewriter. But in fact, the psychic surgeon has come to Padget and disclosed that what the writer really wants is impossible—to love with the purity and fervor of the divine. Such passion is beyond human capacity, for all that man can do is destroy, so the proper end of the novel is the death of the beloved: Agent Scully. Realizing how his story must end, Padget types the last page of

17. *Milagro* means "miracle" in Spanish. It is also the name for petitioning tokens offered to saints, which is the meaning exploited in the episode.

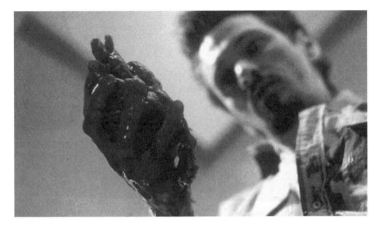

FIGURE 6.8. Video still, "Milagro," *The X-Files*. Created Chris Carter. Episode 18, season 6, 1999. Dir. Kim Manners. Ten Thirteen Productions, 20th Century Fox Television.

FIGURE 6.9. Video still, "Milagro," *The X-Files*. Created Chris Carter. Episode 18, season 6, 1999. Dir. Kim Manners. Ten Thirteen Productions, 20th Century Fox Television.

the manuscript and leaves his room. Mulder chases him into the apartment base-ment, where he finds the writer trying to burn his manuscript, to destroy the words that recount and therefore will bring about Scully's death. Upstairs the psychic attacks her. As she struggles, his fingers probe for her heart, and the blood pools around her throat. In the last shot of the episode, the manu-script is burning in the furnace, and Padget's dead body lies stretched on the floor, his own heart in his hand—a sacrifice to save the woman of his obsession from the fate he had written for her (figure 6.9).

I have described this example in some detail because the very same image—a heart newly ripped from a chest—takes on a stunningly different aesthetic character in the course of a story. The first heart extraction arouses startled disgust as a component of the shock it triggers in the audience. The various murders that take place in the course of the episode are grisly and deploy both disgust and fear, as well as a host of more subtly named emotions, though no other hearts are displayed to us. The heart at the very end *looks* identical to the first one, in the sense that it is visually similar: moist, bloody, pulsing. But in the space of less than an hour it has become far more than disgusting. It is raw and vulnerable, and there is a tenderness and courage surrounding it that induces the audience not to turn away this time but to linger over its sight, pondering and even savoring it.

One might claim that insofar as my description is accurate, the final scene of the heart is no longer disgusting. It is true that one no longer cringes at the image. But I believe it is crucial that the heart prompts that somatic spasm of strong aesthetic apprehension, though now it is disgust of a far more reflective and complicated flavor than is the initial encounter with the heart. The narrative has given the heart meaning, and the doomed passion and mystical overtones lend it unexpected profundity. But it remains a bleeding organ, and the visceral response does not altogether disappear. Rather, it has become the foundation for the final aesthetic apprehension of sacrifice offered for love.

Partly because of the genre of this type of television show—a science fiction adventure with strong tones of horror—episodes such as "Milagro" are unlikely to be taken as seriously as other art forms. Nonetheless, this example demonstrates that what out of context would seem to be simply a revolting image is actually far from that. This eviscerated heart has required no abstraction or prettification, but it has become an object to dwell upon and appreciate. I offer the next examples for consideration of even more profound transformation.

Because the heart is so associated with the self and all it holds dear, it figures widely not only in romance but also in stories of revenge and cruelty. The old folktale of Snow White tells of a girl of such beauty that her jealous stepmother, the queen, schemes to have her killed. In several versions of the story, the stepmother orders that Snow White's heart be brought back as proof of her death. (In other versions the request is for Snow White's lungs or liver.) Although the queen has been deceived by her huntsman, who took pity on the girl and killed a boar instead, she eats the heart with vengeful relish, believing that it belongs to her stepdaughter. The fairy tale includes a cannibalistic episode that is familiar enough from other such stories to indicate that the use of the heart in perverse and violent ways is a recurrent motif in many narrative traditions. Eating a human heart is a fierce act. It may be done for revenge, punishment, conquest, justice, wickedness, or cruelty. In narratives where the heart is eaten, the meal often follows terrible deception, such that the one who

read: 152-58

eats does not realize the nature of the dish until it is too late. He or she has been deceived into devouring an object of love, blindly contributing to an act of grievous destruction. This is a horrific but familiar device that one finds in history, folklore, and literature, and it has been repeated with no diminishment of power for millennia.[18]

Boccaccio's tales from *The Decameron* (c. 1353) include some of the grimmest of narratives. The history of this compilation is complex and need not concern us here, other than to note that Boccaccio took the plots of many of his stories from legends, history, and other narratives, indicating the enduring appeal of the terrible themes. The author's foreword to this work indicates that the stories within will reveal the darker secrets of human experience that are often cloaked by conventions of social propriety.

Seven noble women and three men, with their servants, have fled a Florence stricken by plague. So devastated is their ordinary way of life that not only have they abandoned their homes, but they entertain themselves with stories that under less extreme circumstances they would blush to tell. Promiscuity, adultery, lust, deceit, and chicanery propel the plots, and by the Fourth Day the stories have taken a macabre twist. The stories told on this day are all devoted to disastrous affections: fathers and husbands led by thwarted love to kill and mutilate rivals, the severed head of a lover that nourishes a pot of basil, the blood from the heart of another lover mixed with poison and lovingly drunk, a venomous toad. Here we enter territory where disgust is aroused in a way that so quickly transforms into aesthetic insight that the emotion itself may be scarcely marked.

The Ninth Tale of the Fourth Day presents a love triangle: two noble knights and dear friends, one of whom falls in love with the wife of the other. She reciprocates his love, and they meet secretly. But they are indiscreet, and the adulterous affair is discovered by the husband. His love for his friend turns to hatred, and he kills him and rips the heart from his chest. That evening he gives what he says is a boar's heart to the cook to prepare in the best manner, and it is served to his wife for dinner. She eats with relish, for it is tasty, and when the meal is over this exchange occurs:

> When the knight saw that his wife had finished the heart, he said: "Lady, what did you think of that dish?"
>
> "My lord," she replied, "In good faith, it pleased me greatly."
>
> "God be my helper," said the knight. "I can easily believe you; nor do I marvel that what gave you so much pleasure when alive should please you when dead."

---

18. One finds similar tales recounted by the ancient Greek historian Herodotus in *The Persian Wars*. Milad Doueihi extensively analyzes the theme of eaten hearts in Doueihi, *A Perverse History of the Human Heart*, (Cambridge, MA: Harvard University Press, 1997).

> At this the lady was silent for a moment, and then said: "How? What
> is it you have made me eat?"

She discovers she has just consumed the heart of her lover, and she sits silently
for a time. Then she says to her husband:

> You have acted like a base and treacherous knight. If I, under no com-
> pulsion from him, made him lord of my love and thereby did you
> wrong, I should have borne the penalty, and not he. But, please God,
> no other food shall ever follow a food so noble as the heart of a knight
> so courteous and valiant.[19]

With that she runs to a tower window and hurls herself out, falling to her death.
The husband flees, the story of the doomed lovers is discovered, and they are
buried together in the same grave.

Although the story makes use of several typical disgust elicitors—mutilation,
evisceration, taboo eating—at no level of this story does the emotion operate as
simple aversion. There may be a moment of nausea when we read how the wife
eats the heart, but the visceral acknowledgment runs far deeper than a simple food
rejection. The reader's affective response apprehends the dreadful act that has occurred. The wife does not evince disgust at all; indeed, that would be a relatively
trivial response given the horror she has just discovered. Instead, her initial silence
is a signal that what she experiences is so beyond ordinary emotion as to be utterly
inexpressible. The familiar association of sexual and gustatory pleasure has been
dreadfully combined: the body of her lover is now part of her body—first muti-
lated, then basely chopped and chewed, and now consumed. This is no simple
case of ingesting a foul substance, and there is no way to expel what was eaten and
to restore the self's integrity. The vengeful act has not only destroyed her lover, it
has made her own body an abomination. Her recognition of this condition is indicated in her refusal ever to eat again, as well as in the quick end she makes of her
own life. But whatever psychological state we might imagine for her, for the reader
who comprehends her dreadful state, aesthetic disgust is indispensable, for as an
intimate, physical feeling it viscerally delivers a compressed insight that no other
emotion can ground. The sublate surpasses revulsion. It is a somatic spasm that
registers cruelty, mortality, horror, hate, and lovers united in terrible intimacy.

The First Tale of the Fourth Day in *The Decameron* employs the heart of a
lover with somewhat different emotional valence. The triangle here is among a
father, his daughter, and her lover. The father, Tancred, prince of Salerno, loves
his daughter, Ghismonda, deeply and cannot bear to be parted from her. So
deep is his incestuous attachment that when she is widowed after a brief mar-
riage, he refuses to consider having her marry again. Ghismonda eventually
realizes that she is destined to remain single and takes as a lover a servant,

19. Giovanni Boccaccio (1313–75), *The Decameron*, trans. Richard Aldington (New York: Dell, 1930), 295.

FIGURE 6.10. William Hogarth, *Sigismunda Mourning over the Heart of Guiscardo.*
1759. Oil on canvas. Tate Gallery, London. Tate, London/Art Resource, NY.

Guiscardo, whose noble soul she recognizes. They arrange a series of secret
meetings, which after a time are accidentally discovered by Tancred, who confronts his daughter and charges her with unworthy behavior. Though she recognizes that with his power and distress he could wreak great damage on her
and her lover, Ghismonda stalwartly defends the virtues of her lover and rebuffs
her father's tearful pleas. The following night Tancred has the lover strangled
and his heart cut out, sending it in a golden cup to Ghismonda with this message: "Your father sends you this to console you for what you most loved, even
as you consoled him for what he loved most."[20] Although it is literally Guiscardo's heart in the cup, Tancred also implicitly accuses his daughter of metaphorically tearing out his own heart in her rejection of his loving appeal.

　　This heart is not eaten, and there is no indication that it arouses disgust
among the characters in the story, although it is the object of tremendous grief.
As with the heart in the Ninth Tale, this one carries all the nobility of its owner:
"Gold alone is a fitting burial place for such a heart. Herein my father has done
wisely." Ghismonda weeps over the heart and kisses it repeatedly, to the con-
sternation of her serving maids who are perplexed because they do not know
whose heart it is (figure 6.10). To readers—at least of our own times—the

20. Boccaccio, *Decameron*, 257.

image of a woman kissing the eviscerated heart of her lover probably does arouse disgust.[21] I would surmise that the tale intentionally arouses this response because it is a direct and somatic way to recognize the depth of Ghismonda's love and her terrible loss. She clings to her lover's remains, and it is a portion of his beloved body that symbolizes his very self. No fainter attachment could induce one to place one's lips on a raw and bloody heart.

Ghismonda had prepared a poison for herself, for she had anticipated a bad end to her confrontation with her father. After much weeping and lamentation, she pours the poison into the cup with the heart, watered by tears, and drinks it. The drink is more than poison: it is the essence of her love. The effect of this part of the story also builds upon a visceral response in the reader, for one imagines that the mixture is poison, tears, and heart's blood. Then she arranges herself on her bed, places Guiscardo's heart over her own, and waits for death. Her grief-stricken father repents of his cruelty too late and has the lovers buried honorably in the same grave.

There is no eating of the heart in this story, but it is touched in a way that nature never designed. Ghismonda expresses this very point when she first uncovers the golden cup and sees the heart. Then she declares: "Ah! Thou most sweet dwelling-place of all my delight, cursed be the cruelty of him who has made me look upon you with the eyes of my head! It was enough for me to gaze upon you hourly with the eyes of my spirit."[22] Ghismonda's caressing of the heart is a funerary ritual of sorts. It is followed by an act that, she declares, shall unite their spirits: she places his heart over her own and dies. Although their two hearts can no longer beat as one, the hearts lying together unite their souls after death. The ethereal soul resides in the material heart, and Ghismonda's love is given a solidity and vehemence that are only enhanced by the traces of disgust that undergird the complex aesthetic emotions that this story prompts. In short, although it would be incorrect to describe either the reader's appreciative response or the character's emotional dynamics as being "disgust" in any ordinary sense, the visceral engagement of both readers and characters in the terrible events of these two tales is made all the more profound by the invocation of disgust alongside (or perhaps one should say "beneath") other appreciative affects.

I have noted several times a possible rejoinder to my analysis here, namely, the claim that disgust is culturally and individually variable and therefore not the kind of affect one can reliably attribute either to fictional characters or to audiences. After all, hearts were formerly common fare, as Love in Disguise indi-

21. The Tate Gallery, which holds Hogarth's *Sigismunda Mourning*, attaches this revealing comment to the image of the painting posted on its website: "Remarkably, he shows one of her fingertips touching the exposed, glossy red heart itself." www.tate.org.uk/britain/exhibitions/hogarth/rooms/room9/shtm (accessed March 27, 2010).
22. Boccaccio, *Decameron*, 258.

cates, and what disgusts at one time in one society might be relished elsewhere. It is true that while disgust is a pancultural emotion, its specific objects have a certain variability, especially when it comes to what is considered edible food. I doubt, however, that disgust is so variable that it is aesthetically irrelevant to reading Boccaccio's tales. Rather, it recognizes the unwitting complicity in the destruction of a lover by employing the senses and the triggers where disgust operates. The death of the first lover is not grand or noble. He—or the part of him that signals love, his heart—is mashed into pulp by the teeth of his beloved. Aesthetic disgust apprehends the physical intimacy of this peculiar breed of horror. If its somatic spasm were not recognized across the gulf of time, it would not have the dramatic role that it does in so many narratives throughout history.

These stories also manifest something of the ways that emotions are altered by their aesthetic conversions, for fear and disgust change quite mark-edly—in fact reciprocally—in the sublime and the sublate, though without losing their emotive identity altogether. In its ordinary "real life" occurrences, as Kolnai claims, fear has a double direction and two intentional objects: it is strongly directed outward toward an external danger, and it is almost equally directed inward toward the subject itself.[23] In contrast, he maintains that dis-gust is singly directed outward to its object.[24] The absence of the second inten-tional object permits the allure of disgust and what he describes as the probing intentional character of this emotion. Neither description suits the operation of fear and disgust in their aesthetic modes, both of which require shifts of inten-tional objects. The distance that Burke observes is required for terror to transform into the sublime serves to reduce the reflexive intention from fear. Reciprocally, the somatic recognition that I have labeled sublate requires that disgust assume a second, reflexive intentional object. This is literally the case with the wife of Boccaccio's tale, for her own, contaminated body has become an intolerable object. But my point does not ride on a contestable attribution of a psychological state to a fictional character. Rather, her extreme case drama-tizes that when disgust arises with the sublate it does not permit the subject to feel removed from and superior to the intentional object, as this emotion sup-posedly does in the ordinary instance. Indeed, Kolnai himself acknowledges this element when he notes that disgust signifies "the directedness towards death of our life itself, of our existence as made up of material which is conse-crated to death; one could also say that we are drowned within a material which is already prepared for decay."[25]

The counterpart to the sublime glimpse of cosmic power is the sublate con-frontation with the vulnerability of material nature. Complementary aesthetic

23. Aurel Kolnai, "Disgust" (1929), in On Disgust, ed. Barry Smith and Carolyn Korsmeyer (Chicago: Open Court, 2004), 36.
24. Kolnai, On Disgust, 39.
25. Kolnai, On Disgust, 78.

modes, one is exalted, uplifting, and spiritual; the other intimate and physical, recognizing the lowest common denominator of organic beings. Just as the sublime is not experienced as mere fear, so in the complex, layered apprehensions of the sublate disgust may not be experienced as such. But the aesthetic affect gains intensity from the hallmark visceral repulsion of disgust, which registers the inescapable, dolorous frailty of material existence.

These are not easy truths to grasp—truly to *know*. At one and the same time they are perfectly obvious—organic life is mortal, we are living organisms that will live out our allotted time and then pass from existence. Part of that passing away is a stage where the remainder of our corporeal selves will suffer disintegration and putrefaction. No one is surprised to make this discovery. But like so many existential truths, its magnitude slips through the mind and cannot be held. The sublate aspect of aesthetic disgust permits a moment of sustained recognition, providing a time to dwell upon mortality from a particularly intimate and fragile perspective.

a good reason to be cremated

how can "sustained recognition" take place in "a moment"

7

The Foul and the Fair

This final chapter turns to the subject that seems most incompatible with the uses of disgust in art: beauty. It is the influential philosophies of beauty developed in the eighteenth century that most vehemently exclude disgust from among the emotions that could be portrayed in, or evoked by, artworks that produce aesthetic liking, to use Kant's phrase. While fear, pity, grief, and other discomforting emotions have established credentials in philosophy of art, disgust has no such ancestry. By "aesthetic liking" Kant meant the particular kind of pleasure that became ensconced as the reigning theory of beauty in developing aesthetic theory.[1] While other difficult emotions and subjects might be rendered in art in such a way that they could be made beautiful, when disgust remains among the affects aroused in the perceiver, there is no pleasure, no liking, and no beauty. In other words, disgust is the one emotion that cannot be transformed by means of art into an experience of beauty.

Having already defended disgust against the venerable arguments that deny its aesthetic standing, I now revisit the claims made about its incompatibility with beauty. In a sense, this chapter is a coda of sorts to the preceding argument, prodding consideration of disgust back toward the more traditional values of aesthetics. While

1. Artworks tend to exhibit what Kant called "adherent" or "dependent" beauty because they elicit comparison with some original when we consider their subject matter. "Pure" beauty, for which the criterion of disinterestedness is first developed, is found in the form of an object without consideration for what it is, means, or represents. Paradigm examples are pure designs or objects in nature, which do not prompt the perceiver to compare an object with an original. Overextending the idea of pure beauty to works of art has led many commentators to misinterpret Kant as a formalist.

aesthetic disgust usually takes its worth from values other than beauty, now I want to examine the concept of beauty to argue that in its most difficult and profound forms, it too can sometimes include disgust. I shall argue that some artworks—not many but some—are capable of incorporating the arousal of disgust into an experience of beauty, and that they do so without sacrificing the visceral power of the apprehension. This excursion into beauty will travel again through some of the territory already covered in this study but from a different direction, arriving eventually at the same destination where aesthetic disgust secures its place, vindicated from the charges that have dogged its history. The route I take will also disclose some aspects of beauty that are not always noticed, and it will deepen the complexities of associating beauty with pleasure that were examined earlier.

As already noted, David Hume defends one of the more well-known conversion accounts to address the question of how uncomfortable emotional content is appreciated. While his treatment skirts the really difficult case of disgust, he keeps on the horizon the potential alliance of aversion with actual beauty, so I shall try to recruit him as an ally for my cause. Though he does not always take care to distinguish the depiction of difficult emotions from their arousal in audiences, it is the latter phenomenon that most perplexes him:

> The whole heart of the poet is employed, in rouzing and supporting the compassion and indignation, the anxiety and resentment, of his audience. They are pleased in proportion as they are afflicted, and never are so happy as when they employ tears, sobs, and cries to give vent to their sorrow, and relieve their heart, swoln with the tenderest sympathy and compassion.[2]

Hume invokes the general power of sympathy to account for the ability of a description or an image to infect a reader or a viewer with the emotion portrayed—or with a complementary feeling such as pity for the misfortune of a character. If such events were really to occur, the feelings aroused would only be dolorous, but Hume contends that skillful rendering and poetic eloquence have the power to transform a disagreeable passion into positive enjoyment. So profound is the admiration an audience experiences at a well-done tragedy that it overrides the discomfort of the strong passions aroused. He is not entirely clear about the relation of the different affective components in such experience, but it seems to be that the overall effect of skillfully created and well-executed art not only compensates for the painful emotions aroused but actually transforms the power of those emotions into depth of appreciation. Without the strong feelings involved, the eloquence and artistry would not have so effective an outcome:

2. David Hume, "Of Tragedy," in *Essays Moral, Political, and Literary*, Vol. 1 (1882), ed. T. H. Green and T. H. Grose (Darmstadt: Scientia Verlag Aalen, 1964), 258–59.

By this means, the uneasiness of the melancholy passions is not only overpowered and effaced by something stronger of an opposite kind, but the whole impulse of those passions is converted into pleasure, and swells the delight which the eloquence raises in us. . . . The impulse or vehemence arising from sorrow, compassion, indignation, receives a new direction from the sentiments of beauty. The latter, being the predominant emotion, seize the whole mind, and convert the former into themselves, at least tincture them so strongly as totally to alter their nature.[3]

Hume has been criticized for failing to explain precisely how the all-important conversion is supposed to take place, although I think it is unreasonable to expect that any philosopher could say exactly how this kind of transformation happens. After all, if there were a formula for beauty, its production would be routine. It is consonant with the singularity of artistic excellence that no one can articulate a complete principle for what is going on when beauty emerges from the complexity that is a work of art.

My own criticism of this conversion account is directed to a different problem, which has to do with whether or not the difficult emotions whose enjoyment is being analyzed are *converted* or *erased*. An ambiguity in the preceding declaration leaves this crucial issue up in the air: "The sentiments of beauty . . ., being the predominant emotion, seize the whole mind, and convert the former into themselves, at least tincture them so strongly as totally to alter their nature." If they are so strongly tinctured as totally to alter their nature, emotions such as fear and indignation—let alone disgust—are no longer part of the response to art. Such an outcome just removes the emotion from awareness in the way that one might paint over rude graffiti. This not only would sacrifice the aesthetic power of those emotions, it is not at all clear whether one can adequately describe the art that features them by claiming that they are transmuted "totally" to another nature, arousing entirely different affective qualia. In order for beauty to emerge from difficult subjects, it must convert the difficulty not into something easy but into something significant enough that we do not want to lose the grasp that the emotions supply. In other words, for a conversion account to make sense, the eloquence of artistic rendering must convert a painful emotion into a type of beauty of matching difficulty consonant with the subject.

Hume's position, briefly stated as it is in this short essay, would hardly accommodate the instances when disgust remains loathsome and repellent yet is still profound and worth pondering. It works only for those artworks in which disgust has been deftly rendered into an affect that is strong but no longer disgusting, strictly speaking, which is the very position that was granted by those Enlightenment theorists who ejected disgust from among positive aesthetic emotions. It is

3. Hume, "Of Tragedy," 261.

quite clear that he himself would not have imagined disgust to number among the melancholy passions so transformed into beauty.[4] But it is a conversion for precisely this abhorrent emotion that I want to explore. To understand the nature of beauty that can accommodate such a transfiguration, we must return once more to a consideration of pleasure and all its conundrums.

Beauty: A Brief History

Despite their many differences, most of the theories of beauty to be found in the history of philosophy connect the experience of the beautiful with pleasure—with a positive and enjoyable "aesthetic experience" that rivets attention with delight. Indeed, some theories actually identify beauty as a type of pleasure. George Santayana famously characterized beauty as "pleasure regarded as the quality of a thing."[5] The connection is also articulated in platonic theories that consider beauty a property of objects that is independent of appreciative response, for objective beauty still delivers pleasure when it is recognized. Common parlance commonly connects beauty with pleasure as well, that is, with enjoyment of the presentation of an object to the senses and to the imagination. This all may seem obvious and psychologically uninteresting, for why ever should a positive quality such as beauty not be linked with pleasure, attraction, and allure?

However, on second thought both philosophy and ordinary usage also hesitate about that easy association, for it is evident that beauty is equally present in art that demands confrontation with discomforting subjects such as loss, grief, and death. In other words, while pleasure and beauty are hard to sever, it is also the case that pain mingles with both the subject matter and the affective appreciation of some profound exemplars of beautiful artworks: Shakespeare's *King Lear*, Britten's *War Requiem*, Rodin's *Burghers of Calais*, Donatello's *Mary Magdalene*. Some theorists have tried to reconcile the apparent contradiction between "pleasure" and "pain" by surmising that beauty redeems painful content, sugarcoating a bitter pill. As the Roman poet Horace observed long ago in his theoretical poem *Ars Poetica* (lines 343–44), hard lessons are better learned when they are well expressed, when "instruction" mingles with "delight." Doubtless there is some truth to this insight: a beautiful rendering of a difficult truth can make that truth easier to comprehend, even perhaps to accept. Thus pleasure taken in the beauty of difficult art softens the pain of its message. However, if this suggests that the "pleasure" of beauty is distinct from the "pain" of its subject, it is far from a complete picture, for art can be beautiful not despite its painful import but because of

4. He criticizes a play by Nicolas Rowe, *The Ambitious Stepmother*, for a gratuitously gory scene in which "a venerable old man, raised to the height of fury and despair, rushes against a pillar, and striking his head upon it besmears it all over with mingled brains and gore." This is an example of a scene that, Hume claims, "may excite such movements of horror as will not soften into pleasure." "Of Tragedy," 265.

5. George Santayana, *The Sense of Beauty* (1896) (New York: Dover, 1955), 31.

it. This section explores the perplexing phenomenon of what I shall call "terrible beauty," that is, beauty that is bound up with the arousal of discomforting emotions. In the course of this discussion, I shall try to push the parameters of beauty somewhat further than their usual recognized limits, discovering whether even an aversion such as disgust might find some quarter in beautiful art.

In a way this discussion is a throwback to earlier concerns in aesthetics, for as many have noted, beauty as an artistic value has not been at the center of either art practice or critical appraisal since the mid-twentieth century.[6] But its renewed or continued pertinence is evident in recent books that mourn its departure or revive ways to consider the role of beauty in life and art.[7] Venerable questions about the ontological status of beauty—the kind of quality it is, its relation to aesthetic appraisal, its dependence on other qualities—remain recalcitrant problems for philosophers.[8] And most important for my focus here, beauty presents a zone of puzzlement for our understanding of any art that pains while appealing, no matter when or under what aesthetic fashion it was produced.

As I already indicated two chapters back, some of the puzzle about terrible beauties might be cleared up if we could wean ourselves away from employing the rather crude dichotomy of "pleasure" and "pain" when discussing value and disvalue. As many have noted, overreliance on this pair of terms flattens out the nuances of real aesthetic valuation and neglects the range of qualities and experiences that deliver satisfaction and insight.[9] I have already demonstrated that the term "pleasure" is fraught with problems and misleading implications, arguing that aesthetic engagement is better understood as a kind of affective absorption. However, I shall temporarily revert to the pleasure-pain terminology, for not only is it a continuous thread that binds together disparate theories of beauty, but also it seems to some degree to be inescapable. And one would not want to be committed to the idea that no pleasure issues from encounters with beauty, even if pleasure does not serve adequately to define that concept.

Defining Beauty

Before reaching the subject of terrible beauty, it is necessary to consider the idea of beauty more generally. Defining beauty is a formidable undertaking, some

6. Larry Shiner, *The Invention of Art: A Cultural History* (Chicago: University of Chicago Press, 2001), 221; Peg Brand, ed. *Beauty Matters* (Bloomington: Indiana University Press, 2000), 6.

7. A sampling: Elaine Scarry, *On Beauty and Being Just* (Princeton, NJ: Princeton University Press, 1999); Wendy Steiner, *Venus in Exile* (New York: Free Press, 2001); Arthur C. Danto, *The Abuse of Beauty: Aesthetics and the Concept of Art* (Chicago: Open Court, 2003); Alexander Nehamas, *Only a Promise of Happiness: The Place of Beauty in a World of Art* (Princeton, NJ: Princeton University Press, 2007).

8. Nick Zangwill, *The Metaphysics of Beauty* (Ithaca, NY: Cornell University Press, 2001); Eddy Zemach, *Real Beauty* (University Park: Pennsylvania State University Press, 1997); Mary Mothersill, *Beauty Restored* (Oxford: Clarendon Press, 1984).

9. Kendall Walton, "How Marvelous! Toward a Theory of Aesthetic Value," *Journal of Aesthetics and Art Criticism* 51, no.: 3 (1993): 499–510.

would say doomed. Two assessments feed this pessimistic attitude, one concerning the objects called beautiful and the other concerning those who find them so. Examples of beautiful art are so diverse that the prospect that they share a definable set of beauty-making qualities is dim.[10] This is the case even if we stick with more or less indisputably beautiful art, such as the sculptures of Praxiteles or Bernini, the paintings of Monet or Morisot, the music of Mozart or Dvorak. (I say "more or less" to indicate a reasonable generalization about aesthetic appraisals; there is no such thing as unanimity in aesthetic judgments, despite Kant's efforts to find grounds for universality and necessity for pure judgments of taste.) The multiplicity of beautiful things is one of the main reasons that philosophers often conclude that the only trait beautiful objects share is the ability to arouse a distinctive type of pleasure—which is why, incidentally, it is hard to dispense altogether with hedonic language. Consequently, aesthetic judgments have a necessarily subjective component: they involve reports of responses. Calling something "subjective" does not entail relativism, for it is clearly not the case that all subjective responses are matters of individual preference: the pain of burning flesh keeps most of us from leaning on stoves.[11] But taste for design, fashion, and art does not have the same physiological foundation that governs sensations, and the sheer variety of aesthetic responses bolsters the idea that beauty is in the eye of the beholder. Even so, beholders often see similarly, and there are many examples of beauty that few would disagree with: sunny spring days, the stars appearing at twilight, flower gardens. These things are easy to find beautiful, and they give pleasure to nearly everyone.

While there are certainly diverse preferences for landscapes and objects of nature, it is especially as we enter the worlds of art that consensus begins to shrink and aesthetic judgments to fragment. Consider the range of responses to objects such as Indian raga, Greek tragedy, postmodern architecture; or to individual works within a genre, such as Bartok's music or the paintings of Ad Reinhardt. Tastes for particular kinds of art differ among cultures, historical periods, and individuals. This demonstrable variety of aesthetic opinion might seem to lead to the conclusion that beauty is merely culturally dependent or individually idiosyncratic. A good many philosophers have attempted to establish grounds for standards of taste and warrant for the convergence of critical opinion, although this will not be my focus here. Rather, I shall continue to pursue the arousal of unpleasant emotions as constituents of aesthetic apprehension, which is a major source of divergence of artistic preferences because people differ greatly in their tolerance of art that arouses such feelings. Disgust is but the most notorious of these.

10. Nehamas, *Only a Promise of Happiness*, chap. 3, esp. pt. 4. Umberto Eco reviews the astonishing variety of qualities historically considered beautiful in Umberto Eco, ed., *History of Beauty*, trans. Alastair McEwen (New York: Rizzoli, 2005).

11. On the complexities of subjectivity in the perception of art, see John Hyman, *The Objective Eye: Color, Form, and Reality in the Theory of Art* (Chicago: University of Chicago Press, 2006).

To get to that subject, however, requires an indirect route. Strenuous moments of art (when Antigone hangs herself, for example) do not immediately spring to mind as central examples of beauty, and therefore one might think that a concentration on such "terrible" beauty displaces the discussion to an area that is aberrant or marginal. I do not think this is the case, and indeed I believe that terrible beauties represent beauty in its most profound dimensions. But to make that case I need first to review some other aspects of beauty. I shall start with a subject that might seem to refer to the simplest kind of aesthetic pleasure: formal beauty.

Beauties of Form

Many attempts to correlate beauty with the regular presence of qualities in beautiful objects concentrate on the *form* of objects, such as intricacy and balance of composition or harmony of parts. We can find this approach in mathematical theories of beauty from Pythagoras to the present; we can also find it in empiricist attempts to ground aesthetic pleasure in objective properties. The English painter and engraver William Hogarth, for example, concluded that beauty always has a mathematical basis that is best exemplified in a spiral line twisting around a cone from apex to base.[12] His "line of grace" was invoked by Edmund Burke, who speculated that the appeal of beauty has an erotic origin in the curves of the ideal female body.[13] Somewhat earlier, Francis Hutcheson offered a more flexible formula: the pleasure of beauty is aroused by a "compound variety of uniformity amidst variety," that is, by the balance between complexity and simplicity of design.[14] Such formulae have contemporary versions as well, such as Monroe Beardsley's general canons for aesthetic judgment: unity, complexity, and intensity.[15]

There is nothing wrong with these speculations inasmuch as they describe certain beautiful objects. However, no formula aptly describes all beautiful objects unless its meaning and application are broadened to the point of vacuity. Eero Saarinen's Gateway Arch in St. Louis has a good deal of uniformity but little variety, as it makes only one enormous, sweeping turn. Yet many would single it out as a beautiful architectural gesture. The Church of Santa Maria della Vittoria in Rome is encrusted with so much statuary and decorative detail that by any of these gauges it ought to be a jumble—and it is splendidly beautiful.

12. William Hogarth, *The Analysis of Beauty* (1753), ed. Ronald Paulson (New Haven, CT: Yale University Press, 1997).

13. Edmund Burke, *A Philosophical Enquiry into the Origin of Our Ideas of the Sublime and Beautiful* (1757), ed. James T. Boulton (Notre Dame, IN: University of Notre Dame Press, 1968).

14. Francis Hutcheson, *Inquiry into the Original of Our Ideas of Beauty and Virtue*, (1725), *Collected Works* Vol. I, (Darmstadt: Georg Olms, 1971).

15. Monroe Beardsley, *Aesthetics: Problems in the Philosophy of Criticism* (New York: Harcourt, Brace, 1958).

The availability of counterexamples to the various attempts to ground beauty in objective correlates may seem to defeat the definitional enterprise altogether. But the fact that a single essence of beauty is elusive does not mean that these attempts have failed to identify relevant features of some beautiful objects. The diversity of beautiful things does not entail that beauty is occult or indefinable, nor that it is merely relative to the beholder. Rather, it means that its sources are multiple. The elaborate flower arrangements painted by Severin Roesen fit Hutcheson's compound ratio; a severe, single bud in a vase is more aptly described by the line of grace. These formulae have not defined beauty itself, but they do single out the qualities of various kinds of beautiful things.

This point is illuminated with a culinary parallel, a comparison that is especially apt because the core metaphor for the ability to make judgments about beauty is "taste." (This metaphor is employed in many European languages and in traditions of Indian aesthetics.) All food has taste qualities, and when they are especially pleasing they are called "delicious," which we can understand as a gustatory equivalent of "beautiful." Chocolate is delicious; so is crème brûlée; so is eggplant parmesan; so is cheese soufflé. Note the absence of any theoretical rush to discover some delicious-making property that all these foods share—though admittedly this sensible restraint is probably a symptom of the fact that philosophers traditionally have not considered eating and tasting important enough to merit their concerns. When one enjoys a chocolate mousse, one praises the smooth texture of the pudding, the hint of bitter that deepens the sweet, dark flavor, and so on. When one enjoys the eggplant dish, one notices the creamy texture of the vegetable, the peppery bite of the sauce. From the fact that neither tastes like the other it does not follow that enjoyment is mysteriously subjective and relative, nor that there are no identifiable properties that justify the claim that these foods are delicious. As it happens, the dishes on this list do share a few relevant properties: they are smooth on the tongue, for instance. But it is obviously inappropriate to try to claim that the common smooth texture must be the quality in virtue of which they are all delicious. (Besides, if we did so, we could not accommodate almonds, popcorn, or carrots on the spectrum of delicious things.) The moral of the comparison is this: perceptual values such as delicious and beautiful are subjective inasmuch as they involve positive responses, and often we are moved to try to figure out the basis for those positive responses. But the qualities that make an object beautiful are as various as those that make foods tasty. The fact that there are multiple—indeed myriad—sources of beauty precludes the formulation of general criteria for this aesthetic value. It does not follow that beauty is merely idiosyncratic pleasure, for responses are still dependent on the presence of relevant properties.[16] We may now firmly close two doors opening onto the investigation of beauty: the door that Plato chose—the theory that beauty names a shared trait

16. Zangwill, *Metaphysics of Beauty,* 19.

of all beautiful objects; and the empiricist version of this—that all beautiful objects are correlated with some objective quality that arouses aesthetic pleasure. I shall not search for such commonalities.

This review of formalist theories has been more than a sidebar, for an additional observation about beauties of form leads us closer to consideration of difficult and even painful instances of beauty. Formal properties of objects appeal to sense experience: to the way that an object is presented to its appropriate organ of perception. But even at this surface level of presentation to the senses there are degrees of significance that are relevant to identifying the darker aspects of beauty. Consider these comments by the painter Henri Matisse:

> Supposing I want to paint the body of a woman: First of all I endow it with grace and charm but I know that something more than that is necessary. I try to condense the meaning of this body by drawing its essential lines. The charm will then become less apparent at first glance but in the long run it will begin to emanate from the new image. This image at the same time will be enriched by a wider meaning, a more comprehensively human one, while the charm, being less apparent, will not be its only characteristic. It will be merely one element in the general conception of the figure.
>
> Charm, lightness, crispness—all these are passing sensations. I have a canvas on which the colors are still fresh and I begin work on it again. The colors will probably grow heavier—the freshness of the original tones will give way to greater solidity, an improvement to my mind, but less seductive to the eye.[17]

Matisse deepens the appreciation of his lines and shapes by making them less immediately pleasant and easy to look at. His remarks illuminate a transition between what is merely "pretty" and what marks a more profound visual value, perhaps something that qualifies as beautiful. Evidently part of the transformation of an appearance from pretty to beautiful requires making appreciation somewhat more strenuous, "less seductive to the eye."

A similar point may be observed about the physical beauty of human beings. No one living has ever laid eyes on the disastrous beauty of Helen of Troy, of whom Homer said, "Small wonder men will endure so much for the sake of such a woman, for marvelously is she like the immortal goddesses to look upon" (*Iliad* III:156-58). But in 1971, when Michael Cacoyannis scripted and filmed Euripides' *Trojan Women*, it was the severe-featured Irene Papas who was cast in the role of Helen. Mere prettiness cannot carry the weight of such a role.

17. Henri Matisse, "Notes of a Painter," in *The Problems of Aesthetics*, ed. Eliseo Vivas and Murray Krieger (New York: Holt, Reinhart and Winston, 1953), 257.

Both these examples indicate that formal appearance alone conveys significance and meaning. The more demanding the conveyance, the more that which is sweet, pretty, or charming edges toward the beautiful and delivers an experience that recognizes implicit moral or existential weight distilled into an artwork—or a face. But this also means that beauty begins to move away from the simpler and easier varieties of aesthetic pleasure. And as it moves away, it nears territories of taxing appreciation for qualities that might almost seem to qualify as opposites to beauty: that which is grotesque, harsh, sublime, or even ugly.

Complicating Contrasts

Other attempts to come to grips with the nature of beauty postulate that it might be easier to identify this quality with reference to things that it is not. There is precedent for approaching axiological or normative properties this way, for the idea of the aesthetic itself is classically defined in terms of its contrasting values. By tradition aesthetic pleasure is pleasure taken in the intrinsic properties of objects as they are present to sense and imagination, rather than pleasure in or approval of their moral significance, practical use, appeal to erotic desire, and so forth. Beauty seems to have its own opposites that might help pinpoint just what it is. There are several candidates for being "opposites" to beauty, such as things that are monotonous or dull, insignificant, or ugly.[18] Such qualities either fail to strike up any aesthetic pleasure at all (such as things that are dull); or they arouse aesthetic displeasure (things that are repulsive, perhaps); or the pleasure they arouse needs to be classed in a different category. Certain kinds of ugliness, for instance, can be savored in art that is grotesque—which can be appraised as excellent on its own terms.[19] Indeed, sometimes that which is ugly is wonderful just for being ugly—such as a toad, that small monster beloved of fairy tales. While it is hard to imagine a beautiful toad, that is not the same as denying all aesthetic appeal for toads, a twist of appraisal that turns ugly itself into a positive aesthetic property. This informs us that beauty does not have the monopoly on either aesthetic or artistic excellence, and that not all of the contrasts between the beautiful and the not-beautiful serve to separate aesthetic value from disvalue.

This observation acknowledges a difficulty that freights discussions of beauty, namely, that the scope of the term expands and contracts in different contexts. If we want to consider "beauty" equivalent to "aesthetic excellence," or even to the slightly more focused "artistic excellence," then inevitably it

18. Ruth Lorand, "Beauty and Its Opposites," *Journal of Aesthetics and Art Criticism* 52, no. 4 (1994): 399–406.

19. Matthew Kieran, "Aesthetic Value: Beauty, Ugliness, and Incoherence," *Philosophy* 72, no. 281 (1997): 383–99. Eco, who employs an exceptionally wide concept of beauty, is inclined to include monsters and grotesques. See *History of Beauty*, esp. chaps. 5 and 12.

labels an omnivorous category about which one simply must accept quite a lot of ambiguity and vagueness—for it is shorthand for the entire multitude of aesthetic "goods." The contrast with this usage is just between "beautiful" and "aesthetically discountable." But if we want to think of beauty as a special element of the many aesthetic or artistic excellences that there can be, then we must recognize that there are some contrasts with beautiful that are themselves equally excellent. Indeed, most of the interesting contrasts between beautiful and not-beautiful are contrasts with other aesthetically valuable phenomena. And still, as we are about to see, narrowing our focus just to these does not avoid ambiguity, indeterminacy, or ambivalence.

The competing aesthetic value that has received the most theoretical attention is sublimity. I have already argued that the aesthetic arousal of disgust bears provocative comparisons with the arousal of fear and the experience of the sublime. Pursuing this line of thought further, considering the sublime also helps to instruct the "terrible" elements of beauty. When the standard distinctions between the beautiful and the sublime are lined up, we readily see that the scope of beauty is dramatically restricted. In Burke's representative catalog, that which is beautiful is small, contained, curved, delicate; that which is sublime is vast, unbounded, jagged, and harsh. The sublime presents to the senses and the imagination things that are powerful and terrifying, producing the rapture of the sublime. Because sublimity is so difficult to enjoy, Burke refrains from calling the response to it "pleasure," a tamer appreciation he reserves for beauty. He does, however, claim that it arouses "delight," an experience that eclipses the temperate pleasures of beauty because of the existential significance of its circumstances.

With the sterner category of the sublime available to account for extreme aesthetic value, the scope of beauty shrinks: beautiful things are contained and lovely; sublime things are powerful, unbounded, emotionally challenging. (This separation lends itself to a gender divide as well: beautiful things are feminine; in comparison, sublime things are masculine. Their shapes are stronger and harsher than beautiful things, and their enjoyment is suited for the more robust temperament of males.)[20] It is only a short step further to suggest that beautiful things are less momentous than sublime things. The "merely beautiful" relinquishes to sublimity objects with greater moral and existential significance. Quite apart from the gender asymmetry, which can be examined for its own import, the implications for beauty itself are a problem, for this venerable value is diminished and retreats to something close to pretty. While pretty things have an undeniable aesthetic appeal, they are often avoided by artists because they do not seem able to command attention or to support meaning to the same degree as other aesthetic qualities. (We have already seen

20. Numerous feminist scholars have analyzed gender in the concepts of the beautiful and the sublime, including Christine Battersby, *The Sublime, Terror, and Human Difference* (London: Routledge, 2007).

this suggested in the examples from Matisse's painting and the legendary figure of Helen.) The contrast between pretty and beautiful has been somewhat less explored by philosophers, but it yields as many insights about beauty as do the comparisons between beauty's more familiar counterparts such as the sublime and grotesque. In certain respects pretty and beautiful can be considered points on a continuum of aesthetically pleasing appearance, and considering what goes into assigning an object (or a face or body) its place on this continuum illuminates something of the role of the *difficult* in the formation of beauty.

Easy and Difficult Beauty

In *Three Lectures on Aesthetic* (1915), the English philosopher Bernard Bosanquet identifies two classes of things that are beautiful: *easy* beauty, which is pleasant to almost everyone: simple melodies, pretty faces, things that yield "straightforward pleasure." And *difficult* beauty—in which he includes the sublime—which can present barriers to appreciation "amounting for some persons to repellence." Several features can make beautiful things difficult, including intricacy of pattern that requires attentive focus; tension that "demands profound effort and concentration"; and width of vision present in art that treats unpleasant subjects often considered beneath aesthetic consideration.[21] (Comedy is his chief example of art that challenges with its width, and certainly the uses of disgust in comedy might count as traditionally "beneath" consideration, although Bosanquet does not agree with that sentiment.) While width might encompass qualities that are antithetical to easy beauties, intricacy and tension actually heighten those qualities to a point where they are sufficiently difficult to countenance that their sustained beauty is overlooked. Bosanquet stresses that some beauty puts great demands upon us:

> The kind of effort required is not exactly an intellectual effort; it is something more, it is an imaginative effort, that is to say . . . one in which the body-and-mind, without resting upon a fixed system like that of accepted conventional knowledge, has to frame for itself as a whole an experience in which it can "live" the embodiment before it. . . . In all this difficult beauty, which goes beyond what is comfortable for the indolent or timid mind, there is nothing but a "more" of the same beautiful, which we find prima facie pleasant, changed only by being intensified.[22]

Difficult beauty, because it so often arouses difficult emotions, is as much a physical as a mental response. (Note Bosanquet's unit: body-and-mind, as well

21. Bernard Bosanquet, *Three Lectures on Aesthetic* (1915) (Indianapolis, IN: Bobbs-Merrill, 1963) 47, 48.
22. Bosanquet, *Three Lectures on Aesthetic*, 48–49.

as his incorporation of "embodiment" in aesthetic encounters.) This description of the intensification of aesthetic response will aid later in disclosing the presence of aesthetic disgust in the midst of beauty.

Ironically, the "intensification" of beauty actually propels it toward its opposites. Bosanquet offers a somewhat enigmatic comment about aesthetic pleasure that illuminates the fact that it may be found in the most painful of subjects: "Beauty," he says, "is essentially enjoyed; it lives in enjoyment of a certain kind. But you cannot make it up out of enjoyments of any other kind."[23] Some aspect of this enjoyment stems from the expansion of understanding that takes place in the compressed apprehension that is aesthetic. That is, beauty signals an insight that is of a piece with finding an artwork beautiful and aesthetically moving. It is not a conclusion of research or an inference, but a clarity of vision embodied in art. And this is not only consistent with, but actually required by, the fact that art ponders the most painful subjects.

What I am proposing now as a "paradox" of beauty is a variation on the more familiar aesthetic paradoxes of aversion discussed earlier. Beauty by itself is usually not considered to present a paradox; what is there about beauty that could repel? But in fact it does have an enigmatic side, which becomes evident when we compare the concepts of beauty and prettiness, for we have seen how prettiness gives way to beauty as the more important value. The conversion of pretty to beautiful requires a dose of something difficult that arrests attention and causes it to linger. This might be induced by formal complexities, as both Bosanquet and Matisse observe. But with terrible beauty attention is arrested by elements that strain the heart—and yet they induce us to linger over them and savor them in all their heartache and woe. The language of aesthetic pleasure is especially misleading for terrible beauties; indeed, not all beauties are even enjoyed, strictly speaking, though they are—to use a sadly anemic expression—appreciated. This is the point to look once more at the appropriateness of pleasure-pain language in this discussion, continuing the line of thought defended in chapter 5.

Pleasure and Emotional Depth

Reference to pleasure and pain furnishes a simple way to ground the mysteries of axiological qualities in familiar experiences and to clarify the phenomenon of beauty. Because the nature of beauty is obscure, it helps to think of it as the occasion for a kind of pleasure, because we are clearer about the nature of pleasure. Or so it seems at first. But terrible beauties thoroughly complicate what is meant by "pleasure," and the dichotomy with which we started demands closer scrutiny.

23. Bosanquet, *Three Lectures on Aesthetic*, 51.

As we have seen, there are good reasons for recognizing that pleasure and pain are not the opposites that they might at first appear to be. This is the case even with the most basic uses of these terms to refer to bodily sensations or simple feelings. Certainly we speak of bodily pleasures, and some sensations (such as a caress) are pleasant, but pleasure is ill conceived in sensationalist terms. As I argued in chapter 5, calling an experience a pleasure is not identifying a feeling distinguishable in itself that accompanies an experience or an activity or event. Rather, the locution means that there is an appeal or magnetism or attraction to an experience that sustains absorption and attention.

It is significant that the paradoxes of aversion are largely emotional paradoxes, and that beauty and other aesthetic virtues are tangled in the web of emotional responses to art. I think it is misleading to call strenuous emotions such as sorrow or terror "pains," though it is certainly true that they are uncomfortable and that we tend to avoid them in life, despite their appeal in art. The "pain" of terror is a shorthand way of noticing the stress that terror exerts and—most significantly—the fact that difficult emotions are a means by which we register difficult features of our world. Just as intense pains make us strive to get away from the cause of the pain, uncomfortable emotions lead to recoil and avoidance in practical life. Fear makes us flee; anxiety is so uncomfortable we take pills for it; grief can be unbearable. At the same time, emotions are capable of the same enhancement of attention attributed to pleasures—especially when they are aroused by means of art, with its form and containment. To follow Bosanquet's language, one way to note the emergence of the beautiful out of the merely pretty is in terms of the intensification of experience. Emotions can intensify experience without colliding with some notional opposite.

Emotions are sometimes dismissed as merely sentimental engagement. But some of them—especially those at the center of the great paradoxes such as pity, terror, and dread—are recognized for their own aesthetic weight and the understanding they afford. Understanding demands that one face truths that one would rather be otherwise, but a "painful" emotion cannot be considered negative if it is the only means by which one may understand something important. Fear, for example, is negative insofar as it notices something dangerous and terrible; it is also supremely uncomfortable. But it is positive inasmuch as it alerts one to impending threat. Pity strains the heart, but without it one would not notice the grief of others. Disgust repels as it registers waste and putrefaction, but without it the frailty of mortal existence would be only partially understood. Art does not avoid difficult subjects, and this requires that emotions be part of aesthetic arousal and the recognition of artistic quality. Aesthetic emotions absorb us in rapt attention, with just enough distance supplied by the containment of art that we reap the intense insight available by means of emotion without turning away from that which arouses it. By these observations I do not mean to endorse the perspective according to which disagreeable emotions and perceptions are redeemed by the pleasurable understanding that they enable. Nor do I side with one possible reading of Hume, that beauty requires an affective conversion that leaves the difficult emotion behind. Both positions suggest a separability of the emotion from the insight, as though the aversion were but a regrettable stepping-stone to knowledge. While the aversions aroused by some art may be aptly so described, this account fails to capture the kind of art that is capable of rendering the most awful experiences beautiful—not as a step leads to a destination but as a lens produces clarity.

Can all emotions be transformed by art into a positive aesthetic encounter, perhaps amounting even to beauty? Certainly fear can, and grief, sorrow, and melancholy, as the examples of sublime and tragic art demonstrate. Anger can as well, for anger has a noble side that allies with honor and justice. No one has tested all emotions as they are aroused by art, if one could even come up with a complete list of such multifarious mental phenomena. But as we have seen, for most of the history of debates over this subject, disgust has been deemed incapable of aesthetic transfiguration in beautiful art. This emotion will serve us, therefore, as a test case for the limits of difficult beauty.

In Search of Disgusting Beauties

A good deal of the skepticism meted out to disgust as an apt companion to beauty has to do with the typical targets of disgust and the foul and squalid aspects of life that it registers. The objects that arouse this emotion tend to be incompatible with human dignity and honor, in contrast with the sublime, which is "inseparable from the notions of the dignity of the soul."[24] Most art that trades on disgust is not beautiful, nor is it intended to be. Disgusting aspects of art certainly can be funny, tragic, pathetic, grotesque, arousing, fascinating, and tender—but beautiful? Because not everything artistically worthy is beautiful, it would seem that the line between beautiful and not-beautiful has to be drawn somewhere, and that which is disgusting seems a pretty obvious candidate for the other side of the border. Horror genres, war narratives, the images of hell by Hieronymus Bosch, the excruciating paintings of Francis Bacon, are all examples of art that arouses profound disgust as part of understanding and appreciation. It would be foolish to try to cram all of their immense aesthetic impact into the category of "beauty." I grant that if there is beauty with the arousal of disgust, it has to be located in more plausible cases. And I think there are at least a few.

24. James Kirwan, *Sublimity* (New York: Routledge, 2005), 37.

Insects that feed off human flesh are pretty good examples of disgusting objects. And yet John Donne elevates a flea that bites two lovers into a weirdly compelling image of union:

> Mark but this flea, and mark in this,
> How little that which thou deny'st me is;
> Me it suck'd first, and now sucks thee,
> And in this flea our two bloods mingled be.[25]

Donne's famous and witty poem deliberately exaggerates a common and lowly insect bite into an argument for seduction. This poem, while admired, is seldom singled out for beauty, though perhaps this is because its beauty is taken for granted and its demonstrative argument commands first attention. What but eloquence combined with stunning economy makes this poem so enduring? It seems to me that Hume's conversion account is precisely what we must appeal to for the power of this little verse. Otherwise, we just have a description of a pestiferous bug, squashed in the course of the verse, that doubtless disgusts contemporary readers far more than those sixteenth-century lovers so accustomed to being bitten by creatures residing in their clothing.

Here is another insect, this one scouting out a corpse. One of Emily Dickinson's most disquieting poems speaks from the perspective of a woman who hears a fly buzz as she dies, and who glimpses in her final moment the vermin that will soon consume her corpse. The last two stanzas:

> I willed my keepsakes, signed away
> What portion of me I
> Could make assignable, and then
> There interposed a fly.
>
> With blue, uncertain, stumbling buzz
> Between the light and me;
> And then the windows failed, and then
> I could not see to see.[26]

I find this example a fitting candidate for beauty for its compressed structure and economy of perfectly chosen words that, combined with the eerie presence of the fly, compel a visceral admiration. With its perspective from the dead herself, the poem also borders the sublate, and this is no surprise. With difficult beauty the lines between beauty and sublimity are blurred, and no less so with the sublate when it is expressed with "force of expression and beauty of oratorical numbers" (quoting Hume again), which culminate in a conversion of disgust to beauty.

25. John Donne, "The Flea" (c. 1595), in *Poems of John Donne*, vol. 1, ed. E. K. Chambers (London: Lawrence and Bullen, 1896), 1–2.

26. Emily Dickinson, *The Collected Poems of Emily Dickinson* (New York: Barnes and Noble Books, 2009), 252–53.

Poetry may be especially likely to evidence beauty because of its exacting attention to the form and shape of expression—the eloquence that converts onerous subject matter to beauty. The poem by Wilfred Owen mentioned in chapter 4 suits this description too, for the grisly line—"the blood/Come gargling from the froth-corrupted lungs" —is not only tightly rhythmic itself, but the whole poem is structured to finish with the ironic quotation of Horace's famous line: "Dolce et decorum est pro patria mori," reversing its meaning such that what was an ancient expression of noble sacrifice ("that old lie") becomes a scathing denunciation of war.

We can find passages of prose that equally qualify for consideration as beautiful at the same time that they trade on a spasm of disgust. I offer the example of an episode at the end of Robert Stone's novel *A Flag for Sunrise* (1977) in which a young nun is tortured to death by means of beating and electric shock. It is a harrowing scene that manages to present the sickening effects of torture without flinching, and to do so with an eloquence that I believe qualifies as beauty of the most difficult sort. A short passage:

> When he began, she thought: I must do this, I must finish this, not him. She cast the compassing of her mind as high and wide as she could reach toward strength and mercy. She cried because, at first, there was nothing at all. Only the blows falling.
>
> Though he beat her beyond fear, she kept trying. Until she was awash in all the shameful juices of living and she still kept on. Though she forgot in time who he was and what the pain was about she was able to think of the tears, the blood, and mucus and loose teeth in her mouth: these are not bad things, these are just me and I'm all right.[27]

One can discover in literature other such scenes that graphically present brutality and its wreckage, and some of them we would probably prefer to call powerful, admirable, or vivid rather than beautiful; but with some we may also recognize beauty. Such images transfigure the disgusting into the beautiful just as terror transforms into the sublime. And they become beautiful not just because the rendering is deft or poetic but also because they capture in a breathtaking manner something terrible that we may also recognize as true.

Visual images are powerful vehicles for visceral apprehension. Caravaggio's painting *Doubting Thomas* (figure 7.1) captures an event from the story of Christ just after his crucifixion, when he has returned to his disciples to show them proof of his resurrection. When Thomas heard the news of Jesus's return, he was skeptical of its truth: "Unless I see in his hands the print of the nails, and place my finger in the mark of the nails, and place my hand in his side, I

27. Robert Stone, *A Flag for Sunrise* (New York: Ballantine, 1977), 415–16.

FIGURE 7.1. Caravaggio (Michelangelo da Merisi), *Doubting Thomas*. Oil on canvas.
Stiftung Preussische Schlösser & Gärten Berlin-Brandenburg, Berlin. Bildarchiv
Preussischer Kulturbesitz/Art Resource, NY.

will not believe" (John 20:25). Caravaggio has rendered the apostles a scruffy
bunch with unkempt hair and torn robes, free from any signs of holiness such
as halos. The curious doubting Thomas actually probes the wound in Jesus'
side, inserting his fingers into the gaping skin.[28] Now penetration of the protective covering of the body is one of the standard exemplars of the disgusting
according to psychological analysis. Wounds, dismemberments, and blood all
signal death and the immanence of decay. There is no gore in the painting, but
the sight of dirty fingers intruding into violated flesh quite likely induces a
visceral frisson and a spasm of disgust in the viewer. (When I first encountered
this painting in an art history book years ago, I was appalled, fascinated, and
almost nauseated.) The initial recoil this picture prompts may seem inappropriate for a religious subject. But not only does it render Christ and his followers familiarly human, the aesthetic disgust heightens and enhances
recognition of the mystery of the incarnation: the mortality of Jesus the man
and the Christian doctrine of everlasting life. The disgust component, I believe,
performs the job of intensification that Bosanquet refers to when he says that
beauty is an enjoyment that is not composed of other enjoyments.

28. Some claim this image signifies sexual penetration, though given the subject-matter of the painting,
this strikes me as an extraneous interpretation. Nonetheless, it is not inconsistent with the case I am making for
the participation of aesthetic disgust in beauty.

One may surmise that the absence of gore or decay in this painting controls the disgust response sufficiently that it does not interfere with beauty, but we can find other artworks that push the emotion closer to its trademark grossness. Some, of course, have no claims for beauty, but others do. Artemisia Gentileschi's *Judith and Holofernes* (see figure 4.3), with its glowing colors, pyramidal composition, and a dynamism between the murdering women that is both narrative and formal, is a good candidate for a work in which the "tincture" of artistry overcolors disgust. But not all great pictures are beautiful. We must not fall into the trap of making "beauty" the only synonym for artistic accomplishment. These examples are not intended to reclassify all aesthetic disgust as beauty. Rather, they demonstrate that when beautiful art arouses aversive emotion, the aesthetic effect need not be parsed as a mingling of a negative and a positive affect. There are not two things but one dense and complex phenomenon. And in some cases, even disgust itself lies at the heart of an experience of beauty.

However, these examples also leave some questions dangling. While terrible beauty is fairly obviously distinguished from pretty, what differentiates this aesthetic value from deft grotesquerie or powerful horror? The border between terrible beauty and the grotesque or horrid is hazy. Just as pretty shades into beautiful, so terrible beauty shades toward horror and other difficult aesthetic categories. The examples I have offered here hover at that border, and one might object to calling all of them beautiful. (Perhaps Donne's "Flea" is just too weird and amusing for beauty.) The complexity of aversive emotions bound up with artistic beauty creates a zone where horrid, beautiful, sublime, and sublate can be difficult to distinguish. But that is why some beauty is truly terrible.

It is also why there will be perennial borderline cases where some will find beauty and others will not. Earlier I noted that some commentators find Jenny Saville's paintings beautiful, while others emphasize the expressive power of their disgusting qualities. I myself fall in the latter camp, for I think that the meaning of her work—including *Host*—is compromised with an emphasis on beauty. However, as I indicated in the earlier discussion, I am also inclined to read this painting in existentialist terms, and to displace existentialist sentiments from their links with uncompromising disgust would dilute the central vision of that philosophy. Sartre's aptly named novel *Nausea*, for instance, is full of revolting images designed not only to describe the feelings of the main character but also to evoke the same state of mind in the reader. To mix Roquentin's revulsion at the facticity of Being with the "sentiments of beauty" would be a variety of bad faith that tries to hide from the foundational insights of his philosophy.

The discovery that disgust can perform such divergent intellectual tasks—that it can either illuminate the meaninglessness of the universe or present a deftly expressed insight that approaches beauty—demonstrates that this emotion can also propel philosophical commitments. We have encountered many examples that confirm that disgust reactions vary with the particular objects classed as "foul" and "contaminating" according to historical and cultural frameworks. And in the worlds of art the tenor of disgust varies with style, narrative structure, and the different meanings that the emotion signifies. All this follows from the fact that it is not only a type of object that triggers emotion but also its presentation in a certain manner. Added to the contextual elements that influence the tenor of disgust, there is the overall philosophical framework where the emotion is assigned a place and value. To a philosopher such as Sartre for whom the very fact of existence is mindless and random, disgust is an important and unavoidable loathing that confronts this realization. In his writings he deploys disgust as a persuasive device to disclose features of existence that his readers would doubtless rather ignore. It is thereby a tool of truth.

But there are many perspectives on truth at this abstract level, and another philosophical framework might serve as an instrument by which disgusting objects are regarded in a way that converts them into beauty—not by denying their nature but by accepting it as part of a whole. To a philosopher for whom death—even one's own—should be inconsequential, objects that would ordinarily arouse onerous emotions take their place in nature and all its wonders. The most eloquent of Stoic philosophers, Marcus Aurelius, achieves this vision in his *Meditations*, and it is his words that will close this protracted excursion into disgust:

> Even the small characteristics of things produced according to nature have something in them pleasing and attractive. . . . Figs when they are quite ripe gape open; and ripe olives when they are near to rotting are particularly good to look at. And ears of corn bending down, and a lion's eyebrows, and the foam which flows from the mouth of a wild boar, and many other things—though they are far from beautiful, if one examines them separately—still, because they are characteristics of things formed by nature, help to adorn them, and please the eye. Thus if a man has a feeling for and deep insight into the things produced in the universe, there is hardly one of their characteristics that will not seem to him of a sort to give him pleasure. So he will look on the gaping jaws of living wild beasts with as much pleasure as on those which painters and sculptors depict in imitation; and in an old woman and an old man he will perceive a certain ripeness and comeliness; and will look on the attractive loveliness of young persons with chaste eyes. Many such beauties will show themselves, not pleasing to every man, but to him who has become truly at home with nature and her works.[29]

Disgust profoundly recognizes—intimately and personally—that it is our mortal nature to die and to rot. Acquiescing to this terrible truth and finding beauty in the overall pattern that gives it shape is both an artistic and a philosophical accomplishment. And—not surprisingly—it is rare.

29. Marcus Aurelius, *Meditations*, trans. George Long (New York: Walter J. Black, 1945), 26.

Bibliography

Adams, Charlotte. *The Four Seasons Cookbook*. New York: Ridge Press/Holt, Rinehart and Winston, 1971.

Ahmed, Sara. *The Cultural Politics of Emotion*. New York: Routledge, 2004.

Alston, William. "Pleasure." In *Encyclopedia of Philosophy*. Vol. 6. Ed. Paul Edwards. New York: Macmillan, 1967.

Ames, Kenneth. *Death in the Dining Room*. Philadelphia: Temple University Press, 1982.

Andrews, Edmund. *The History of Scientific English*. New York: Richard R. Smith, 1947.

Angyal, Andreas. "Disgust and Related Aversions." *Journal of Abnormal and Social Psychology* 36 (1941): 393–412.

Aristotle. *Nicomachean Ethics*. Trans. W. D. Ross. Revised J. O. Urmson. In *The Complete Works of Aristotle: The Revised Oxford Translations*, ed. Jonathan Barnes. Princeton, NJ: Princeton University Press, 1984.

———. *The Poetics*. Trans. Stephen Halliwell. London: Duckworth, 1986. Excerpts in *Aesthetics: The Big Questions*, ed. Carolyn Korsmeyer. Malden, MA: Blackwell, 1998.

Aydede, Murat. "An Analysis of Pleasure vis-à-vis Pain." *Philosophy and Phenomenological Research*. 61, no. 3 (2000): 537–70.

Ayto, John. *The Diner's Dictionary: Food and Drink from A to Z*. Oxford: Oxford University Press, 1993.

Barnes, Donna R., and Peter G. Rose. *Matters of Taste: Food and Drink in Seventeenth-Century Dutch Art and Life*. Albany/Syracuse, NY: Albany Institute of History and Art/Syracuse University Press, 2002.

Barthes, Roland. *The Empire of Signs*. Trans. Richard Howard. New York: Hill and Wang, 1982.

Bataille, Georges. *Oeuvres Complètes*. Vol. 2. 1922–40. Paris: Gallimard, 1970.

Battersby, Christine. *The Sublime, Terror, and Human Difference*. London: Routledge, 2007.

Beardsley, Monroe. *Aesthetics: Problems in the Philosophy of Criticism*. New York: Harcourt, Brace, 1958.

Beauvoir, Simone de. *The Second Sex*. 1949. Trans. H. M. Parshley. New York: Random House, 1989.

Bencivenga, Ermanno. "Economy of Expression and Aesthetic Pleasure." *Philosophy and Phenomenological Research* 47, no. 4 (1987): 615–30.

Ben Ze'ev, Aaron. *The Subtlety of Emotions*. Cambridge, MA: MIT Press, 2000.

Bergson, Henri. *Laughter: An Essay on the Meaning of the Comic*. Trans. Cloudesley Brereton and Fred Rothwell. Copenhagen and Los Angeles: Integer Books, 1999.

"Bits and Pieces." http://www.historic_uk.com/HistoryUK/England_History/BitsandPieces.htm. July 14, 2009.

Boccaccio, Giovanni. *The Decameron*. Trans. Richard Aldington. New York: Dell, 1930.

Bosanquet, Bernard. *Three Lectures on Aesthetic*. 1915. Indianapolis, IN: Bobbs-Merrill, 1963.

Brand, Peg, ed. *Beauty Matters*. Bloomington: Indiana University Press, 2000.

———, ed. *Beauty Revisited*. Bloomington: Indiana University Press, 2011.

Brentano, Franz. *Psychology from an Empirical Standpoint*. 1874. Ed. Linda L. McAlister. New York: Humanities Press, 1973.

Brillat-Savarin, Jean-Anthelme. *The Physiology of Taste*. 1825. Trans. M. F. K. Fisher. New York: Heritage Press, 1949.

Burke, Edmund. *A Philosophical Enquiry into the Origin of Our Ideas of the Sublime and Beautiful*. 1757. Ed. James T. Boulton. Notre Dame, IN: University of Notre Dame Press, 1968.

Calder, Andrew J., Andrew D. Lawrence, and Andrew W. Young. "Neuropathology of Fear and Loathing." *Nature Reviews: Neuroscience*, May 2001: 359–60.

Carroll, Noël. *The Philosophy of Horror, or Paradoxes of the Heart*. New York: Routledge, 1990. Excerpts in *Aesthetics: The Big Questions*, ed. Carolyn Korsmeyer. Malden, MA: Blackwell, 1998.

Carroll, Noël, and David Bordwell, eds. *Post-Theory: Reconstructing Film Studies*. Madison: University of Wisconsin Press, 1997.

Chapman, H. A., D. A. Kim, J. M. Susskind, and A. K. Anderson. "In Bad Taste: Evidence for the Oral Origins of Moral Disgust." *Science* 323 (February 27, 2009): 1222–26.

Cornelius, Randolph R. *The Science of Emotion*. Upper Saddle River, NJ: Prentice-Hall, 1996.

Creed, Barbara. *The Monstrous Feminine: Film, Feminism, and Psychoanalysis*. London: Routledge, 1993.

Crowther, Paul. *Critical Aesthetics and Postmodernism*. New York: Oxford University Press, 1993.

Currie, Gregory. "Imagination and Simulation: Aesthetics Meets Cognitive Science." In *Mental Simulations*, ed. Martin Davies and Tony Stone. Oxford: Blackwell, 1995: 151–69.

Curtis, Valerie, and Adam Biran. "Dirt, Disgust, and Disease: Is Hygiene in Our Genes?" *Perspectives in Biology and Medicine* 44, no. 1 (2001): 17–31.

Damasio, Antonio. *Descartes' Error: Emotion, Reason, and the Human Brain*. New York: Avon Books, 1995.

———. *The Feeling of What Happens: Body and Emotion in the Making of Consciousness.* San Diego: Harcourt, 1999.

Danto, Arthur C. *The Abuse of Beauty: Aesthetics and the Concept of Art.* Chicago: Open Court, 2003.

———. "Bad Aesthetic Times." In *Encounters and Reflections: Art in the Historical Present.* Berkeley and Los Angeles: University of California Press, 1990: 297–312.

———. "Beauty and the Beastly." *Nation* 272, no. 16 (April 23, 2001): 25–29.

Darwin, Charles. *The Expression of Emotion in Man and Animals.* 1872. Chicago: University of Chicago Press, 1965.

Davidson, Richard J. "Complexities in the Search for Emotion-Specific Physiology." In *The Nature of Emotion*, ed. Paul Ekman and Richard J. Davidson. New York: Oxford University Press, 1994: 237–242.

Davies, Stephen, ed. *Art and Its Messages: Meaning, Morality, and Society.* University Park: Pennsylvania State University Press, 1997.

———. "Responding Emotionally to Fiction." *Journal of Aesthetics and Art Criticism* 67, no. 3 (2009): 269–84.

De Bolla, Peter. *Art Matters.* Cambridge, MA: Harvard University Press, 2001.

———. "Toward the Materiality of Aesthetic Experience." *Diacritics* 32, no. 1 (2002): 19–37.

Deigh, John. "Cognitivism in the Theory of Emotions." *Ethics* 104 (1994): 824–54.

———. "Primitive Emotions." In *Thinking about Feeling*, ed. Robert Solomon. Oxford: Oxford University Press, 2004: 9–27.

Derrida, Jacques. "Economimesis." *Diacritics* 11, no. 2 (1981): 3–25.

De Sousa, Ronald. *The Rationality of Emotions.* Cambridge, MA: MIT Press, 1987.

Dickinson, Emily. *The Collected Poems of Emily Dickinson.* New York: Barnes and Noble Books, 2009.

Donne, John. *Poems of John Donne.* Vol. 1. Ed. E. K. Chambers. London: Lawrence and Bullen, 1896.

Doueihi, Milad. *A Perverse History of the Human Heart.* Cambridge, MA: Harvard University Press, 1987.

Douglas, Mary. *Purity and Danger: An Analysis of the Concepts of Pollution and Taboo.* London: Routledge and Kegan Paul, 1966.

Dumas, Alexandre. *Dumas on Food: Selections from Le Grand Dictionnaire de Cuisine.* Trans. Alan Davidson and Jane Davidson. London: Folio Society, 1978.

Eagleton, Terry. *The Ideology of the Aesthetic.* Oxford: Blackwell, 1990.

Eco, Umberto, ed. *History of Beauty.* Trans. Alastair McEwen. New York: Rizzoli, 2005.

Ekman, Paul. "Biological and Cultural Contributions to Body and Facial Movement in the Expression of Emotions." In *Explaining Emotions*. ed. Amélie Oksenberg Rorty. Berkeley and Los Angeles: University of California Press, 1980: 73–101.

———. "Facial Expressions of Emotion: An Old Controversy and New Findings." *Philosophical Transactions: Biological Sciences* 335, no. 1273 (1992): 63–69.

Ekman, Paul, and Richard J. Davidson, eds. *The Nature of Emotion.* New York: Oxford University Press, 1994.

Ekman, Paul, Robert W. Levenson, and Wallace V. Friesen. "Autonomic Nervous System Activity Distinguishes among Emotions." *Science* 221 (September, 1983): 1208–10.

Erickson, Robert A. *The Language of the Heart, 1600–1750*. Philadelphia: University of Pennsylvania Press, 1997.

Even, Yael. "The Loggia dei Lanzi: A Showcase of Female Subjugation." In *The Expanding Discourse: Feminism and Art History*, ed. Norma Broude and Mary Garrard. New York: HarperCollins, 1992: 126–37.

Faulks, Sebastian. *Birdsong: A Novel of Love and War*. New York: Vintage, 1997.

Feagin, Susan L. "Monsters, Disgust, and Fascination." *Philosophical Studies* 65 (1992): 75–84.

———. "The Pleasures of Tragedy." *American Philosophical Quarterly* 20, no. 1 (1983): 75–84.

———. *Reading with Feeling: The Aesthetics of Appreciation*. Ithaca, NY: Cornell University Press, 1996.

Floyd, Keith. *Far Flung Floyd*. New York: Citadel Press, 1994.

Fodor, Jerry. *The Modularity of Mind*. Cambridge, MA: MIT Press, 1983.

"Food for Thought: Paul Rozin's Research and Teaching at Penn." *Penn Arts and Sciences*, Fall 1997. http://www.sas.upenn.edu/sasalum/newsltr/fall97/rozin.html. February 2, 2010.

Formations of Pleasure. London: Routledge and Kegan Paul, 1983.

Frazier, Charles. *Cold Mountain*. New York: Atlantic Monthly Press, 1997.

Freeland, Cynthia. "Against Raunchy Women's Art." In *Art and Social Change*, ed. Curtis L. Carter. International Yearbook of Aesthetics 13. Milwaukee, WI: Marquette University Special Editions, 2009: 56–72.

———. "Art and Moral Knowledge." *Philosophical Topics* 25, no. 1 (1997): 11–36.

———. *The Naked and the Undead: Evil and the Appeal of Horror*. Boulder, CO: Westview Press, 2000.

———. "The Sublime in Cinema." In *Passionate Views: Film, Cognition, and Emotion*, ed. Carl Plantinga and Greg Smith. Baltimore: Johns Hopkins University Press, 1999: 65–83.

Freud, Sigmund. *Beyond the Pleasure Principle*. 1920. Trans. James Strachey. New York: Norton, 1961.

———. *The Complete Psychological Works of Sigmund Freud*. Vol. 7. 1901–5. Ed. James Strachey. London: Hogarth Press and the Institute of Psycho-analysis, 1953.

Frijda, Nico H. *The Emotions*. Cambridge: Cambridge University Press, 1986.

Gardiner, H. M., Ruth Clark Metcalf, and John G. Beebe-Center. *Feeling and Emotion: A History of Theories*. New York: American Book Company, 1937.

Gaut, Berys. "Art and Cognition." In *Contemporary Debates in Aesthetics and Philosophy of Art*, ed. Matthew Kieran. Malden, MA: Blackwell, 2006: 115–26.

———. *Art, Emotion, and Ethics*. Oxford: Oxford University Press, 2007.

Gazzaniga, Michael S. *Human: The Science behind What Makes Us Unique*. New York: HarperCollins, 2008.

Goldie, Peter. *The Emotions: A Philosophical Explanation*. New York: Oxford University Press, 2002.

Goodman, Nelson. *Languages of Art: An Approach to a Theory of Symbols*. Indianapolis, IN: Bobbs-Merrill, 1968.

———. "Reply to Beardsley." *Erkenntnis* 12, no. 1 (1978): 169–73.

Gordon, Robert M. *The Structure of Emotions: Investigations in Cognitive Philosophy.* Cambridge: Cambridge University Press, 1987.

Greenspan, Patricia. *Emotions and Reasons: An Inquiry into Emotional Justification.* New York: Routledge, 1988.

Griffiths, Paul. "Are Emotions Natural Kinds?" In *Thinking about Feeling,* ed. Robert Solomon. Oxford: Oxford University Press, 2004: 233–49.

———. *What Emotions Really Are.* Chicago: University of Chicago Press, 1997.

Grosz, Elizabeth. *Volatile Bodies: Towards a Corporeal Feminism.* Bloomington: Indiana University Press, 1994.

Guyer, Paul. *Values of Beauty: Historical Essays in Aesthetics.* Cambridge: Cambridge University Press, 2005.

Haidt, Jonathan, Clark McCauley, and Paul Rozin. "Individual Differences in Sensitivity to Disgust: A Scale Sampling Seven Domains of Disgust Elicitors." *Personality and Individual Differences* 16, no. 5 (1994): 701–13.

Haidt, Jonathan, Paul Rozin, Clark McCauley, and Sumio Imada. "Body, Psyche, and Culture: The Relationship of Disgust to Morality." *Psychology and Developing Societies* 9 (1997): 107–31.

Harrell, Jean. *Soundtracks: A Study of Auditory Perception, Memory, and Music.* Buffalo, NY: Prometheus Press, 1986.

Hjort, Mette, and Sue Laver, eds. *Emotion and the Arts.* New York: Oxford University Press, 1997.

Hogarth, William. *The Analysis of Beauty.* 1753. Ed. Ronald Paulson. New Haven, CT: Yale University Press, 1997.

Houser, Craig, Leslie C. Jones, Simon Taylor, and Jack Ben-Levi. *Abject Art: Repulsion and Desire in American Art.* New York: Whitney Museum, 1993.

Hume, David. "Of Tragedy." In *Essays Moral, Political, and Literary.* Vol. 1. 1882. Ed. T. H. Green and T. H. Grose. Darmstadt: Scientia Verlag Aalen, 1964.

Hurwitz, Daniel. "Pleasure." In *Encyclopedia of Aesthetics,* vol. 4, ed. Michael Kelly. Oxford: Oxford University Press, 1998.

Hutcheson, Francis. *Inquiry into the Original of Our Ideas of Beauty and Virtue* (1725). *Collected Works* Vol. I. Darmstadt: Georg Olms, 1971.

Hyman, John. *The Objective Eye: Color, Form, and Reality in the Theory of Art.* Chicago: University of Chicago Press, 2006.

Iseminger, Gary. "How Strange a Sadness." *Journal of Aesthetics and Art Criticism* 42, no. 1 (1983): 81–82.

Izard, Carroll. *Human Emotions.* New York: Plenum Press, 1977.

Jacobs, Carol. "The Critical Performance of Lessing's Laokoon." *Modern Language Notes* 102, no. 3 (1987): 483–521.

Jager, Eric. *The Book of the Heart.* Chicago: University of Chicago Press, 2000.

"Jenny Saville: Contemporary Artists: Host." http://www.saatchi-gallery.co.uk/imgs/artists/saville. February 17, 2009.

Kahane, Claire. "Freud's Sublimation: Disgust, Desire, and the Female Body." *American Imago* 49, no. 4 (1992): 411–25.

Kant, Immanuel. *Critique of Judgment.* 1790. Trans. Werner S. Pluhar. Indianapolis, IN: Hackett, 1987.

Kass, Leon. *The Hungry Soul: Eating and the Perfecting of Our Nature*. New York: Free Press, 1994.

Kekes, John. "Disgust and Moral Taboos." *Philosophy* 67 (1992): 431–46.

Kenny, Anthony. *Action, Emotion, and Will*. London: Routledge and Kegan Paul, 1963.

Kieran, Matthew. "Aesthetic Value: Beauty, Ugliness, and Incoherence." *Philosophy* 72, no. 281 (1997): 383–99.

———. *Revealing Art*. London: Routledge, 2005.

Kirwan, James. *Sublimity*. New York: Routledge, 2005.

Kitty Litter Cakes. http://allrecipes.com/Recipe/Kitty-Litter-Cake/Detail.aspx. February 20, 2010.

Kolnai, Aurel. *On Disgust*. 1929. Ed. Barry Smith and Carolyn Korsmeyer. Chicago: Open Court, 2004.

Korsmeyer, Carolyn. "Delightful, Delicious, Disgusting." *Journal of Aesthetics and Art Criticism* 60, no. 3 (2002): 218–25.

———. "Disgust," In *Aesthetics as Philosophy: Proceedings of the XIV International Congress for Aesthetics*. Ed. Aleč Erjavec. Ljubljana, Slovenia: 1999.

———. "Fear and Disgust: The Sublime and Sublate." *Revue Internationale de Philosophie* 62, no. 246 (December 2008): 367–79.

———. *Gender and Aesthetics: An Introduction*. New York: Routledge, 2004.

———. *Making Sense of Taste: Food and Philosophy*. Ithaca, NY: Cornell University Press, 1999.

———. "Terrible Beauties," in *Contemporary Debates in Aesthetics and Philosophy of Art*, ed. Matthew Kieran. Marsden, MA: Blackwell Publishers, 2005.

Kristeva, Julia. *The Powers of Horror: An Essay on Abjection*. Trans. Leon S. Roudiez. New York: Columbia University Press, 1982.

Kuehn, Glenn. "Food Fetishes and Sin-Aesthetics." In *Food and Philosophy: Eat, Think, and Be Merry*, ed. Fritz Allhoff and Dave Monroe. Malden, MA: Blackwell, 2007: 162–74.

Lamarque, Peter. "Cognitive Values in the Arts: Marking the Boundaries." In *Contemporary Debates in Aesthetics and Philosophy of Art*, ed. Matthew Kieran. Malden, MA: Blackwell, 2006: 127–39.

LeDoux, Joseph. *The Emotional Brain*. New York: Simon and Schuster, 1996.

Lessing, Gotthold Ephraim. *Laocoön: An Essay on the Limits of Painting and Poetry*. Trans. Edward Allen McCormick. Indianapolis, IN: Bobbs-Merrill, 1962.

Levenson, Robert W., Paul Ekman, and Wallace V. Friesen. "Voluntary Facial Action Generates Emotion-Specific Autonomic Nervous System Activity." *Psychopathology* 27, no. 4 (1990): 363–84.

Levinson, Jerrold. "Emotion in Response to Art: A Survey of the Terrain." In *Emotion and the Arts*, ed. Mette Hjort and Sue Laver. New York: Oxford University Press, 1997: 20–34.

———. *The Pleasures of Aesthetics*. Ithaca, NY: Cornell University Press, 1996.

Lorand, Ruth. "Beauty and Its Opposites." *Journal of Aesthetics and Art Criticism* 52, no. 4 (1994): 399–406.

"Love in Disguise." http://www.pbs.org/kqed/demonbarber/recipes/loveindisguise.html. November 4, 2003.

Lyons, William E. *Emotion*. Cambridge: Cambridge University Press, 1980.

Lyotard, Jean-François. "Presenting the Unpresentable." *Artforum*, April 1982: 64–66.

MacClancy, Jeremy. *Consuming Culture: Why You Eat What You Eat*. New York: Henry Holt, 1992.

Mackay, James A. *Robert Bruce King of Scots*. London: Robert Hale, 1974.

MacKendrick, Karmen. *Counterpleasures*. Albany, NY: State University of New York Press, 1999.

Marcus Aurelius. *Meditations*. Trans. George Long. New York: Walter J. Black, 1945.

Matisse, Henri. "Notes of a Painter." In *The Problems of Aesthetics*, ed. Eliseo Vivas and Murray Krieger. New York: Holt, Reinhart and Winston, 1953: 255–61.

McGinn, Colin. *The Meaning of Disgust: Life, Death, and Revulsion*. New York: Oxford University Press, 2012.

McNally, Richard J. "Disgust Has Arrived." *Anxiety Disorders* 16 (2002): 561–66.

Meagher, Michelle. "Jenny Saville and a Feminist Aesthetics of Disgust." In "Women, Art, and Aesthetics," ed. Peg Brand and Mary Devereaux. Special issue, *Hypatia* 18, no. 4 (2003): 23–41.

Mendelssohn, Moses. "On Sentiments." In *Philosophical Writings*, trans. Daniel O. Dahlstrom. Cambridge: Cambridge University Press, 1997.

Menninghaus, Winfried. *Disgust: The Theory and History of a Strong Sensation*. Trans. Howard Eiland and Joel Golb. Albany: State University of New York Press, 2003.

Meyers, Diana Tietjens. "Jenny Saville Remakes the Female Nude." In *Beauty Revisited*, ed. Peg Brand. Bloomington: Indiana University Press, 2011.

Miller, William Ian. *The Anatomy of Disgust*. Cambridge, MA: Harvard University Press, 1997.

Monroe, Dave. "Can Food Be Art?" In *Food and Philosophy: Eat, Think, and Be Merry*, ed. Fritz Allhoff and Dave Monroe. Malden, MA: Blackwell, 2007: 133–44.

Morreall, John. "Amusement and Other Mental States." In *Philosophy of Laughter and Humor*, ed. John Morreall. Albany: State University of New York Press, 1987.

Morris, J. S., A. Ohman, and R. J. Dolan. "Conscious and Unconscious Emotional Learning in the Human Amygdala." *Nature* 393 (1998): 467–70.

Mothersill, Mary. *Beauty Restored*. Oxford: Clarendon Press, 1984.

Mulvey, Laura. *Fetishism and Curiosity*. Bloomington: Indiana University Press, 1996.

Nead, Lynda. *The Female Nude*. London: Routledge, 1992.

Nehamas, Alexander. *Only a Promise of Happiness: The Place of Beauty in a World of Art*. Princeton, NJ: Princeton University Press, 2007.

Neill, Alex. "Fiction and the Emotions." *American Philosophical Quarterly* 30 (1993): 1–13.

———. "On a Paradox of the Heart." *Philosophical Studies* 65 (1992): 53–65.

Ngai, Sianne. "Afterword: On Disgust." In *Ugly Feelings*. Cambridge, MA: Harvard University Press, 2004.

Nussbaum, Martha. *Hiding from Humanity: Disgust, Shame, and the Law*. Princeton. NJ: Princeton University Press, 2004.

———. *Upheavals of Thought: The Intelligence of Emotions*. Cambridge: Cambridge University Press, 2001.

"Oh, Yuck!" *Discover*, December 2002, 32–34.

Outram, Alan K. "Hunter-Gatherers and the First Farmers." In *Food: The History of Taste*, ed. Paul Freedman. Berkeley and Los Angeles: University of California Press, 2007: 35–61.

Owen, Wilfred. "Dolce et Decorum Est." In *The Oxford Book of War Poetry*, ed. Jon Stallworthy. Oxford: Oxford University Press, 1984.

Pangsepp, Jaak. "The Basics of Basic Emotions." In *The Nature of Emotion*, ed. Paul Ekman and Richard J. Davidson. New York: Oxford University Press, 1994: 20–24.

Partridge, Eric. *Origins: A Short Etymological Dictionary of Modern English*. New York: Macmillan, 1958.

Paterniti, Michael. "The Last Meal." *Esquire* 129, no. 5 (May 1998): 112–17, 138.

Peterson, T. Sarah. *Acquired Taste: The French Origins of Modern Cooking*. Ithaca, NY: Cornell University Press, 1994.

Picard, Rosalind. *Affective Computing*. Cambridge, MA: MIT Press, 1997.

Plato. *Republic*. Trans. G. M. A. Grube. Revised C. D. C. Reeve. Indianapolis, IN: Hackett, 1992.

———. *Republic*. Trans. Paul Shorey. In *The Collected Dialogues of Plato*, ed. Edith Hamilton and Huntington Cairns. Princeton, NJ: Princeton University Press, 1973.

Prall, David. *Aesthetic Judgment*. New York: Crowell, 1929.

Prinz, Jesse. "Embodied Emotions." In *Thinking about Feeling*, ed. Robert Solomon. Oxford: Oxford University Press, 2004: 44–58.

———. *Gut Reactions: A Perceptual Theory of Emotions*. Oxford: Oxford University Press, 2004.

Pym, Barbara. *No Fond Return of Love*. New York: Harper and Row, 1984.

Ragland, Ellie. *Essays on the Pleasures of Death: From Freud to Lacan*. New York: Routledge, 1995.

Redding, Paul. *The Logic of Affect*. Ithaca, NY: Cornell University Press, 1999.

Revel, Jean-François. *Culture and Cuisine: A Journey through the History of Food*. Trans. Helen R. Lane. New York: Da Capo Press, 1984.

Robinson, Jenefer. *Deeper Than Reason: Emotion and Its Role in Literature, Music, and Art*. Oxford: Oxford University Press, 2005.

———. "Emotion: Biological Fact or Social Construction?" In *Thinking about Feeling*, ed. Robert Solomon. Oxford: Oxford University Press, 2004: 28–43.

———. "Startle." *Journal of Philosophy* 92, no. 2 (1995): 53–74.

Rorty, Amélie Oksenberg, "Explaining Emotions." In *Explaining Emotions*, ed. Amélie Oksenberg Rorty. Berkeley and Los Angeles: University of California Press, 1980: 103–26.

Rose, Peter G. *Matters of Taste: Dutch Recipes with an American Connection*. Albany/Syracuse, NY: Albany Institute of History and Art/Syracuse University Press, 2002.

Rozin, Paul. "Food for Thought: Paul Rozin's Research and Teaching at Penn." *Penn Arts and Sciences*, Fall 1997. http//:www.sas.upenn.edu/sasalum/newsltr/fall97/rozin/html.

Rozin, Paul, and April E. Fallon, "A Perspective on Disgust." *Psychological Review* 94, no. 1 (1987): 23–41.

Rozin, Paul, Jonathan Haidt, and Clark R. McCauley. "Disgust." In *Handbook of Emotions*, ed. Michael Lewis and Jeannette M. Haviland. New York: Guilford Press, 1993: 575–94.

Rozin, Paul, Jonathan Haidt, Clark McCauley, and Sumion Imada. "Disgust: Preadaptation and the Cultural Evolution of a Food-Based Emotion." In *Food*

Preferences and Taste: Continuity and Change, ed. Helen Macbeth. Providence, RI: Berghahn Books, 1997: 65–82.

Ryle, Gilbert. *Dilemmas*. Cambridge: Cambridge University Press, 1954.

Santayana, George. *The Sense of Beauty*. 1896. New York: Dover, 1955.

Sartre, Jean-Paul. *Being and Nothingness: An Essay in Phenomenological Ontology*. Trans. Hazel Barnes. New York: Citadel Press, 1956.

———. *Nausea*. Trans. Lloyd Alexander. Norfolk, CT: New Directions, 1949.

Scarry, Elaine. *The Body in Pain: The Making and Unmaking of the World*. New York: Oxford University Press, 1985.

———. *On Beauty and Being Just*. Princeton, NJ: Princeton University Press, 1999.

———. *Resisting Representation*. New York: Oxford University Press, 1994.

Schaper, Eva. "The Pleasures of Taste." In *Pleasure, Preference and Value*, ed. Eva Schaper. Cambridge: Cambridge University Press, 1983: 39–56.

Scherer, Klaus R. "Toward a Concept of Modal Emotions." In *The Nature of Emotion*, ed. Paul Ekman and Richard J. Davidson. New York: Oxford University Press, 1994: 25–31.

Schimmel, Annemarie. *The Triumphal Sun: A Study of the Works of Jalaloddin Rumi*. Albany: State University of New York Press, 1978.

Schopenhauer, Arthur. *The World as Will and Representation*. Vol. 1. 1859. Trans. E. F. J. Payne. New York: Dover, 1969.

Sharpe, R. A. "Solid Joys or Fading Pleasures." In *Pleasure, Preference and Value*, ed. Eva Schaper. Cambridge: Cambridge University Press, 1983: 86–98.

Shellekens, Elisabeth. "Towards a Reasonable Objectivism for Aesthetic Judgments." *British Journal of Aesthetics* 46, no. 2 (2006): 163–77.

Shiner, Larry. *The Invention of Art: A Cultural History*. Chicago: University of Chicago Press, 2001.

Shorto, Russell. *Descartes' Bones: A Skeletal History of the Conflict between Faith and Reason*. New York: Doubleday, 2008.

Shusterman, Richard. "Somaesthetics and Burke's Sublime." *British Journal of Aesthetics* 45, no. 4 (2005): 323–41.

Smith, Barry C. "The Objectivity of Tastes and Tasting." In *Questions of Taste: The Philosophy of Wine*, ed. Barry C. Smith. Oxford: Signal Books, 2007: 41–77.

Smith, Martin Cruz. *Havana Bay*. New York: Random House, 2008.

Smith, Richard Gordon. *Travels in the Land of the Gods: The Japan Diaries of Richard Gordon Smith*. Ed. Victoria Manthorpe. New York: Prentice Hall, 1986.

Smuts, Aaron. "Art and Negative Affect." *Philosophy Compass* 4, no. 1 (2009): 39–55.

Solomon, Robert C. "Emotions, Thoughts, and Feelings." In *Thinking about Feeling*, ed. Robert Solomon. Oxford: Oxford University Press, 2004: 76–88.

———. "Facing Death Together: Camus's The Plague." In *Art and Ethical Criticism*, ed. Garry L. Hagberg. Malden, MA: Blackwell, 2008: 163–83.

———. *The Passions*. Garden City, NY: Anchor/Doubleday, 1976.

———, ed. *Thinking about Feeling*. Oxford: Oxford University Press, 2004.

Sophocles. *Elektra, Antigone, Philoctetes*. Trans. Kenneth McLeish. Cambridge: Cambridge University Press, 1979.

Spinoza, Benedictus de. *Ethics*. Trans. Samuel Shirley. Indianapolis, IN: Hackett, 1982.

Steiner, Wendy. *Venus in Exile*. New York: Free Press, 2001.

Stoller, Paul. *Fusion of the Worlds: An Ethnography of Possession among the Songhay of Niger*. Chicago: University of Chicago Press, 1989.

Stone, Robert. *A Flag for Sunrise*. New York: Ballantine, 1977.

Summers, David. *The Judgment of Sense: Renaissance Naturalism and the Rise of Aesthetics*. Cambridge: Cambridge University Press, 1987.

Sweeney, Kevin. "Alice's Discriminating Palate." *Philosophy and Literature* 23, no. 1 (1999): 17–31.

Sylvester, David. "Areas of Flesh." In *Jenny Saville*. New York: Rizzoli, 2005: 14–15.

Talon-Hugon, Carole. *Goût et dégoût: L'art peut-il tout montrer?* Nîmes: Éditions Jacqueline Chambon, 2003.

Tate Gallery (Hogarth). http://www.tate.org.uk/britain/exhibitions/hogarth/rooms/room9.shtm. March 27, 2010.

Telfer, Elizabeth. *Food for Thought: Philosophy and Food*. London: Routledge, 1996.

"Thomas Hardy." http://www.britainexpress.com/History/bio/hardy.htm. July 14, 2009.

Thomasson, Amie L. *Fiction and Metaphysics*. Cambridge: Cambridge University Press, 1999.

Tso, Natalie. "Edible Excretions: Taiwan's Toilet Restaurant." *Time*, March 2, 2009. http://www.time.com/time/arts/article/0, 8599, 1882569,00.html. February 20, 2010.

Vermersch, Peter. "Introspection as Practice." *Journal of Consciousness Studies* 6, nos. 2/3, 1999: 17–42.

Visser, Margaret. *The Rituals of Dinner: The Origins, Evolution, Eccentricities, and Meaning of Table Manners*. New York: Penguin, 1991.

Wallace, Alfred Russel. *Borneo, Celebes, Aru (from The Malay Archipelago)*. London: Penguin, 2007.

Walton, Kendall. "How Marvelous: Toward a Theory of Aesthetic Value." *Journal of Aesthetics and Art Criticism* 51, no. 3 (1993): 499–510.

———. *Mimesis as Make-Believe: On the Foundations of the Representational Arts*. Cambridge, MA: Harvard University Press, 1990.

Wilson, Robert Rawdon. *The Hydra's Tale: Imagining Disgust*. Edmunton: University of Alberta Press, 2002.

Zangwill, Nick. *The Metaphysics of Beauty*. Ithaca, NY: Cornell University Press, 2001.

Zemach, Eddy. *Real Beauty*. University Park: Pennsylvania State University Press, 1997.

Žižek, Slavoj. "Grimaces of the Real, or When the Phallus Appears." *October* 58 (1991): 45–68.

Index

the pleasure pain contrast
which occupies a good deal of this
book (special pleasure)
is a problem that comes out of
Pepper. category of
<u>Mechanistic</u>

aesthetics

In pragmatist (Continental)
and "grooming" aesthetics
it is not a major
sticking point. But what
about Organicism? — e.g
Bosanquet does in his
book — "invincible ugliness"
is a concept

I wonder if my "Emilio" attributes to
Hamlet crosses into this
books'n discussion

Batiess gust pk] – w ow

VALENCE *define* 97=

no quality ~~has a~~ something is felt

= felt quality